A CONFLUENCE
OF RIVERS

A Memoir Through Digital
Love Letters

Katherine S. Hansen

Cover and interior designs by Farrukh Khan.

Printed in the United States of America.

For more information, or to book an event, contact:
Lydian@KatherineSHansen.com
http://www.KatherineSHansen.com

ISBN - Paperback: 979-8-218-69631-3
ISBN - eBook: 979-8-218-69632-0
Library of Congress Control Number: 2025912982

To all who carry a Rivers story in their hearts.

"Being deeply loved by someone gives you strength, while loving someone deeply gives you courage."
(Lao Tzu)

CONTENTS

VOLUME I: As I Recall

VOLUME II: The Box

VOLUME I
As I Recall

PART ONE
Meeting Through Email

ᚤ CHAPTER 1

NEVER ENDING STORY

In my basement sits an old cardboard box, perched a few inches from the concrete floor on a wooden-pallet pedestal to protect it from water that seeps in during spring rainstorms. A beat-up corrugated office box with an ill-fitting lid, it is a plain container for a thing of extraordinary beauty, stored in obscurity. I've lugged that box through moves of two-plus decades, safeguarding it like an ark of the covenant for my heart. In all that time I've never reexamined its contents.

As our present ceaselessly becomes our past, the mementos of the noteworthy - in basements, attics, closets, hearts - we store in order to preserve. To shield them from view if they hurt, to protect from harm the ones that hold joy, to know exactly where they'll be when we feel ready to meet them again.

Why have I never reopened the box? It's complicated.

This Box is loaded with old papers, but not just any old papers.

These are pages of text from an inkjet printer, email messages arranged in manila folders tabbed with the months of 1998. They comprise the record of a sublime relational adventure, from its earliest seed-speck to its petals of promise unfolding - all before we met in person. Our digital correspondence began in the early years of the medium and, being a preserver by temperament, I printed every message. Many hundreds of pages.

They tell of a chance encounter in the budding internet age, a bond formed through the written word and deepened from a distance.

Though the story's origins are only twenty-some years behind us, evolving technology has already rendered it archaic, a modern analog of a Victorian romance conducted through ship-carried letters.

How well I remember the soaring joy, the bursting open of life's possibilities, the wildly unlikely rendezvous across the ocean… The giddy in-love-ness, creased with desperate hopes, that gave out under the weight of heart-wrenching hindrances.

These are more than memories. The story is seared into my psyche. The story *is* me.

And yet… I find my faculty of memory at odds with itself.

The tale as I've retold it through the years leaves blank spaces and bewilderments. Before now I haven't felt ready to let the Box's clarities soothe me. I'm not sure they will.

I do know how wrecked I felt when the dream crumbled, as surely as I know its ecstasies, in time, eclipsed the distress of its demise. The wretched ache of mourning testified to the inestimable worth of the encounter. Had it not been so wondrous an experience, letting go couldn't have hurt so much - making even the pain a privilege. What remains among the pangs those misaligned stars still inflict is the undying amazement.

Whenever I pause to ponder it all, tears well up instantly. They're ready to spill again at this writing.

Telling this or any story involves contemplating the nature of story itself. It takes a thousand decisions (some unconscious) about weaving its filaments, which to highlight, which to consign to background. I want you to know the winnowing presented here fictionalizes nothing. This means certain scenes remain indistinct and light on dialogue - and I may use "as I recall" too often for some readers' tastes. I do realize sharper details make better stories.

But beyond authenticity, I have a further justification for the soft focus, the indeterminate lines. The long carried chronicle naturally became abridged over time, and now that I'm prepared to revivify it at close range, by bringing into service the Box's contents, *I want to tell the story from memory first.*

You'll see the spasmodic uncertainty of my recollection. That's ok… it won't stay that way. In Volume II, I'll finally pry open the treasure chest - that is, I'll gingerly flip the flimsy cardboard cover off the old Box - to see what I learn and how it feels. If you keep reading, you'll learn along with me.

But first: the adventure as my heart remembers it begs to come out. As I begin to commit it to paper for the first time, I sense new discoveries await from this retelling alone.

Every Day Is A Winding Road

Discoveries abounded in the months before this odyssey began, when I'd turned a huge corner in life. Well, "corner" doesn't begin to capture it; a better word is transformation. While there was a sparkling newness to who I was becoming, I was in another sense simply coming into my own, able to unfurl my truer self for the first time. From the moment I'd been married off barely out of high school, my individuality had been put in the shade throughout the ensuing fourteen years by that partner and by the fundamentalist set of beliefs that surrounded our pairing.

Five years after being liberated by a tumultuous divorce, 1997 found me and my two little boys settled into a dinky yet comfortable apartment in a rural town. In the intervening span I had become, in my thirties, a first-generation college graduate.

Formal education wasn't valued in the sect that molded my adolescent thinking, nor was it available within the sect-approved traditional marriage. No one in my family of origin had earned a post-secondary degree. In my girlhood visions for what my future might hold, it had never even come up.

When I found myself starting over, it did come up - a suggestion from a counselor - and it constituted a true moment of illumination. I immediately began laying the groundwork. With support from various quarters, I managed to earn a bachelor's degree with two majors and a perfect grade point average. College turned out to be the most resonant and inspired act of unfurling yet.

Deeply gratified by guiding my young sons' growth, I felt exhilarated too by the life of the mind, ideas and study. And if that weren't enough transformation for a 30s-aged single mom, a minor medical crisis the year after graduation fostered a revolution in physical health as well; seventy pounds lighter, I experienced new levels of energy and wellbeing.

Have you noticed, when people describe an accident, or any sudden life-altering experience, they often say the instant before impact became frozen in recall? I like to think, similarly, that the backdrop I've just outlined became crystallized by the breathtaking events that followed.

How to Save a Screen

Those events began with an "accidental" purchase. Remember the screensavers of the 1990s? With the advent of home PCs, they were developed to preserve the condition of the monitor. An image held in place too long could leave a permanent discoloration or ghost imprint on the screen. To prevent this, screensavers began playing moving images after so many minutes, continuing until the keyboard or mouse was tapped, or until the monitor powered off. The Windows operating system came preloaded with a selection of them; some of us purchased non-Windows designs, just for fun.

How I initially came across my favorite screensaver collection I no longer recall. My best guess is it was sampled on a shareware CD I got from an electronics store. Mesmerized by designs based on infinitely repeating patterns called fractals, I ordered the full version.

As I recall (there's your first of those), when I loaded the program onto my PC, some of the designs were accessible but not others, so I contacted the tech support email address in the software - hardly expecting to hear back. When I did, I envisioned some tech nerd at a fancy workstation in a fancy office, fielding inquiries for the company.

The response was prompt, clear and helpful, the respondent knowledgeable and patient. It wasn't an instant fix; further diagnostic steps were needed. In the process, it became apparent that this "Thomas" was himself the creator and programmer - the screensavers what we'd call today his side hustle. Efforts at resolving the issue over email proved unsuccessful, and the friendly programmer offered to snail-mail me a fresh copy of the program on floppy disk.

Our problem-solving exchange was flecked with cordial asides, some of which dabbled in unrelated topics. I supposed he was based in the technology hotspot of the Pacific Northwest. (Didn't all the best programmers migrate there because of Microsoft?) The moment I learned otherwise is still a source of supreme delight. That sound you can't hear is my half-smiling face wagging in disbelief, even after all this time.

I've often wished for a crisper recollection of those early exchanges - I sure remember how they made me feel. Corresponding with this smart, easygoing, eminently likable programmer utterly charmed me! How fortunate my email keepsakes are safe and available in the Box; I never thought it would take this many years to reopen it. Knowing it was there was enough.

I didn't want to excavate the intense emotions until I felt certain of my readiness. I'm choking back tears just thinking of telling you what happened. How could I not expect to be overcome going back to it in print - up close, word by word, right in my face?

The essential components of the chronicle never left me, yet I'm bracing for startling revelations because I know that, chiseled by years of intervening experience, even deeply imprinted episodes can lose pieces and look different later. I'm prepared to discover what time, sentimentality, and fallible memory have done to the details. Because I printed and saved the emails, I'll be able to compare them with the heart-held version to learn what shifted or got lost.

For now, I rely on my inner archives, faded by time and smudged by tears.

I can peg my tech support inquiry to January of that year because of a sports event. Among the irrelevancies in the exchanges with Mr. Programmer was my mention of the NFL team near my Wisconsin hometown heading to the Super Bowl. When I asked if he planned to watch the game, he replied, "That's the big American football event, isn't it?"

I recall seeing those words on my computer screen, wrinkling my eyebrows and cocking my head, like a puppy hearing an unfamiliar noise. That would've been an odd question for a fellow American to ask. Naturally, I replied, "Where are you located?"

"Near Cologne, Germany."

The major European city was unfamiliar, and the French-looking spelling threw me off. Germany I had heard of! How far away it sounded - and how exciting to realize my new pen pal was not merely a long-distance acquaintance, but an international one. *Pen pal: a person with whom one keeps up an exchange of letters, usually someone so far away that a personal meeting is unlikely.* The term used to be common; I just pulled up that definition online. The unlikelihood of a personal meeting certainly fits, but with electronic communication, would we still call them letters?

Thomas had lived in the area his entire life - as I had in mine. I told him his written English was so fluent I wouldn't have guessed it was his second language. He often listened to British radio, he said, adding, "Sometimes I even understand what they're saying." I distinctly remember his quirky way making me smile. His professional title was software developer, but he liked to refer to himself as a techie or hacker.

When the promised floppy disk turned up in my mailbox, I was elated to have this tangible testament to his existence in my very fingers, the postal markings confirming his far-flung locale.

It just hit me: that airmail envelope must be in the Box!

With the updated screensavers installed and working properly, their creative programmer met his objective - another satisfied customer. But if that had marked the close of our contact, you wouldn't be reading this.

ϓ CHAPTER 2

TRUE COLORS

It was evident Thomas and I enjoyed our emailing. In this narrative, by the way, I mean to speak only for myself. Here my collective assertion is backed by the simple fact that we both kept responding amicably and with interest.

With the problem solved, we carried on the conversation for its own sake. Music became a running theme, computer technology too. Of course, I soon became eager to know what he looked like. At the time, sharing photos digitally was a clunky endeavor requiring some technical knowledge. In Thomas's case, all he had to do was point me to the URL for the website he'd designed to promote his software creations.

I was so impressed! The light gold-toned home page was crisply organized, and included buttons to switch between German and English. One page featured samples from the screensaver collection I'd purchased, called *2000 Lights Go Down*, an apparent marketing tie-in to the approaching turn of the century.

Photos were posted in a section titled *Rogue Gallery*. Thomas was shown in various settings, with captions referencing his profession ("Long-haired programmer," and one as a boy: "Not yet a programmer"). Two leap to mind now. In one he was crouched on a small sailing vessel nearing a wooden pier. I remember the calm focus in his blue eyes, and his flowing blondish mane. In the other - always my favorite - he stood against an indoor wall, eyes directed off to the side, dressed in a smart bold-blue blazer and an unruffled half smile.

His expression in every sandy-haired shot, at various stages of beard length, reflected a playfully self-effacing personality - exactly how I was experiencing him in writing. Yes, I printed the photos too.

I don't recall how I showed him what I looked like, but it would've required Thomas's tech support, even if I had a scanner then (I'm not sure). Could I have snail-mailed them?

While I hesitate on this and other conundrums, scanning corrupted files in my mind - as if furrowed brows and determined concentration will yank the details to consciousness - a galvanizing insight diffuses through me, displacing the unknowns. This saga, in pieces and as a whole, at once *expressed* and *shaped* who I was. The epiphany magnifies the sheer delight of these early steps, and reinforces how completely mine the story is. A few blank spaces don't diminish that or keep me from reliving the heart's flutter.

Whatever method I used to transmit photos, an associated memory is unusually distinct. Thomas acknowledged receiving them, but without added comment. I can think of two reasons this sliver stayed with me. First, as an indication of his reserve - barely knowing each

other and not expecting the contact to last - it proved consistent with the Thomas I later came to know. The second reason says more about me. By contrast, my nature predisposed me to express compliments (as I had about his photos), and his reticence made me aware I'd hoped for (expected?) one from him.

My private speck of reflection didn't hinder the conversation. I wrote about parenting and my part-time work, of my college experience and career aspirations. Thomas told of his background in software development, about his day job and home business. He said he lived alone and liked to stay up late. His calling himself "shy" is a vivid recollection; another was his phrase, "I smile a lot" - the fragment has always been essential to my early impressions of him. To this day, it's as appealing a self-description as I've heard from anyone.

We recounted day-to-day doings and interests, and compared perspectives on current events from our separate continents. It was stimulating to discover a fair amount of overlap between our general frames of reference, considering the geographical distance and divergence in background. This intersection extended to the shared enthusiasm for collecting and listening to music. Anyone with a musical sensitivity to match mine, and with as eclectic a taste, would intrigue me on that score alone. Thomas was six years my junior, yet most of his favorites came from several years earlier, a period I was well versed in: perfect match.

Another area of compatibility stemmed, naturally enough, from verbal acuity. Thomas was obviously fluent in his second language; I had just completed a degree in mine (Spanish). I recall such delight in our multilingual toying with terms and phrases, applying semantic cleverness to make each other laugh.

He had a way of making trenchant points with a light touch. I suspect he often cracked me up without necessarily aiming to. And when he *was* trying, he sure succeeded. Without doubt, my most prominent memory of his emails is simply the laughter they induced.

A phrase he might've assumed I'd heard - "the other side of the pond" - amused me to no end; it was my first exposure to it. When I expressed gladness at befriending someone overseas, he countered, "I consider you to be the one overseas." Ok, the hilarity might not come through to you, but I was quite charmed.

The better acquainted Thomas and I became, the more the enjoyment grew - yes, I'm telling you *I* felt the mutuality - and the more frequently we emailed. I realize sample lines would help you grasp this, help you *feel* it. They will come when I open the Box; for now, my recollections are largely impressionistic.

A sense of closeness developed through this vehicle, one which suited each of our dispositions well but for disparate reasons. An extrovert who thrived on eye contact in person, I relished self-expression through the written word too - especially, as far back as I can remember, through letter writing. Getting to know someone by email uniquely satisfied that penchant.

My take on why relating through email fit Thomas so favorably is based on all I later experienced of him. He wouldn't put it in these terms, and I can't swear he would concur - but I suspect he might. It's because the sparkle of his confident and courteous intellect, suffused with natural affability, shone through in writing more readily than his introversion allowed for in person.

Above all, there never seemed to be a question of false presentation from either of us. I knew my most authentic self was on offer; it felt reasonable to suppose the same was true of him. This may sound naive

given the burgeoning of online dating since then, with its well understood hazards. I was aware, of course, of the potential for deception; nothing in Thomas's written manner or his web presence raised red flags. But there was a larger reason for being persuaded of his authenticity: our remote acquaintance had come about altogether by chance.

I've always considered this the paramount feature of our entire convergence. We didn't meet through an online forum or dating service; neither of us used them, neither actively sought a connection.

And yet, my path crossed with Thomas's when we both happened to be in a singularly open-hearted and receptive life-moment - as borne out by the random encounter's unfolding. This helps explain why a transitory business exchange between a product peddler and his customer could come to encompass such reciprocal comfort, enjoyment and desire.

Shiny Happy People

We became part of each other's routines. After several weeks, I was trading emails with Thomas nearly every day, always aware what time it was for him. Clearly some late-night hours he usually devoted to programming were now spent writing to me. Germany is seven hours ahead of Wisconsin; I knew if I didn't receive a message by 6 p.m., I wouldn't hear from him anymore that day, as he typically went OTB (off to bed) around midnight.

He loved to use, and coin, acronyms like that one; we had such fun with them. He once sent a long list of initialisms then coming into popular use, and explained that transmission costs at the dawn of digital messaging were calculated on a per character basis - hence the usefulness of brevity. Two he favored were IOW (in other words) and OTOH (on the other hand). Another was AFAIK (as far as I know), which he sometimes tactfully deployed even when he was certain. Once, I incorrectly named the band members of ZZ Top - unaware Thomas was an avid fan. Setting me straight, he began with "AFAIK..." It was a hallmark of his personality: an unassuming self-possession free from a need to gloat.

Because of Thomas, I learned new technical uses for old words, such as *chat* and *thread*. Novel terms he clued me in to included *search engines* for the World Wide Web (capitalized back then). I used my home PC mainly for word processing and my boys' learning games; now I could take my *techie* questions to him, reaping added benefits from his expertise.

I'd set up my first email account during my final semester of college, because my Chaucer professor required it - she was also responsible for my inaugural exposure to the internet. To encourage the class to take advantage of this vast new resource, an entire lecture period was held in the library, students huddled around a computer station, as a young tech-savvy researcher demonstrated navigating websites. I recall finding it confusing.

At the time, AOL and other email providers routinely blanketed postal mailboxes with free CDs. That must be how I came across Juno, the one I chose for class and kept for several years. How could I have imagined where this new convenience would take me? Less than a year later I sent my first email to Thomas.

My weekdays in early 1998 consisted of getting the boys off to grade school, then putting in hours at my part-time job (helping coordinate a domestic violence awareness program), while trying to stay on top of household tasks and keep our little family well and content as possible. Evenings, when the after-school hubbub subsided, I logged onto the computer and dialed in - if I wasn't expecting a phone call, that is. When the modem was in use, it monopolized the landline. Imprinted on my aural memory are the several seconds of beeping and blurping that emanated from the device springing to life to check my email inbox or browse the web.

Spare weekend moments found me perched on our second-hand office chair, before a boxy PC monitor on a wooden table that served as our computer desk, a set of speakers alongside the keyboard and mouse. This "office" space of our tiny apartment bled into the cramped kitchen it faced toward. Behind me the boys watched TV or roughhoused in the living room, if they weren't away with their dad or with friends. A large casement window to my right overlooked our building's parking lot, beyond which lay a grassy field that flooded when there was too much rain.

How vividly I recall fixing my gaze on the thick horizontal line filling in as the email software performed its mysterious process. If there were no incoming messages (and none being sent), that left-to-right progress bar fluidly zipped over in no time. When a message was being received, the bar would hesitate partway across for a split second before completing its path.

I lived for that hesitation.

⅄ CHAPTER 3

HALF A WORLD AWAY

The microsecond's delay would bring a happy little gasp because it usually meant I was hearing from Thomas. Our digital penpalship - I truly believed that's all it would ever be - added a ray of sunshine to full and taxing days.

It was an unexpected prize which nestled itself into my prosaic reality. Having a friend on the other side of the pond stirringly expanded my small-town existence - giving me a taste of connection with the wider world, a fresh grasp of my orientation in it, and the privilege of viewing it through another's perspective. These *grew* me.

And I had Thomas to thank for them. A well-known Maya Angelou quotation springs to mind: *I've learned that people will forget what you said, people will forget what you did, but people will never forget how you made them feel.* Yes, that gets at something relevant. Although I recollect few specifics of my email conversations with Thomas that spring, crystal clear in the remembrance is the absolute delight his messages brought me. How could I *not* imagine what meeting him would be like? It could never happen, I knew. I can see myself shrugging, dismissing the notion with a wave of the hand.

Decades of technological advances since, it's become commonplace to make contact first in cyberspace - even within your own neighborhood, via security-conscious apps - and then contemplate meeting IRL (in real life). With high enough hopes, it's not so unusual either to arrange a F2F (face-to-face) across a considerable distance.

Not then. It was inconceivable, crossing an ocean to meet a friend for the first time. Except that Thomas and I, I contend, had indeed *met* - in written conversations that penetrated more deeply (and came about sooner) than they might've in person. Emailing lent itself to disclosing selves and stories less guardedly, from the comfort of home and security of distance.

The discourse with Thomas turned into a fixture I couldn't imagine doing without. His playful banter and flourishes of intellect elicited the same from me, and we soon became emotional confidants. It was that kind of harmony which kept me daydreaming quixotically about meeting him.

By May, and by an inner progression I can no longer explain, those musings crossed some formless border - and the idea no longer sounded categorically impossible.

When the preposterous notion was first broached - I don't remember how or by whom - we entertained the question of who would travel. My part-time work afforded me some flexibility; his programming job provided more. Not only could he take more time off, he could complete some tasks online while abroad.

Also in favor of Thomas visiting me: he had no children to be away from. But one factor outweighed all those considerations. My sheltered background made travel (especially to Europe), a more exotic prospect for me. The sights in Germany would be more compelling than anything I could show him in Wisconsin.

I would be the one to venture forth. Well, at this point, that meant nothing more than... taking a step toward... looking into... possibly contemplating... just maybe... whether I could even *consider* it.

Once the fanciful conception took root - still an implausible dream - I had to determine whether I could afford it. The funding for my nonprofit position was about to end, but I had a lead on a full-time admissions post with the college I'd graduated from. The modest child support from the boys' father went to their needs alone. I did live quite frugally though, thrift-shopping for clothes and furnishings, only occasionally splurging for books and music. I carried no debt on my credit card, so I could manage limited travel expenses that way - especially since my German friend offered lodging at his home for no cost. The wild idea inched toward doable. That left the cost of the flight as a potential deal-breaker.

This sounds funny now, but I physically visited a local travel agency to research costs. Braced to learn the airfare could put the trip beyond reach, I left there surprised and exultant: the expense could indeed be absorbed.

Next matter to tackle: care for Sam and Ben (ages 9 and 7) during my hoped-for week's absence. Their regular schedule placed them with their father part of every week, but it wasn't workable for them to stay there, or with my sister nearby, for the entire time. Next-door friends of hers, though, with two sons roughly the ages of mine, gladly agreed. My boys knew the family, and this way they could hang out with their cousins and keep their dad visits. I could hardly imagine a more favorable arrangement.

One by one, potential obstacles to the trip fell away, clearing a tentative path from fantasy to reality.

From Here to Uncertainty

Every Memorial Day, the boys spent the long weekend with their father. The *me time* it offered that year seemed providential. The preliminary trip research was done, theoretical groundwork laid; I needed to make up my mind whether to go for it. The rare extended solitude would give me time to weigh things out. Did I feel ready to commit to this fantastical pursuit, or would wisdom dictate pulling back and letting it go?

At the usual Friday time, I dropped the boys off at their dad's. We hugged and waved our goodbyes, as usual, and I headed home to ponder. That afternoon found me gleeful, tantalized, a little giddy - and quite uncertain. When I reunited with them (as usual) on Monday, I still felt gleeful and giddy - but no longer uncertain. There was nothing usual about the plans I was making. Why not see how far this ride would take me?

Just as each year's Super Bowl brings Thomas to mind, Memorial Day evokes the momentous decision to go meet him. Both bring the same happy tears and wistful smile writing about them does now.

My decision made, Thomas and I explored what the decidedly platonic visit would entail. As part of the discussion, he emailed a dictionary definition translated from German: *Platonic love: the purely intellectual / mental / spiritual love between two persons searching for virtue and beauty.* I printed an extra copy of that page, to clip and display those words on my refrigerator. That's how profoundly they moved me, and how central they were to my thinking about meeting Thomas.

Readers would be right to suspect my level of detail on this; I have an explanation. Separate from the Box of printed emails, I've safeguarded (also without revisiting) a photo album and a shoebox of keepsakes from the trip. Upon deciding to write this story, I dared to unearth those first. The shoebox holds the receipt for the airline ticket - that's why I know the trip's cost and exact dates. The *platonic love* definition is there too. I knew we'd discussed the term by email, but I'd blocked out posting the clipping - until I held it again in my hands.

Thomas and I also agreed on the wisdom of exercising skepticism, no matter how much our written familiarity inclined us to trust each other. Weren't we the sage ones - approaching with such rationality an encounter based on such affection!

Since I'd be traveling alone to an unfamiliar locale, Thomas offered advice to his inexperienced, small-town friend. If an unsavory character were to harass me, he said a simple "F— off" would be understood in Germany.

A slightly more elaborate contingency plan involved a friend of mine, closely connected with a couple living in Germany. At her request, they agreed to act as a resource in case of a disruption in plans during the trip, even offering me lodging should I decide not to stay with Thomas.

Of course, I didn't anticipate taking them up on their kind offer, but felt it important and reassuring to have in place. My aim to be prudent about this enormous step held hands with my conviction that Thomas and I already shared a profound friendship. Simply put, we believed each other. I could tell.

Yes, this would be a loftier leap than I'd ever taken. But only after I planted my feet, eyed the terrain, checked my gear - making sure I balanced confidence with caution. The moment of springing forward was coming into view.

To my friends, the trip to meet Thomas looked like an insane risk to take; I assured them it was informed by careful deliberation and backup plans. They came to understand I was neither blinded by attraction nor harboring unfounded expectations. Besides, the opportunity to *travel,* because of Thomas, represented more than they immediately grasped. The contemplation of it alone felt immensely consequential.

I was keeping my head - while letting my awakened heart have its say too.

The frame around my decision to fly to Germany was this: the choice was mine to make, the consequences would be mine to own. I was ready.

Walking On Sunshine

The inner assessment that I *could* take the trip constituted in itself the most pivotal act of all. It was a threshold I crossed with a daring part of myself I hardly knew - and the *having crossed it* influenced how I saw myself and every decisive moment from then on.

I pressed forward with the bold endeavor.

Thomas and I had been writing each other, with growing fondness, since January. Shoebox receipts inform me I purchased the airline ticket on June 8th: departure July 28th, return August 5th. Seven weeks sounded a long way off; I could barely contain my perpetual excitement.

The planning that preoccupied our correspondence only enlarged my affection for him. Inwardly, I knew whatever our connection meant, I could call my side of it love.

All the major puzzle pieces - time off work, child care, flights - had fallen into place with barely any pushback from the universe. And I had those seven weeks to let it sink in that I was really doing this. Once the plans were in motion I never harbored any serious doubts. My friends were excited for me, but a little wary.

Some who'd known me from my mousy married days or pre-college years just could not believe the metamorphosis they witnessed. Even those who'd come into my life since were stunned I would take such a step. I too was astounded by my own flowering confidence, the readiness to jut out into a wider world. And yet, it all felt right. Intoxicating, not without uncertainties - and completely fitting.

My sister and closest confidant supported my plans, with understandable reservations. "You sure about this?" she probed. "I'm sure." Have I mentioned we're twins? That summer found us settled in the same small-town neighborhood, after many years living hours apart, each recently divorced with two young children. While I was getting ready to meet Thomas across the pond, Deb was preparing to move to the West Coast for graduate school.

One of our diversions in that life-season was performing as a musical duo at local coffee shops. We called ourselves HeartSong; I played guitar and we sang folked-down arrangements of pop songs we found meaningful. In anticipation of Deb's move away, and spoofing our purely casual musical aspirations, we announced a "farewell concert" on the small stage of the community college she attended. I made a rare brand-new clothing purchase for the occasion. The solid-colored dress, of an eye-catchingly bright azure shade, had an intricate gathered-stitch design at the top and a wide-cut swirling hemline. These combined to give it visual interest up close, while making it ideal for stage attire as well. The performance took place amid the seven-week period between purchasing my airfare and taking flight.

That dress (still in my closet) would become a tangible symbol of the brightness and blue skies of that summer. Not until after the concert did I realize it could perform a pragmatic function in addition to its aesthetic one - as an easy way to pick me out of a crowd at a busy international airport.

As departure day neared, when I wasn't occupied with work or summertime activities with my sons, I could think of little else. Reveries of Thomas and traveling infused my everyday existence with spirited charm, like a drop of sun-yellow food coloring - in one of the boys' kitchen table "science experiments" - spreads through a glass of water in playful mesmerizing curlicues. (Hey, that would make a cool screensaver.)

It's difficult to convey how audacious yet perfectly reasonable making plans to meet Thomas felt. Heady adventurousness fused with rational groundedness. Not only had I never traveled internationally, I'd never formed a friendship through writing alone and only later met in person. And I was just so damn happy! My heart brimmed with gratification and gratitude about where I'd landed in life and where I was heading.

ɤ CHAPTER 4

A LYRICAL TIME

That expansive season - I'm picturing time-lapse blooms opening - was marked by emotional potency. Minor disappointments sunk deeper, elation soared higher, and every sensation in between, against the backdrop of my Thomas adventure, was outlined more keenly. Music sounded more musical, and my lifelong responsiveness to it felt heightened.

Dancing alone in my apartment, or on drives I took expressly to give utterance to the soul, I cocooned myself in music and motion and cranked up the volume. In the car no one could hear me scream-singing *Walking on Sunshine* or *Everybody Hurts*, exploding in joy and anguish. Hand-heels pounding the steering wheel in time, body bobbing and oscillating in my seat, I laughed while I cried and cried while I laughed

- because old griefs can lie dormant and then blindside you when you feel the most healed and happy.

This may not be true for everyone, but for me sunny times always hint at their shadows. The more brightness I revel in, the more aware I am of its contrast, of low times weathered to get me here. Music has a way of drawing all that out, bringing to the surface what waits inside to be faced and felt - the whole jumble from mourning to dawn.

My musical tastes range wide. When a song's energy suits my state of mind, any slice of lyric can be molded into pertinence. My favorite example from that summer was hearing REO Speedwagon's 1978 hit *Time for Me to Fly*. The title alludes to leaving a bad relationship, as I'd done years before. But now when I belted out its determined vitality, I was gleefully celebrating a literal flight toward a good relationship.

When I conceived of sharing this narrative, aware of the towering role music played in the experience, I granted readers would miss something of that dimension because of music's subjectivity. Not only is there no accounting for taste, words can't adequately convey a song's effect. Even if they could, I can't expect the song to have the same effect on someone else, so naming titles and artists could, rather than add rich overtones to this telling, make it sound a little tinny - like hearing a moving masterpiece on a cheap stereo.

I'm taking my chances. Maybe the same holds true of the story itself, of any deeply felt experience we hope to relay well enough for others to feel something too. And yet... When an experience does connect, just enough, it makes the sharing so worthwhile that, well, it means we won't stop telling stories or making music anytime soon.

A 1990s song that connected with me - I could not refrain from singing along with intoxicated glee - was *Dreams* by the Cranberries:

Oh my life is changing every day in every possible way. Unlike the REO song, its lyrics echoed my circumstances and sentiments as though it were written just for me, just for then.

The quoting of song lyrics was a perennial feature of Thomas's and my emails, most often in subject lines or postscripts, as a title-and-artist quiz. (We didn't stump each other often.) From June on, I anticipated nothing more ardently than the times we would spend listening to music *together.* As we narrowed down ideas for how we might spend the week, with no shortage of sights to see, building in ample time for music was a shared priority.

I explained my limited mental associations with Germany, despite coming from an area with deep German immigrant roots. What came to mind were the Alps of *The Sound of Music,* and the harsh language from old Hitler newsreels. Thomas assured me German doesn't sound like "the mental pygmy's" speeches. As to Bavarian scenery I anticipated seeing, Thomas noted, with his typical economy of words, "No mountains here."

Needless to say, it was Thomas himself I most looked forward to seeing.

Six months after my opening plea to Tech Support, everything was in place for an excursion thousands of miles from home to meet the man who'd become a cherished and intimate email friend. We were, as I've told you, on the same page as to circumscribing the platonic relationship, but for my part it wasn't hard to imagine an attraction that could tempt us beyond it - so I made a contingency plan for that too.

In accordance with my moral persuasion at the time, I made myself a promise (just in case) to forswear sleeping together. As a bon voyage gift, one of my good friends gave me a set of cute silky pajamas to take along; I resolved that Thomas would not see them.

Time for Me to Fly

Do you know the sensation, an exciting event looming, of time passing too slowly and too fast - all at once? Part of you feels the object of your anticipation can't come soon enough, while another senses its speeding approach and wonders if you'll be ready in time.

That's not what I was feeling as I awaited the trip.

Instead, time passed at a Goldilocks pace, neither dragging nor rushing. Come to think of it, this dovetailed with the trip itself seeming both absurd and rational.

Departure day arrived.

My travel agency purchase included transport from my apartment to the Chicago airport, a three-hour drive. A favorite snapshot of that era was taken by my sister, who saw me off that morning (the boys, goodbyes exchanged earlier, were already with friends). If Deb was uneasy, it didn't show; I saw only her excitement on my behalf. She captured my beaming smile out on the front sidewalk, preparing to bid farewell, my ride expected any minute. The photo is emblematic of my bright adventurous self, on a bright sunny day, in my bright blue dress. Once I hopped into that shuttle, the trip was truly in motion.

At the end of the ride, the driver would deposit my luggage and me at the proper terminal, and I would have to find my own way from there. Terminal, gate - the parlance was unclear; navigating an international airport was itself foreign to me. I managed to check in and to locate the assigned gate, where I parked myself in the general vicinity until boarding time. No more decisions to make. All I had to do was get myself onto that airplane for the direct flight - to depart from my world and disembark in Thomas's. I awoke that morning in my home, and would go to bed in his!

Was this really happening? Was this small-town woman who in all her years had barely left her home state actually headed across the ocean? And was I actually about *to meet Thomas*?

As we'd arranged - by email alone, I remind you - he would be there to meet me at the Düsseldorf airport, a 90-minute train ride from his home. If all went well, nothing stood in the way of looking into Thomas's eyes but nine hours time.

As I handed my ticket to the boarding agent, I felt excited, confident, sparkling, awake - and completely unafraid.

There were no surprises about the flight - other than how I came to be flying at all. I drew in with purposeful keenness every facet of the experience - the cozy comfort of my seat, the chilly air of the cabin - while imaginings of the Thomas moment soon to unfold twirled behind every other thought.

Well prepared for passing the time - with books, magazines, a notebook for jotting thoughts (no personal electronics back then) - I carried these and other small necessities in my favorite college book bag, medium-sized, of muted orange suede. I also carried with me confidence in the preparations I'd orchestrated. The assurance my sons were well cared for, and the contingency-plan phone number in the book bag's pocket, allowed me to soak up every moment. I don't recall the hours seeming long; some would've been passed in dozing.

Apart from that, memory furnishes me with only episodic impressions, the feeling and flavor of it all. That happens with a story you carry long enough. At first you remember every little thing and you're sure you always will. Then time wears down the lucidity, until only linchpins and tartest slices remain.

What I remember best about the flight is the paradox of calm exuberance I felt.

It may have seemed to loved ones like I was about to dive from a cliff's edge. It looked like a cliff's edge to me too, but I expected to soar - safety-harnessed and paragliding over all kinds of amazing scenery.

PART TWO

Face to Face

MEETING MR. WRITE

The computer that linked me to Thomas was off, and so was I. On that late-July day I flew high over the Atlantic to meet him, with no trepidation or second-guessing. I didn't jot my emotional state in the notebook I carried, so you're left to take my word for it - as am I, for that matter.

The landing was uneventful; I must've dozed through the descent. Deplaning, shuffling through the jetway with the passenger scrum, shoulder-slung orange backpack, these come back in shards. I have no memory of going through Customs or retrieving checked luggage. Nearly fifteen hours would elapse between last looking into my family's faces and first looking into Thomas's, yet I clearly remember being unconcerned over appearing bedraggled.

Ebullient yet composed, not nervous (imagine that!), I paused to get my bearings, then prepared myself to wait, in case of a train delay for Thomas. Three years before 9/11, it was no great inconvenience for him to pass through security and meet me at the gate area, using the flight number I'd emailed. Worth noting too is that we had no other way to get in touch inside the busy airport.

Equipped with images memorized from emailed photos, we would each keep a sharp eye out for a person who was keeping an eye out for us. (Wouldn't almost everyone at an airport gate be out to spot someone?)

As dearly as I long to *feel* myself in that scene again, even a memory as distinctive as this one foregrounds only certain components, like an incomplete painting, rich colors alternating with faded grays. I do remember (in color) first taking in the capacious space. The brightly lit ceiling seemed to reach forever, above a polished floor so shiny it reflected the determined motion of travelers of all kinds.

I surveyed the gate area for the most suitable perch, then planted myself to watch the hustle and bustle. There were fewer people than I expected. The seat I found for my lookout was ideal for casting a hawk-eyed gaze toward folks approaching newly arrived passengers, affording them a line of sight toward me too. Of course, I had only one folk in mind.

There I was, in my striking azure dress, expectant, self-assured, feeling attractive and ready. (When I searched just now for a synonym for azure, *cyan* came up, a word I've only heard in reference to ink cartridges for color printers; a little on the nose for meeting a techie.) An unruffled vivacity prevailed. Even now, from the perspective of age, I insist the dearth of fearfulness didn't come from foolhardy ignorance of what could go wrong. Rather, it sprang from dual roots: the bond

Thomas and I had developed in writing, and the conviction that I would be capable of coping if something did go awry.

In that conviction lies the starkest contrast to my earlier life. I'd been taught I needed protection, that as a woman I was particularly vulnerable to being misled and preyed upon - a mindset that conditioned me to be fearful. In that airport in Germany, that conditioning no longer held the sway it once did. I even felt, if you can believe it, comfortable. Rather than treating my instincts as inherently suspect, I was giving my intuition credence. If something had gone seriously amiss, doubtless I would've had to deal with a rearing of old anxieties. But nothing did.

Whenever I recount key elements of the adventure - by heart indeed - four uber-highlights flash to mind, its most emblematic moments start to finish. All persist purely as mental snapshots; for these, no photographs exist.

The topmost of them is the instant I first laid eyes on Thomas.

Right Here Right Now

Free and alive. That's how my heart felt, scanning the strangers for a tall thin man in his thirties with sandy blond hair, medium-length beard and kind blue eyes.

It couldn't have been more than a few minutes before my eyes landed on a figure, maybe 30 yards out, who fit the profile. The wait had barely been long enough to check my wristwatch. Amid a sparse stream of travelers on the move at cross trajectories, the figure was headed in my general direction. Initially I could make out only the appropriate build and facial hair. I distinctly remember by the time I pegged him as a candidate, waiting for the spark of hopeful recognition to morph into certainty, his view was already fixed toward where I sat. Thomas had recognized me first.

My memory-window into this scene is dual-paned. Through the first I see, vivid as any other of my life, his appearance in motion as I watched him approach: the slender frame, mellow demeanor, determined yet unrushed stride. Through the second pane is a still portrait of how I would've appeared to him: alone and alert in my seat, bookended by backpack and suitcase, expression as bright as the blue dress that identified me.

When not a shred of doubt was left, I rose.

"Katherine?"

His voice was silvery and sure. I replied evenly, an effort to contain my gleeful wonder.

"Hello, Thomas."

Dressed in solid off-white t-shirt tucked into crisp blue jeans, his bearing was affably unflustered, though timid. My irrepressible grin met his retiring smile. I'll never forget that first eye contact; the moment is rapturous to replay. It instantly demarcated all other experience into before meeting Thomas and after.

We knew so much about one another's inner selves; now we took in the physical presence. It would take a bit to feel at ease in this realm. This explained, I think, the ever so slight disquiet I detected on his kind-eyed face - that, and his pressing concern to help me feel as comfortable as possible.

In my countless pre-imaginings, I saw us throwing our arms around each other; I couldn't conceive we wouldn't, given what we'd shared. But when the dreamed-of moment came, we didn't embrace. Right then, it clicked for me that despite our close writing relationship, in person we were still new to each other. There was no discomfort for me in that awareness. We were both a little self-conscious; he didn't initiate the gesture, so I didn't either.

That was the first surprise of the trip.

Beyond initial greetings and determining our next steps, few words were spoken, or needed; there would be plenty of time for conversation later. I was feeling my way through this mix of knowing yet not knowing Thomas - starting with not hugging. (Only later did the cultural ingredient occur to me: American informality versus German reserve.) I lifted my backpack as Thomas reached for the suitcase, and we were on our way.

The task at hand, with a full week to cultivate the friendship in real life, was to decide on our first day's plan. It was about 9:30 a.m. local time when we left the airport; to my body clock it was the middle of the night. But any jet lag was overridden by amped up fascination. The train ride to his town would take an hour and a half, but there was no hurry.

The next scene I recall after our moment of encounter is stepping into the sunny street. Thomas pointed out a fancy shopping center, in case it might be of interest to me to browse there. It wasn't. I doubt he was surprised.

Remember the notebook in my backpack? I still have it: half-standard size, metal spiraled, thick burgundy cover. I didn't write much in Germany, so what's recorded there is especially significant. A single page, consisting of nothing more than a few keywords scribbled for each day, constitutes the only chronology of how Thomas and I spent our time.

In the entry for Wednesday, the day I landed, I find a hint about that morning. Scrawled after *Düsseldorf* is *deck of airport*, which suggests

Thomas and I took in the view from the observation deck before exiting the airport. I would've been awestruck by the tableaux, by viewing it alongside Thomas - yet no recollection of this remains.

I'm having trouble getting over the implications. Apparently I have limited influence over what stays in the memory and what gets lost - I would certainly have chosen the cityscape to have endured. That the instance from the same hour (unrecorded in my notes) of declining to window shop stayed with me I find utterly baffling.

The next clip on my memory screen has us standing beside each other at a busy train station. I'd never even been near a passenger train, and I watched, captivated, as Thomas scrutinized the inscrutable, deciphering with ease the complex data for innumerable trains and tracks, constantly updated on gigantic displays.

I might remember more about navigating the train system had I needed to learn the logistics for myself. Instead, in contrast to the plucky independence that got me there, I simply followed Thomas's lead. From one hectic station to the next, one platform to another, on and off cars: this was second nature to him. He didn't expect me to pick up on the how-to's - all part of hosting his American visitor.

During most train rides, my attention oscillated between the scenery as it breezed by and Thomas himself. I stared at him for as long as I could get away with whenever he looked out the window. The clean, odor-free railway carriages had sturdy yet comfortable fabric-covered seats; rows facing forward alternated with rows facing rearward, two or three seats on either side of the aisle. I remember only one very crowded ride; most often we had empty seats around us and sat facing each other. Riding was quieter than expected, allowing for conversation without raised voices, but we didn't talk much on the way home.

The introverted nature I'd sensed in his writing was evident in person - and again, words could wait. You might notice I didn't say "on the way to *his* home" a sentence ago. It didn't take long to feel comfortable with Thomas; soon I would also feel at home where he lived. Physically present, moving through shared time and space, connecting through facial expressions, body language, gestures… everything about him fit exactly the Thomas I'd come to know through email.

Take, Take Me Home

On the afternoon of my arrival, I met a few of Thomas's friends. He'd cleared his calendar for my visit, with one exception - he hoped I wouldn't mind - a meeting at an office in Cologne. I was thrilled to listen and observe, despite comprehending next to no German.

Its purpose, as I recall, had to do with exchanging goods and services, the group of ten or so bartering colleagues convening around a conference table. When the meeting began, he presented me as his friend visiting from the United States, and I beamed. But before folks had taken seats, Thomas introduced me individually to someone whose name I actually recognized from our emails: the girlfriend who he'd said had moved out several months earlier.

She was small-framed, a bit taller than me, not as slight as Thomas. Close-cropped dark hair and oval black wire-rimmed glasses graced a round face I found pleasant but less than expressive. Thomas hadn't mentioned Gretchen ahead of the meeting; I didn't expect to meet her during my visit. I was glad, though, to make her acquaintance, eager to experience the people, places and doings of his everyday world, especially those he'd written me about. It was good to see that although they were no longer together they seemed on amiable terms.

After the meeting, Thomas and I walked to the train station to head home, a half hour's ride at most. When we disembarked on an underground level at his town, I remember being surprised by the unpleasant odor of urine. Concrete stairs led up to the street and we emerged into fresh mild air, the bright afternoon winding down.

Thomas carried my suitcase as we strode through a quaint, neatly kept neighborhood. Surrounded at first by small stores and restaurants, we left the traffic behind after a few blocks and turned onto a wide paved footpath, edged with shrubbery. Partway up the curved moderately sloping lane, we stopped at a foliage-framed rickety wooden gate.

Thomas's was the second of four row houses on the other side. The three-story dwelling had once belonged to his parents, the family home during part of his childhood. Now it belonged to him. From the gate he latched behind us, a narrow sidewalk led along the multi-hued facades - a few more steps and we were home.

The memory of that view, facing Thomas's front door from the walk, later became buried. But unlike the airport deck panorama, it was preserved in a snapshot. After the trip, I painstakingly labeled and arranged my 200-plus photographs in an album with a light green Old World map on the cover. When I inventoried the mementos shoebox to kick off this project, I cracked open the photo album for the first time too.

Perusing visual testimony to the many spectacles - of scenery, architecture, companionship - only a single snapshot provoked a spontaneous burst into tears. It portrays none of those. I couldn't have guessed it would be the one to elicit such emotional release, and I never would've recalled the view otherwise. That itself added to the emotion.

It was the sidewalk photo of Thomas's house.

The tan stucco facade, dappled by shadows of tree leaves in sunlight, is broken up by a plain brown entry door and a small window, ornamented with a white lace curtain and a box planter on the outdoor sill, filled with ivies crowding around blossoms of purple and pink.

Remember the four uber-highlights I told you of? This isn't one of them, precious as it is to reflect on arriving there. The moment represents, in a way, their inverse. They have no depiction outside my mind, whereas this highlight I couldn't have accessed were it *not* for the snapshot.

The image quintessentially evokes the warmth and welcome I felt - an icon for the sights we took in, talks we had, meals we shared, music we played - and I am overcome once more by the simple eloquence of a doorway into home.

AS I LAY ME DOWN

Our first moments in Thomas's home didn't last long. It was suppertime, so we dropped off my bags and walked to the neighborhood grocery store. He'd waited to shop until we could go together and get foods I'd like, the domestic task occasioning more conversation than the train ride had. Thomas's spoken English carried only a faint German accent, over a distinctly British cadence. At times, he wasn't entirely confident in his wording, but as with his written English, I told him he underestimated his speaking skills too.

According to my old notebook, we cooked potatoes and broccoli. On a day of firsts, it was the first undertaking of our first evening - in the first room of the house. The kitchen sat to the left of the entry, at the near end of a hallway leading farther in. The sidewalk photo's lace-curtained window looked into this modest but adequate cooking and dining area.

The hallway led into the largest space of the house, a rectangular living room, site of my most beloved remembrances of enjoyment and comfort with my friend - yet I took no snapshots there. These mental pictures, in contrast with the forgotten facade, have always remained distinct. As I conjure them, a peaceful warmth envelops me, comingled with the amazement that never diminishes.

To the right from the entry, opposite the kitchen doorway, stairs led to the second floor, where a wide central space was flanked by a bedroom to the right and a closed door to the left. Between them, straight across the landing, was the bathroom.

Behind the closed door was Thomas's computer room, where he'd created the screensavers that had so implausibly brought me there - an inner sanctum I did not breach. Some nights he spent time there after I retired for the evening, perhaps fielding emails from customers. To the right, exiting that room, another flight of stairs took Thomas to the third floor where he slept. I never went up there either.

The room he'd arranged for me was the one opposite the computer room. My door was lockable from inside, as was the bathroom door, mere steps from it. After we retreated each night to separate rooms on separate levels, the second floor was mine in privacy and security until morning.

Unpretentiously furnished, the cozy room was to me the height of luxury. My only indoor photo at Thomas's place shows the neatly made single bed (sans headboard), topped with a comforter whose fabric mimicked a handmade quilt, with repeating heart shapes in varicolored prints and bordered in solid navy. On the plain wood chair that served as a nightstand (with a clip-on lamp for a nightlight) are my belongings: burgundy notebook with green pen, an apple, and in a mini stand-up frame, a photo of my sons. My summer robe - white with paint-splatter pattern in primary colors - hangs on one chairback corner. Nothing but the vintage beige-gray wallpaper (textured, I believe) adorns the walls, an interlocking motif of rounded shapes pointed at top and bottom like retro-style Christmas tree ornaments.

As he showed me around his home, I studied Thomas himself, charmed by the same reserved self-assurance that appealed to me since our earliest email exchanges. There was a soft-spoken gentleness in his interacting with me that never varied during my time there, and I could tell he'd gone out of his way to make me feel safe, comfortable and undemanded upon.

By the time I turned in for the night, more than twenty-four hours had passed since waking in my Wisconsin bed - what amazing thresholds I'd crossed! I nestled under the covers, jubilant about the unfolding so far. Preceding intuitions about meeting my email friend were borne out; I didn't regret heeding them. Snug and drowsy, I took a long look at the bedside picture of my boys, restful knowing they could reach me if they needed to. I yawned, clicked off the light - and slept exceptionally well.

The next morning - and every morning - breakfast time with Thomas was a quiet joy. His spartan tastes and lifestyle extended to choices of cuisine, which overlapped comfortably with mine, though only he was vegetarian. We drank fennel tea, which I hadn't heard of and liked quite well. He heated the water in separate mugs, dipping into them an electric coil device I'd never seen either - an immersion heater, I later learned.

Breakfast consisted of thinly sliced dark bread - it reminded me of "brown bread" my mom baked when I was little, but this was even denser. Buttered lightly, topped with slices of hard white cheese, the fare ideally suited my taste. Over the simple meal in the small kitchen, Thomas initiated morning conversations about our plans: "We could go see A, or visit B. Would you like to do one of those today?" My thoughtful host made suggestions, offered options, and handled the arrangements. I usually answered, "Both sound wonderful! Do you have a preference?" It never took much to decide on the day's excursion.

Of my eight days in Germany - both Wednesdays taken up with arriving and departing - we visited on each of the six others at least one landmark, and always left time for unwinding at home. We split sightseeing, transport and dining costs; he paid as we went along, with a plan to settle up on my last day, when I'd withdraw from my credit card the total I owed him. I still have my bundle of receipts, only a few of which I can decipher and attach to specific activities and expenses. My notebook's keywords are more useful for calling back the outings by day.

But Thursday's I don't need help with. On the first morning I woke in Thomas's home, we went to the Cologne Cathedral.

Roam If You Want To

Since I hadn't heard of Cologne before Thomas, I was equally ignorant of its renowned landmark. He had been born in the city and still commuted there for work; the famously twin-spired cathedral was our natural starting point.

About to tell you of it, I become aware of a phenomenon worth pausing on. Alongside scenes already in memory's focus, forgotten ones abruptly reappear - as though I needed to stare into those I do recall in order for some on the periphery to unveil themselves.

Is this another inkling about the operation of memory? Had I not undertaken to write this story, I'm convinced some formerly obscured fragments would not have come back to me. I can therefore thank you for this gift.

Just such a fragment pops into mind now. One morning as we prepared to leave, Thomas's phone rang. He picked up the landline receiver in the entryway and answered with his surname - a cultural distinction from Americans' "Hello." Watching him from a short distance, attentive to his lilting German (I couldn't be said to be eavesdropping), I vividly recall finding his speech melodious. The splinter of recollection feels new, as though it hasn't replayed since.

It could've taken place on Cologne Cathedral morning. Our visit to the largest Gothic cathedral in northern Europe was my first up-close confrontation with the sheer scope of European history. There I tried to wrap my mind around numbers like 1248, the year its construction began - my trip coincided with the 750th anniversary - and the 600+ years until final completion in 1880. Displayed in my writing room today is the t-shirt I bought, emblazoned with a large *750* over the Cathedral's image and the years *1248 / 1998*.

Outspread before the entrance was a broad square, visitors coming and going in all directions. We paused there, dwarfed by the monumental and inconceivably ornate edifice, and Thomas probably watched my face as I gazed skyward, spellbound by its immensity and grandeur. For him the sight was a lifelong mainstay of everyday existence. (A favorite tidbit he shared went back to his youth: he and his buddies called it "the church across from McDonald's.") But for me, well... I was positively carried away, entranced.

The church building's impact on me had nothing to do with religious experience; it was all about the exquisite achievement of architecture and culture. How could anyone not be moved? I marveled at the uncommon manifestation of a common human impulse: to transcend the earthly and material through art and creativity. From this perspective it struck an overpoweringly harmonic chord. It *filled* me.

I must've stared a long time before Thomas and I entered the hushed interior. I remember little from inside other than the access to the bell tower. An enclosed spiral staircase - the narrow passage's stone walls scrawled with graffiti - took us, in close quarters with the stream of visitors, up the 533 steps to the lookout. That vista over the sprawling city is still with me - in memory and in photos. The headiness is impossible to imagine without experience; I drank it in, straining to memorize it. In my favorite picture from the tower, the cityscape, split by the Rhine River, is partially framed by the stonework opening through which I snapped it.

That day's encounter with the Cathedral is foremost among many indescribable gifts I received through Thomas, and it would take on a depth of significance well beyond our relationship, lasting throughout my life. Those moments fused themselves with the idea of travel itself. Never had I seen anything so far from and so unlike my everyday surroundings. I had no cathedrals to compare to; it may as well have been the only cathedral that existed. This was my initiation to seeing the world - and I took it all in like a wide-eyed girl far younger than my age who could not get enough.

Getting In Tune

The Cathedral loomed over Cologne's frenetic central train station; the ubiquity of such intertwinings of ancient and modern never ceased to stir this novice traveler's spirit. Of the sightseeing ideas Thomas and I had considered by email, only two were definite plans, as I recall. The Cathedral, of course, and the massive record store not far from it - yet another juxtaposition of old and new.

Four days after our foray to the church across from McDonald's, Thomas and I returned to the city to browse (with its pre-internet meaning) at Saturn Records, a favorite haunt of the avid record collector I was in Germany to visit. Boasting of "thousands of square meters of inventory," the store provided a memorable afternoon's enjoyment, as we leisurely pawed through countless CDs. From the start of our email friendship, our common pastime of collecting music had been a persistent theme. Now we engaged in the pursuit together.

The Saturn spree netted me eight CDs (the receipt is in my shoebox): Cat Stevens, Falco, Del Amitri, etc. It won't surprise you to read they're the most treasured of my collection. Track lists of some European releases differed from those available in the U.S., making my souvenirs all the more distinctive. One other band important to name (you'll see why soon) may be less familiar: Slade. That day I'd planned to buy *Slade In Flame*, but it was out of stock.

Some of my newfound gems were by longtime favorite artists; others I'd only been introduced to that week. These introductions took place in Thomas's living room - one reason the space figures so prominently in my memories.

Thomas kept his collection on shelves built like he was, tall and narrow. I recall the obvious delight on his otherwise placid countenance when he pointed them out my first evening there, in one corner of the room. The location of the stereo is fuzzier to me, but I remember clearly where we sat for the best listening.

Along one of the rectangle's walls was a plain chocolate-brown sofa, pushed into the corner opposite the shelves, but we didn't listen from there. The other long wall was largely made up of built-in dark wood cabinets with glass doors. The shorter side, across from the room's entrance, was "wall" only from waist level down, its top half consisting of a huge picture window that looked out onto a garden.

When we listened to music, Thomas and I sat side by side on the floor, leaning against the half-wall beneath the window. Something about his sound system must've favored that spot. In one of the most indelible mental clips from my time there, I see us passing CD cases back and forth - I'd brought a few from home too - while Thomas played assorted tracks, one after another, and we talked about what we liked, and didn't, and why.

Scribblings in my burgundy notebook list some selections from each evening. Of the artists unfamiliar to me, Slade turned out to be my best-loved musical discovery. To this day, hearing *Run Runaway* takes me back to those evenings as nothing else can - their sound as emblematic of the week as the Cathedral. Our music sharing was the pinnacle expression of the easy and natural friendship we erected over our written beginnings.

AMERICAN GIRL

A longside the notebook's musical mentions are daily keywords denoting our restaurant meals, *Spanish lunch* and *Italian penne* among them - no social-media-style food pictures in my photo album. It's funny to me now, for as few notes as I took, that I bothered to record them. What I remember most about dining with Thomas was his predilection for vegetarian pizza, a thin-crust affair he ordered more than once and ate with knife and fork - as he did the day we went to Bonn.

Less than half an hour's train ride from home, we visited a historical museum there on Friday. It's confounding I don't have among my keepsakes a museum brochure or any photos taken that day, but three exhibits are still with me. One was the first Volkswagen automobile ever manufactured, black and Beetle-shaped. Another, more affecting, was a graffiti-embellished chunk of concrete, tall as me, a remnant of the Berlin Wall demolished nine years before. The third consisted of a screen replaying 1940s newsreels of the destruction Germany suffered from World War II bombings. The Cologne Cathedral I'd met only the day before was included in the black and white footage, damaged but still standing, surrounded by devastation.

It turns out I do have one photo snapped that day. It shows Thomas from the shoulders up, seated next to a train window in his cream colored t-shirt, eyes on the picture-taker, as we rode in facing seats. The shot is a favorite because of his peaceful pleasant smile; he looks so happy. It could have been from any of our train rides - except when I pull the print from its pocket, I find written on the reverse: *Thomas, on the train ride to Bonn: Friday, July 31, 1998.*

Touring the museum and stopping for pizza couldn't have kept us out more than a few hours - so that must've been the day Thomas's mother dropped in. Bookshelf-shaped like Thomas, with business-like short gray hair, she struck me as stern and purpose-driven; I never learned her purpose that day, or whether she knew I would be there. She wasn't unfriendly when Thomas introduced me, but neither could I perceive much interest. He remained standing, I recall, leaning against a table, arms crossed, while they conversed in German. They didn't seem very warm toward each other, though I didn't sense outright antagonism. I don't think he commented on her brief visit afterward.

The following day was more eventful. Thomas's former girlfriend (whom I'd met at the meeting) joined us for Saturday's sightseeing at Aachen. I'm not sure whether Thomas presented this as an option or simply informed me; I wouldn't have minded either way. The city lies west of Thomas's town, but we must have gone north first to link up with Gretchen, because I have a nice photo of them at the Cologne station.

They didn't converse much in my presence, which hit me as normal enough based on their personalities (she seemed as naturally withdrawn as him) and long familiarity. When they did, it was in German. I felt only openness toward her and didn't perceive discomfort on her part. My overtures toward polite discourse, though, bore limited success - owing to her reserve and limited English, I surmise, rather than indifference.

I never learned how (or when) Thomas told her of his American customer's visit. As far as I knew, in keeping with our email commitment, Thomas regarded me platonically, as I did him (what-ifs deeper down didn't count). I doubt he elaborated beyond that for Gretchen. Their manner with each other came across as relaxed and non-romantic, and her presence didn't detract from my enjoyment of the day.

The three of us fit in quite a few sightseeing stops, including the foremost historical attraction, Aachen Cathedral. With this second cathedral under my traveling belt, maybe I shouldn't use "the Cathedral" to refer solely to the one in Cologne. I will anyway. Cologne's uniquely carries the heart-piercing intimation of how I got there - as though its treasury holds my contemplative tears among its relics.

Pages of Aachen day's photos bring back forgotten highlights, among my favorites the narrow cobblestone street where we lunched outdoors, and the panoramic view from a hill overlooking the city.

Composing these paragraphs, I feel a little blocked. It ultimately occurs to me this isn't because my subject matter is nudging at deeper feelings; it's precisely because it is not. Although I gratefully engaged with Saturday's experiences, they are for some reason backgrounded emotionally in favor of scenes from other days.

Paradoxically, however, the most iconic snapshot by far from the entire adventure was taken that day - my most cherished image of Thomas and me. Two friends stand placidly beside each other, not quite touching, with pleased expressions but not quite smiling - the moment a zenith of their improbable bond.

That's not all the photo has to tell.

Keep Feeling Fascination

It's not easy to tell on a given day which scenes will stay with you. My photo souvenir from Aachen locked that moment in my heart forever. Each with our own arms behind us and eyes on the camera, we pose at the edge of a plaza fountain - Thomas in his customary light t-shirt and jeans, me in a patterned sleeveless jumper of gold geometrics against royal blue. The midday sun causes us to squint a little and blends my gold-toned wire rim glasses into my slightly upturned face. His posture and expression convey ease and inner independence, as do mine, and perceptible between us is an unstressed vibe of flourishing friendship.

Attuned to my mounting feelings for Thomas, I didn't presume upon his. The picture evokes this too: behind my benign half-smile, I was unreservedly beaming - with contentment. I had no designs on pressing the friendship's direction beyond the marvel it already was.

Back home after parting from Gretchen, enough of the day remained for Thomas and I to enjoy our regular music time. These sessions invariably provided a satisfying capstone to the days' outings; both spheres augmented the harmony I felt between us. That evening marked the halfway point of my time in Germany, an equation I relegated to the back of my mind: three full days in, three to go.

I was in this don't-let-it-end frame of mind when Thomas and I took the hour's train ride to Koblenz the following morning. It was Sunday, just the two of us again. On each day's excursion, at his side and thanks to his kindness, my astonishment never faded at the *anciency* all around. (I like the archaic term.) That year my home state of Wisconsin celebrated its sesquicentennial. One hundred fifty years becomes marginally less impressive when everywhere you turn in Europe, you encounter antiquities hundreds or thousands of years older.

Sunday's day trip promised further variations on the theme: Koblenz is among the oldest German cities (as are Bonn and Cologne). It's also the site of the one natural wonder we visited. Our first stop, however, was Ehrenbreitstein, the second largest preserved fortress in Europe, constructed, like the Cathedral, over hundreds of years - with origins dating back to 1000 CE.

Measurements of altitude are difficult to fathom, so when I learn Ehrenbreitstein is perched seven tenths of a mile up the Rhine riverbank, it doesn't help take me back there. My pictures remind me we rode a ski-style lift and toured the stronghold unguided. What comes back clearest is that traversing the sprawling grounds felt like an expedition in itself. Stoney sand pathways walled by an artful patchwork of brick and stone (the interlacing of centuries) drew us from one courtyard to the next along curves, corners and passageways, and through arched gateways with hinged iron-spindle barriers held open for tourists.

A few years ago I happened to read *Moby Dick* for the first time. There Melville names Ehrenbreitstein as a metaphor for fortification. It marked the first time I'd met the appellation in print since I stashed my captioned photos decades before, and it drew a gasp of recognition - one of many such startlings through the years. I still react that way to surprise encounters, visually or in print, with German landmarks I got to see, the Cathedral above all. It gets me every time.

On outings with Thomas, I occasionally amused myself by snapping furtive shots of him, from a short distance and outside his view - some while he himself took photos. A couple classics of the genre are in my Ehrenbreitstein pages, a trivial diversion to note in conjunction with the locale's most striking feature: the spectacular view of the waterway.

I haven't said enough about the River Rhine. Well, I could never say enough about the Rhine! Majestic, breathtaking, enthralling - these echo descriptors plenty of writers have applied. All true, yet they don't quite get at the River's effect on me, an oddly intimate, profound and enduring one. In my mind's eye, I'm seeing myself looking out over the River - absorbing its magnificence and beauty into my being. I remember trying to make the sensation itself into an amulet I could wrap my fingers around and never lose, so that my stunned tears could nourish my spirit again whenever I imagine myself back there.

There are other majestic rivers, just as there are awe-inspiring cathedrals besides Cologne's - but *this* is the one I got to *feel*! More than that, I felt it alongside and because of a cherished friend I met purely by chance. Thomas could have been from anywhere, but because he came from *here*, I got to experience the Rhine every day I was with him.

At Koblenz the Rhine is joined by the Mosel River, forming a confluence. The point of land between the two rivers is called the *Deutsches Eck*, the German Corner, and the high riverbank which attracted the fortress builders provides an astounding view over the dramatic natural attraction. There are other river confluences; this one instantly became *mine*.

I can't say how long Thomas and I stood looking down over the confluence, arrested by the riverscape on that mild day, beneath thin gray clouds that coasted along with just enough breaks between to leave the sky bright. The barest breeze made me mindlessly brush away the same stray hairs from my face time after time, never detracting from my sense of awe.

After we broke ourselves away, we rode the lift down and hopped a bus across the bridge to the opposite bank. From a busy Koblenz street, we sauntered along the walkway out to the Corner. On that day, players batted a volleyball on a sand court near the point - captured in my photo album, watched over by the enormous monument of Kaiser Wilhelm on horseback.

A scrap of conversation from that hour would congeal into a lifelong memory, word for word. As we strolled around the tip of land, I didn't grasp how my sense of direction and perspective had become momentarily unmoored. In the distance, the shape and shade of a structure I didn't recognize caught my eye, intriguing me. Gesturing in that direction, I asked Thomas, "What's that?"

I will never forget his eyes as he focused on mine when he answered. His mellow expression matched the evenness in his voice: "That is where we have been."

It was Ehrenbreitstein I pointed to. Recognizing my "error," an intense feeling of foolishness - all out of proportion, rooted in age-old insecurities - washed over me. It must've spilled onto my face, despite efforts to suppress it.

His stilted syntax still reverberates - but not as loudly as his gentleness with my fleeting embarrassment. My inner disquiet evaporated with the pale drifting clouds, replaced with consolation that only my old self-consciousness had precipitated it. I perceived not a shred of even playful mocking from him, only the constancy of kindness. He wouldn't, of course, have made light of my feelings; the point is how perfectly his natural response fit what I needed.

I love to ponder that day, living out my friendship with Thomas at the corner between two rivers. Much would follow to entwine us further, for a time; you already know we couldn't stay that way. But once waters intermingle, they're never the distinct streams they were before, even if they later diverge.

All our experiences, entwinings that come and go, become part of who we are - the places, the friends, the lovers. They ripple through our stories long after the partings. Before I went to Koblenz, I'd never heard of river confluences; there, I was *living* in one - dynamic and magnificent as the natural wonder.

THAT GLORIOUS YET WRINKLED WEEK

For all the wonder that never left, all the images etched, some finer points have faded. This retelling, as predicted, is recovering some mini-scenes even before I break into the Box. But it's also giving rise to confusion over a particular link in the chain of events. I'm starting to think my subconscious may have tinkered with the story at the margins in a way I hadn't accounted for, massaging memories outside my volition.

Since the perplexity bears on my time in Germany, I'm not sure it'll be cleared up by the printouts - I hope so. It concerns Thomas's relationship with Gretchen.

Early in our email acquaintance, Thomas said his girlfriend had recently moved out after a few years together, and that they were on civil terms. When I was introduced to the quiet dark-haired Gretchen at the meeting, and when she joined us for Saturday's sightseeing, it didn't throw me. As you've read, I appreciated the chance to interact with her, and told Thomas so.

On Monday, she joined us again. That was the day Thomas and I returned to Cologne for CD shopping at Saturn; I'd forgotten we met up with Gretchen afterward and went to the cinema. *As Good As It Gets*, which I'd seen at my local theater, was my favorite film. (It also happened to be the in-flight movie on my way to Germany.) I was delighted to watch it, subtitled in German, as a trio.

After the movie, Gretchen came with us back to Thomas's place. Shortly after arriving, the two of them - speaking in German, of course - got drawn into a serious discussion, so I slipped upstairs to my room to give them privacy. I didn't understand a word but sensed their agitation, and soon overheard the exchange develop into an unpleasant argument. Waiting alone, I became increasingly uncomfortable - for my sake and out of concern for their upset. I honestly don't recall whether I suspected their point of contention could've had to do with me.

Eventually their voices quieted and Thomas came upstairs to tell me Gretchen left. I never saw her again. He offered no explanation; I didn't expect one. My old notes show we proceeded with our evening - cooking supper, looking at pictures, listening to music.

The isolated, short-lived incident was never explained, and I didn't keyword it in my daily chronology. It was the only time that week I felt real anxiety. Until this writing, my retellings have never mentioned it.

As I pause, however, to leaf through neighboring pages, I'm caught off guard by a jarring discovery. Before I elaborate, let me tell you about me and notebooks.

My practice for storing thoughts on paper has sometimes been not exactly linear. (These days I take most notes digitally.) When the impulse would strike - to make a list, sort out a problem, muse over an idea - I'd flip open a notebook to any virginal page and have at it, if not in paragraphs, then in bullets of incomplete phrases, always finishing off with the date. The burgundy storehouse which accompanied me to Germany contains jottings from before and after the trip (some unrelated to it), and only a few written while I was there.

Now a half-filled sheet far from the keywords page snaps me to attention and roils disjointed recollections, unexpected emotions, fresh questions. Dated Monday, August 3rd, 1998, its contents show me working through agitated thoughts - possibly written while Thomas and Gretchen argued. My jaw literally drops when I come to one phrase: "drawn to someone already taken…" Evidently I had inklings about them I later suppressed. If I was confused about their relationship then, it's hardly surprising I'm befuddled in the present.

The amazing and glorious week, it appears, was not without its wrinkles.

Castles and Cafes

It was impossible to process that summer's events, as they encased themselves in my heart over time, without ordaining certain interpretations of what happened. Some of those meanings and memories, I'm coming to realize, may need reconsidering.

Others won't. There is nothing unclear about how I felt as the week wound down. By Tuesday I could no longer ignore how soon the goodbye would come - all this was almost over. But I dearly missed my little boys too; the yearning to return to them churned incongruently with wishing I could stay.

A swirl of sentiments leaks from my eyes. When I used to rehearse emotional songs with my sister, we'd sometimes pause to give in to tears. Getting the feelings out beforehand helped us to not choke up on stage. Something akin to that happens as I approach the coming chapters. Every so often I need to set the laptop aside and *go there* for a while, and then I'm ready to take up the thread and go on without drowning.

On the morning after the brief unpleasantness between Thomas and Gretchen, dawn broke on my last full day in Germany. Thomas and I filled our Tuesday to the brim - starting with a train ride to Königswinter, the city on the Rhine nearest the Drachenfels, or Dragon's Rock. On a ridge atop the thousand-foot hill rest the remains of a 12th century castle, in fragments of stone walls and rubble. One fragment is taller than the rest, visible from miles away. Locals call it *Backenzahn*, the Molar.

The railway took us most of the way up, leaving about 200 feet of elevation to reach on foot along a black paved path. I remember our leisurely pace on the curving, climbing walk which took us under a couple of stone gateways and offered a glimpse of "wildlife" along the way: a few woolly dark-brown sheep grazing off to one side. As I recall, we didn't take terribly long exploring the summit's ruins. I blame it on the Rhine. The River below engrossed me anew, and I dared not squander my final opportunity to drink in its enchantment from this lofty perspective.

Also visible from the ruins, on the hill farther down, was the castle Thomas and I toured next, actually a late 19th century private villa styled as a palace. Elegant, complete, opulent - everything the Molar wasn't. I remember my astonishment at its decor's extravagance and time-travel quality; its exterior profile looked exactly like a fairytale castle. The most practical souvenir I purchased on the trip was a cloth tote bag imprinted with that image. Far deeper imprints would be left by two more adventures that afternoon.

I like the word *adventure* for the next stop we made. Making our way back down, we came to a cafe alongside the path and went in for a snack. That's it. The adventure was in the conversation.

My single snapshot inside the cafe shows four small tables, tablecloths and chair pads coordinated in light maroon; we were the only patrons. A half height wall, wide-paneled in pine, divided ours from a second dining area, its ledge so broad it was lined with potted plants. Dark wood crossbeams supported a low ceiling, which between them was covered with a fancy lattice-patterned wood of a lighter tone.

We sat facing each other, always such a delight in itself. My notebook tells me I ordered kuchen, a custard-topped German cake.

On that sunny afternoon, in an empty hillside cafe at Königswinter, over unrushed dessert and coffee, Thomas and I had a wholehearted talk about us. I wish I could tell you every word. In truth, I can't distinctly recall even one. And yet, they resound so deep in my being I can reimagine their essence for you faithfully.

I went into the conversation quietly ecstatic about our comfortable companionship. Any notion of openness to more, were it even possible, was held so tightly in reserve I barely acknowledged it to myself - preferring to accentuate what I was already grateful for. This would be the occasion, I sensed, for facing the fact together: I would have to leave the following day.

Thomas's introverted nature coexisted with a quality of

plainspokenness. A quiet man, when he did speak his words were simple, direct, and the product of forethought. I had this in mind when he spoke first, and I hung on every syllable as we looked straight into each other's eyes:

"Tomorrow we will need to leave for the airport at 8 in the morning."

"I can hardly imagine having to go!"

"I have enjoyed having you here."

"I can't even begin to say how wonderful it has been for me."

"You are special to me, Katherine, and I hope our relationship continues."

"I want that too, Thomas!"

"Then we will see where it goes from here."

Tilted head and puckish eyes complemented his dulcet cadences.

Now, if I were attempting to write fictional dialogue, I hope I could do better than that. But with my archeological dig into heart-memory, I mean to reflect our genuine styles of expression. Were Thomas to read this, he might remark, "I would not have worded it that way." I can only trust I'm not too far off from what he'd remember feeling.

Whatever the exact words that tumbled out and where else they took us, they unambiguously affirmed how much we enjoyed being together and expressed hopes for building upon our bond. I remember we both spoke freely and openly, yet didn't use the word *love*. It wasn't an explicitly romantic exchange - though a lively warmth radiated through me, and does again as I relive it now. Our attraction had deepened in person; verbalizing this to each other passed a poignant milestone.

On the way up the hill, our growing mutual fondness was as yet unuttered. By the time we descended, these feelings were out in the open. The evolution felt natural and exhilarating - as if a spinner of tales were hiding in the bushes whispering, "Of course."

ϓ Chapter 9

River of Dreams

O ur cafe colloquy was followed by an adventure *from* Königswinter.

Thomas and I cruised the Rhine!

Until this moment, I've never framed it this way: our riverboat ride, taking us *home*, could not have more perfectly punctuated our heart-baring talk.

Oh, the simplicity of it! Of wordlessly looking out over the water while we floated together through it. How could I know that very simplicity would bring forth the deepest, sweetest emotions pouring out of me now?

There were no racing thoughts, no angsty bracing myself for leaving. No keyed-up wild elation either. Just the widest possible wakefulness to the gifts of the moments as they passed. The timeless tranquility of the Rhine, the sunny warm day, the nearness of the dear friend I loved.

Thomas and I stood abreast on the main deck, right at the bow, for the entire two-plus hours - I didn't keep track of time. The River rippling beneath and stretching out ahead, I occasionally stared straight down into the water, enjoying the intentional disorientation. I'm seeing now the steep sloped banks dotted with castles and quilted in angled rows of grapevines - the mental playback borrows and blurs scenery from riverside train rides. Yet the most emblematic visual, repeated often and preserved in a snapshot, is of Thomas's smiling sideways glance when I turned my face to look up at his.

(A neighboring album photo resurfaces a forgotten trifle. Remember Melville's mention of Ehrenbreitstein? On our River ride, we passed a novelty vessel painted to look like a whale and lettered *Moby Dick*.)

The vastness of the Rhine tempts me toward the phrase *at sea*. It doesn't fit, of course, but neither does it sound right to say, *After we'd been at River a long while...* Thomas pointed to Bonn as we passed it. The next major city would be Cologne, but I was so in the moment - wakefully serene, alive, floating! - I wasn't watching for it.

With shimmering clarity I recall idly eyeing the horizon - when there it was, my Cathedral! I was wholly unprepared for the sensation. From far off its dual spires were unmistakable, together with the scalloped outline of the Hohenzollern Bridge over my River. I felt a surge of belonging, attachment, *homeness.*

Only later did I comprehend all that these feelings betokened. That instant of recognition enfolded who I was becoming, who Thomas was becoming to me - and the powerfully improbable origin story behind both. The moment's rush of sentiment, an intangible souvenir, would

prove inseparable from the fascination with travel the Thomas story became forever intertwined with.

The picture I snapped of the Cathedral as we glided toward Cologne - my heartbeat picks up as I replay the approach - preserved exactly what I hoped it would. One week earlier I'd caught sight of Thomas for the first time, already a beloved confidante, already a part of me. I knew nothing of the Cathedral he would give me, but by the time I spotted it from the River, it had become a part of me too.

We came ashore at Cologne; the train took us the last leg home. It was dusk when we got to Thomas's place for my last night there. In a single day, we'd gazed down at the Rhine from the Drachenfels, toured a fairytale castle, expressed our feelings for each other, and - buoyed by the freedom and release of that - we got to feel the River up close for hours. And the evening was just beginning.

Every time I reprise the adventure, at exactly this point the same thought re-arises. My experience with Thomas that week vindicated all my reasons for choosing to go to Germany. This was, in one sense, the highest gratification of all.

In my photo album, the snapshot of Cologne's skyline from the Rhine rests beside the bedroom picture I snapped the morning I left his home. How ideal. Thomas's gracious welcome there remains as revered to me as my adopted River and Cathedral. And yes, now that it's nearly time to write about leaving, you just caught me calling it *his* home.

Save Tonight

During the time away from my sons, my sister assured me by email they were having a blast with the neighbor family. My anticipation of reuniting with them fluttered furiously with thoughts of how much there would be for us all to tell. At the same time, it was becoming harder to imagine parting from Thomas and from Germany.

I keep saying this, I know: being together in real life only deepened my feelings for him. On my last full day there, I learned Thomas felt the same. Gone from my mind were misgivings over his Gretchen quarrel the late afternoon before - dissipated into irrelevance by dawn, then supplanted by our tender cafe talk and cruise home.

Back at the house after our enchanting day, Thomas and I contemplated our final evening while we prepared supper, the sublime followed by the mundane. Well, even the mundane was sublime to me. With evening closing in, our time together was winding down. I had trouble conceiving how my heart would withstand the next morning's farewell.

My notebook's keywords for Tuesday skip from *boat* to *night*. No annotation as to meal or music - nothing else until Wednesday's *flight*. The interlude that played out in the hours between would become more cherished than any other. Remember the first uber-highlight, when my eyes met Thomas's at the airport? The evening I'm about to recount comprises the second.

Thomas and I settled in the corner of the sofa, near the garden's picture window, leaning cozily against each other - our first real physical touch. In time he snaked a long soothing arm around my shoulders. In that position we simply rested in silent lucidity.

It's impossible to summon the scene, to fully reenter it, without dissolving into tears - but these are not solely tears of joy/loss, of love remembered, of nostalgia. They are translucent with the inexpressibility of having *felt* at that *depth*. If there were any single interval of my life I could make last forever, it would be this one, with its supreme comfort and profound connectedness.

Neither of us spoke for a long time. I expected, as I'm certain he did, we'd eventually retire to our individual rooms to rest up for the following day's difficult parting. But until then, togetherness was all we needed or wanted.

Evening's shadows rolled in, progressively seizing territory over the room and over my thoughts.

I'm pausing at this line to listen keenly to the silence.

I wonder which of us broke it.

Here in the midst of this full-hearted serenity, pierced with the awareness it could not last, we opened our souls.

One of us probably said, "What do we do now?" - and then we talked and talked as we snuggled, imagining a future together. We parsed hurdles and hardships, posed questions and broached issues that had not become seriously relevant until that day. In this unguarded exploration the mutual ease I'd felt with Thomas in writing reached its highest expression in person. How far we had come!

Miles had been traversed just since Saturday's photo-moment at Aachen, and the door Thomas and I unlatched at the cafe a few bright hours ago we now threw open wide in the living room half-light. What would it mean to care this deeply for each other? We faced the prospects squarely. What did we each desire and believe possible - and what were the ramifications of our answers?

How I wish I could replay the night and its discourse with flawless recall - but I can draw only from the repository of imperfect memory.

Like an airplane awaiting an open landing strip, our conversation came to circle over twin fields. For Thomas and I to dare try for togetherness, only two impediments left us in the air - but they were doozies.

Paramount was, obviously, the distance, the fact that we carried out everyday existence on separate continents, 4,000-plus miles in our way. The other hindrance arose from our dissimilar beliefs. The first was *our* problem; the second, strictly speaking, was mine.

Wasn't I getting a little ahead of myself there? Before I explain, it will help you to know that in my faith group of the time, the notion of casual dating was frowned on. Relationships were treated from the start as a sort of screening process pointing toward marriage. Unless you could imagine yourself permanently working out as a couple, you backed off and stayed just friends.

Thomas and I were undeniably more than friends. He saw no need to agree on beliefs, yet tried to understand my convictions on that point. At issue was the compatibility of Thomas's atheism with my evangelicalism - not the *fact* that we differed, but rather the implications, an example of which was at hand in our pleasing sensual closeness in that moment. You'll recall I'd set myself a limit before I went to Germany, believing full physical intimacy was to be saved for marriage. Well, cuddling with Thomas I now grappled with whether I could consider marrying an atheist.

Up to then, I'd never *not* held that couplehood ought to be formalized by marriage and that the commitment must rely on some measure of commonality as to faith. That evening, I was trying to figure out how to apply these principles to this new context.

Thomas's lifelong and non-strident atheism generated, in itself, no discomfort for me. It sounded perfectly reasonable as he characterized it. Not only did I enjoy everything about him, I was sure I'd never met anyone - religious or otherwise - more kindhearted and authentic.

He displayed nothing but respect toward my points of view, as I did toward his.

"Do you think I will go to hell?" he asked.

"No, I don't..." was the reply I remember. I elaborated in some way I don't. I'd evolved beyond the literal-hell fundamentalism of my upbringing, but as for what I did believe by then, I must've fumbled in my attempts to articulate it, leaving something unclear.

As I recall, our conversation in shadows spent fewer words on the distance dilemma, maybe because its solutions seemed even more remote.

Dusk had darkened into nightfall, and our talking petered out. Neither of us expected resolution; it was astounding enough that we'd aired all this. Nothing was left to do but revel in nearness while we still could.

We stayed nestled together in the quiet, still and speechless. I listened to heartbeats and breaths in the dark. Outside, the early August elements were calm and toasty as we were. I wonder if the plumeria scent I wore wafted enough for Thomas to notice it. As desperately as I wished otherwise, my glowing wristwatch kept ticking - I refused to look at it. We each waited for the other to stir and head upstairs, but neither of us ever did.

All too soon, dawn lit up the picture window, finding us still wrapped together, and rudely reminding me of what had been blissfully blotted out by sleep.

KIND AND GENEROUS

My resplendent week in Germany, the incredible culmination of our chance crossing, was near its end. The adventure with Thomas was not.

A far-fetched story brought us to this moment; we were well aware our future hopes were far-fetched too. We'd blanketed them with hours of words in our evening colloquy - now spoken, not written.

The bond itself, the comfort of our togetherness, required no words, cliche as that sounds. I've lived a long time since, and simply waiting out that night, close and quiet, remains the sweetest, most beautiful thing I have ever experienced.

In the brightness of morning, when I finally headed upstairs, it was to pack my belongings and ready myself for leaving. That's when I snapped the bedroom photo, bed still made.

The day following my return flight would be Thomas's birthday. Before going down to the kitchen where he was already dressed and brewing tea, I scribbled a few lines in a card I'd brought from home and surreptitiously tucked the envelope into the frame of the bathroom mirror. For all the crispness of that micro-memory, I don't recall my lines or what the card looked like - I wonder if Thomas still has it. What I wouldn't give to know what I wrote.

Groggy and somber, we ate our usual breakfast with little conversation.

To lessen last-minute time pressure, we'd squared up financially the day before, when we disembarked from the cruise. There'd been no trouble arriving at a figure, neither of us being fussy about the numbers. He was, I knew, being more than generous in this and so many other ways. I remember how sunny it was at the street corner ATM in Cologne, where he hung back a few steps while I pulled out my credit card to withdraw the German currency.

Feeling pleased with my planning skills as a rookie pond-crosser, I waltzed up to the machine - and was promptly stymied. The credit card was accepted, but I'd neglected to note the PIN, ignorant it would be required. This was the first cash withdrawal I'd ever attempted. I only used the card for in-store and online purchases - maybe even for a set of screensavers once.

Mortified about appearing careless or clueless to Thomas, above all I didn't want him to have to wait until I figured out how to reimburse him from stateside. I knew exactly where the code was in my home files - after all, I was so on top of these things, right? It hit me maybe I could get my sister to retrieve it. A phone booth was nearby (remember those?) and, mentally calculating the time difference, I dialed Deb, muttering, "pick up pick up pick up."

She did! It was late morning in Wisconsin and, on summer break from classes, she gladly zipped over to my place; when I redialed her minutes later, the PIN she provided was my rescue. In short order, the alarming hitch was easily dispensed with.

Had Thomas and I saved the ATM stop for departure morning, the fix wouldn't have been so easy; it would've been middle of the night for Deb. Now we had one less task to concern ourselves with over our final breakfast on our final morning together. Maybe if I stop saying *final*, it'll avert the tears making it difficult to see what I'm typing.

It's easy for my mind's eye to see Thomas and me leaving his home. He set down my suitcase, turned and locked the door behind us, and we started down the walk. I asked him to give me a minute to snap a picture of the facade - the photo that precipitated a gush of tears decades later.

Nothing about the train ride to Düsseldorf is with me. The screen is blank between waiting on the train platform near his home, on yet another sunlit day, and ambling together through the airport. We would've transferred trains in Cologne, giving me a final glimpse of the Cathedral (oops, another final) - easy to imagine, but I can't honestly say I remember. It's gone.

If in writing this book I hoped to discover a formula for how intense feeling influences recall, well, it's not working out. Clearly some moments laden with emotion became for that reason accentuated in memory. But with others - passing the Cathedral the morning I left Germany, for one - it makes no sense that the experience became obscured by clouds. After all, my inner response must've been intense. Photographs plainly aid in cementing some memories, yet trivial flashbacks remain despite not being thus memorialized. I surrender.

Remembrances of our second time at the airport are deeply imprinted and readily resurrected. There were extraordinary sweetnesses in my final hours (there I go again) spent with Thomas.

He intended to stay with me, of course, until I boarded. We'd allowed ourselves ample time so we wouldn't have to rush at the airport. Were our imminent separation playing out today, we would check-in online before leaving Thomas's place and confirm the departure time. But in 1998, we didn't learn until arriving at the terminal that my late-morning flight would be delayed by three hours. Wonder of wonders! A reprieve, temporary though it was. Bleary eyes suppressing tears, my dropped-jaw grin couldn't have adequately conveyed my elation at being granted a little extra time with Thomas.

We wandered around some, though no shops or attractions interested us. Eventually we landed at a small square table where, once again, we sat face to face, raw-hearted and grateful. I don't recall having a snack or drink; I do recall him reaching into his tote and sliding several items across the table toward me.

Thomas presented me with gifts! I was stunned. The thoughtfulness they reflected overwhelms me to this day.

First were two chocolate bars, one for each of my boys. (I still have a folded wrapper among my shoebox keepsakes.) Next were German coins he thought Sam and Ben would like too. Europe was set to switch to Euros soon and these Deutsche Marks would become obsolete.

Last, Thomas gave me a CD. Not just any CD - the musical discovery that had instantly became my runaway favorite. I'd been intent on buying it at Saturn Records, but as you'll recall, they were out of copies that day. Now Thomas gave me *Slade In Flame* from his own collection! I still remember gasping and choking up; I'm moved to tears now. It remains my most prized memento. The best gifts have nothing to do with monetary value - it's the *knowing* of the person that makes them priceless.

As the time for togetherness dwindled, there remained one more task I'd set for myself. I wanted my last souvenir to be a picture of Thomas and me at the airport. With my old-school camera, this required the involvement of a third party. (Cell phone selfies wouldn't become a thing until several years later.) I began scanning the scramble of travelers for someone I might ask to snap one.

Back when we discussed languages by email, Thomas told me German students studied English as part of their secondary education. This came to mind when I spied a pair of older teen girls chattering nearby in German and whispered to Thomas why they'd be the first I'd approach. Looking impressed, he said, "You are very clever." I swelled with pride - the converse of my abashed moment at the German Corner.

Until I began writing this scene, I'd never thought about why my German companion didn't make the request himself. Maybe my bold side preemptively deferred to his introversion. I only remember him leaving me the mission of recruiting a photographer; I was probably too distracted by his compliment to second-guess his reluctance.

Our airport farewell photo is another perfect capture. I'm staring at it thinking of our relational ascent in the four days since the Aachen shot. Its optics are hardly pleasing - harsh lighting, our backdrop a bank of Lufthansa kiosks along a drab wall - yet it's beautiful because this time we're not just side by side but entwined, each with an arm around the other's back.

Me in jeans and maroon t-shirt with my college's logo, Thomas in his ever-present ensemble (t-shirt untucked this time), our tired eyes and weak smiles hint at how poorly rested we were - for reasons I couldn't have been more euphoric about.

The wall clock behind us reads ten minutes to two, a retro timestamp proving the picture was taken shortly before the delayed departure, since my shoebox itinerary gives the original takeoff time as 11:20 a.m.

With the loudspeaker's blare that it was time to board, no further reprieve was forthcoming. I don't remember the height difference inhibiting our impassioned embrace - a far cry from our airport encounter eight days before - as I held on with all my strength for as long as I could.

It could not be long enough. At last we loosened, stared into each other's eyes one last moment, and whispered goodbyes as I turned toward the gate. My god, how I loved Thomas!

I walked *away* from him and *toward* everything else I loved back home. Every few steps, I glanced back to see Thomas watching me - until we couldn't see each other anymore.

I Wish the Real World...

That was it.

In my mind I'm seeing nothing but a white wall. A bright blank barrier as of that instant sealed off the deepest sweetness I'd ever known.

I've never bought into fairy tales - but my week with Thomas came close. My character in this tale, though, wasn't helpless or distressed. No, I was a joy-filled independent woman who got to venture to an enchanting faraway land. Met and respected by a man of kindness, together we reveled in the *knowing* of each other. And its physical expression is what I had to leave behind. Despite daunting obstacles and the pain of leaving, when I parted from Thomas that day, everything else about our romance felt thrilling and hopeful to me.

Only a single recollection of the long flight home, from the first minutes after takeoff, is still with me. The wave of emotion that accompanies recounting it - I'm trying to unscrunch my face, to keep typing through watery eyes - merges with a craving to understand why the feelings are this strong after so long. Maybe it'll become clearer to me in coming chapters.

On that airplane, I found myself in a deluge unlike any I'd ever cried. Sure, I'd wept with woundedness years before when my marriage disintegrated, and often choked up with wistfulness over my sons' milestones as they grew.

This was different. The unrestrainable torrent was let loose by reflecting on the blissful presence with Thomas - and knowing this plane was taking me away from him.

Ensconced in the window seat, torquing my frame so I could push my face right up to the pane, I hoped my inundation wouldn't disturb seatmates as I suppressed the sobs the best I could. As a further measure toward isolation, I placed the radio headset over my ears. While I waited for the plane to lift off, my heart quaked and shoulders heaved. I blocked the side of my face from view with a hand clenched around tissues.

The song playing in the headphones might've become a discarded detail were it not for this uncanny lyric: *I wish the real world would just stop hassling me.* Matchbox 20's fluffy pop song became forever embedded with those wrenching tears and memories - aren't they so often the same thing?

My river of tears displaced defined thoughts. Staring down through the glass, constantly wiping my eyes, I could not tear my gaze from the ground. Gray buildings and green trees shrank and dropped from view as I watched Germany fall out from under me.

That visual, with its real world soundtrack, loops on my mental screen as if it lasted hours rather than minutes, and it's the third of the four uber-highlights of the adventure. So much was contained in it: becoming and discovery, attachment and farewell - and the up-in-the-air-ness of it all. The only certainty was the longing that could not be fulfilled.

The crossroads and its bounty came about because of Thomas, but they weren't tied to him alone. My all-consuming upheaval came down to this: Would I ever see Thomas or Germany again?

PART THREE
Back to Email

MY WORLD IS A FLOOD

The rest of the flight back from Germany is gone, along with the ride home from the airport. In the early evening of Wednesday, August 5th, I arrived back at my apartment, where my sister waited with my sons and their cousins for our tender and gleeful reunion. I saw them through fresh eyes and took such delight in their excitement, all of us bursting with stories.

I presented the boisterously ecstatic boys with souvenirs - matchbox-size metal cars with German lettering, one a green and white police car, the other a red firetruck - along with the chocolate bars from Thomas. (The cars are in my shoebox too.) Hard to say which they enjoyed more.

Spent from reuniting, ready to call it an amazing day, I emailed Thomas to let him know I'd arrived safely, that the boys enjoyed his gifts, and that we wished him a happy birthday.

Wet weather greeted my return and continued into the following day. Why would I remember that? The August 1998 newspaper clipping in my hands (stored with the shoebox) describes the downpour. More rain fell on my hometown in a 24-hour span than had ever been recorded. On my first morning back from Germany, the boys and I woke to the worst flooding in our area in generations.

At least three feet of water flooded the basement of my sister's home; the water that covered her street came within inches of flowing through her front door. I lived in a split-level building consisting of four apartments, the lower two partially in-ground. Ours was an upper unit. The downstairs neighbors had to evacuate; we didn't. Next to the computer desk where I composed emails to Thomas, the large window facing the field out back now overlooked a watery expanse. Our next door neighbor Duffy got out his little fishing boat and rowed Sam, Ben and other neighborhood children around what had been his well-kept yard - the predominant flood memory our family shares.

My emailing with Thomas in those first days back would've been replete with updates on the once-in-a-lifetime catastrophe, but from those messages I can give you only a single quote, and it had nothing to do with the flood. It's not even a full sentence - just his signoff: "Luv, TH." It was the first such declaration from either of us, and I clearly recall gasping, tearing up, and springing from my chair to happy-dance.

The other major development of the time I remember less vividly.

A misunderstanding was uncovered that we'd both been oblivious to. The passages I can muster only in murky outline are among those I'm most impatient to locate in the Box. The best I can do for now is surmise that Thomas alluded to our being unable to be a couple, that it confused me, that I asked him to explain, and that he answered by citing our final evening's conversation. See? Pretty cloudy. Something I'd said - maybe about being with an atheist, or in the jumble on the hell question? - came across as closing the door to a romantic relationship.

My mindset as we snuggled and talked had been the opposite, but now I learned my ruminations had come out muddled. Yes, I was pondering aloud the relevance of certain tenets I held, in light of our being more than friends, but I thought I'd conveyed by my transparency that I was open to continuing the love story - while *I* worked out things for myself. My landing point was that I hadn't landed yet.

With the crossed signals exposed, it took only a little trouble to untangle them. How well I remember both the short-lived alarm and the profound relief.

Another reprieve!

The revelation cast our final airport moments in a new light. Thomas didn't realize I was open to staying sweethearts; I didn't know he thought I wasn't. He was saying farewell to me *and* to romance. My farewell was filled with tantalizing hope *for* it.

The way my heart quivers as I write suggests it won't be easy or peaceful to reread those emails.

Even Walls Fall Down

With the clouds cleared, Thomas and I took steps toward the dream of seeing each other again. We had to find out how far our serendipitous encounter would take us. I felt sure the strength of our feelings would enable us to find the common ground to satisfy my spiritual boundaries - and to cope with the ocean between us.

We weren't children. We'd lived long enough to know we needed to keep our heads in the midst of our in-love-ness. Yes, I'm aware of the presumptuousness of *we*, but this I remember, and the emails will prove it.

Thomas planned to visit me over the holidays. Spending an extended amount of time in Wisconsin with me and the boys would give us a better idea as to real-life compatibility. He aimed for a three-week trip, three times as long as I'd stayed with him. I remember being impressed by his rational process, probably because I thought the same way.

Just now, a new memory flashed to mind - of hearing him repeat that rationale over the phone. As soon as I got back, we arranged a live talk, by landline, my first ever international call from home. We probably waited for the flood's upheaval to subside, then set a time when the boys were away. I have a clear image of myself with the receiver up to my ear, in my bedroom where the phone jack was, thrilling to Thomas's voice from afar.

I remember joking that I was smiling so wide he could hear it. Since long-distance charges were metered, we limited ourselves to twenty minutes. I bet he dialed, now that I think about it, to save me the expense. Another crystal clear recollection: as we ended the call, I blurted, "I love you!" - and he quickly echoed, "I love you too."

When we next spoke by phone, we touched on the earlier call's wrap-up. I so enjoy this remembrance, because I saw it as indicative of a kind of radar we had in common, a heightened sense of verbal dynamics. We agreed that uttering "I love you" creates a momentary pressure to reciprocate. We, on the other hand, loved each other *and* wanted to free each other from convention and veiled demands. How lovey-dovey is that?

Our brief phone calls amounted to mere backdrop to the relational strides we took through email, as before. We spoke once more, I believe, when the boys were around to say hello if they wanted; by then they understood Thomas was my faraway sweetheart, and seemed to get a kick out of the idea. Knowing my sons, only the 9-year-old would've chosen to speak to him.

After finishing the paragraph above, I checked whether Sam (now in his 30s) recalls this. He texted back, "It happened! I thanked Thomas for the Haribos and Milka bar." Sweet confirmation - and I'd forgotten Thomas's gifts included gummy bears.

I could hardly wait for him to meet my sons and experience our family life. Planning for our Wisconsin rendezvous ran parallel with trying to dismantle the obstacles we'd named. Deliriously in love, yet intent on facing all aspects realistically, we worked at the pressing issues involving faith and distance. I suppose those email conversations alternated, as before, between funny and serious - I only remember the seriousness.

We contemplated whether one or both of us could live partial years abroad. This would've been a formidable dilemma for me given my sons' split time with their dad; they were just too young. Even if I could've stomached putting that distance between them for months at a time (I couldn't have), the idea would've met legal resistance, just as I'd have resisted if I were in their dad's position. Unfettered by parenthood, Thomas could consider such an arrangement with fewer complications. Additionally, during his upcoming visit he could test the feasibility of working at his software job from abroad.

As for the divergence of beliefs - the other ocean between us - that obstacle rested on my own shoulders to hash out.

Heaven Is A Place On Earth

My faith dilemma pointed to a truth I could not fully comprehend until much later: Thomas had become part of my story at a sharp point in it.

A keener comprehension of the wider physical world and the world of ideas, bestowed by my recent college experience, had provoked questioning about how I would move through them both. What did I see as my core identity, what did I really believe, where did I hope to be headed? These were coming into focus in newfound contexts. Some answers drew on inherent traits recognizable since childhood. Others pointed to leanings now up to me to chisel and refashion as I pleased.

All of this was in motion when I went to Germany. Now, writing about the adventure ossifies that summer's exact stage of becoming, a time-bound composite of identity and experience. An educational toy from my sons' boyhood comes to mind: a rock tumbler. In 1998 I couldn't know which of my planes and corners weren't through being tumbled and polished. I met Thomas on one of the angles.

I returned home with facets of self affirmed in ways I could not have predicted, and aglow with deep urgent love for Thomas. But faith was an important facet of my identity too - and I wasn't sure I could smooth the edge between.

The notion of entering a union with an atheist created inner dissonance, as I've described. While resolute in my convictions, I was also an evangelical in flux. My beliefs were already moderating, but the process was incremental, and each gradation looked like a landing to me.

On our last night together, Thomas was clear about his desire to pursue an intimate relationship, and he understood that for me - we were merely what-iffing - this would mean eventually getting married.

Not something he would need, he said, but he wasn't opposed to it for my sake.

Now back in my everyday life, it was up to me to work out how I could say yes to him - yes to what *I* so desperately desired. The binary choice before me, as I saw it: discard long-held precepts altogether or persuade Thomas of some bare-minimum kernel of faith.

I debated exhaustively over what that kernel would need to be. Precisely what would I ask Thomas to accept so as to quiet my spiritual conscience? Hearing myself tell it now makes me squeamish. I counter this with a dual reminder. First, evangelicalism by definition insists adherents try to win others to their faith. Second, more critically, a reluctance to toss one's convictions aside for an untested relationship is, in principle, a good thing. I was doing the best I could with who I was at the time.

I couldn't have known I would soon lose Thomas regardless.

Striving for integrity in the throes of romance, I arrived at a stripped-down pair of tenets I hoped Thomas could bring himself to avow, one of which wasn't even strictly Christian. The first was the soul's existence after death, the second that Jesus was divine. If he could muster this sliver of overlap, I assured him, no other faith-oriented discrepancy (such as differing on social issues) would block our pairing from my perspective.

I thought I was being so minimalist, but now I know how very much I was asking.

Naturally, I sensed the problem with trying to change someone, even with laudable loving motives - and mine were certainly mixed (though not entirely consciously). Let me reiterate: to my mind I was taking the soundest approach, given what I genuinely believed. I admit feeling desperate; I was in deep. Love and hope urged me on. No doubt the desperation was evident to Thomas, a pull that could not have felt entirely pleasant to him.

Thomas's conviction was equally firm that he couldn't generate beliefs he wasn't actually convinced of, no matter how fervently he wished for us to work out. Religious faith, he'd explained as we walked along a Cologne street, never felt relevant to his life. He recalled feeling this way by age twelve, affected by the realization that the Cathedral's claims to house supposed saints' relics couldn't be logically or scientifically supported. How could he take seriously their other claims? His nonchalant atheism was summed up with a shoulder shrug and these words: "I just never felt I needed to be led." The theme of that casual July talk between friends now became central to our impassioned missives as summer faded into fall.

There were other topics, none as consequential. The faith question's bearing on our future came to overshadow everything. My fondest hopes hinged on it.

WHICH FLOWER'S GONNA GROW

The position I'd staked out was rooted in self-respect and honesty, and it expressly honored the same attributes in him. I never doubted Thomas. We fiercely hoped to be together, but neither of us would sacrifice our principles to get there. Ironically, having these qualities in common was one sign of compatibility. Yet clouds were gathering.

Inwardly working through complex feelings, I unburdened myself to my sister and closest friends. All offered versions of this: *No matter how much you love each other, if you throw away your beliefs for him, it won't work out in the long run and you'll regret it later.* That was my fear too. Still, I felt driven to take my advice-seeking beyond my immediate circle.

I turned to two outside resources - one from my faith community, the other a past connection from college. An analogy will help explain why I chose them.

The fundamentalism of my early life could be likened to growing up in a secluded corner of a huge mansion. The walls of the small space delineated all truth for me; I didn't know there was a whole house beyond that room. Gradually, well into adulthood, I learned of stairs and hallways leading to other wings, religious ways of thinking vastly different from mine.

Of the people I looked to for guidance in my Thomas quandary, Jerry represented an outlook somewhat closer to the corner room. A counselor and pastor who'd helped me through the dissolution of my marriage six years before, his counseling emphasized making open-eyed choices and owning the consequences.

Before I made the decision to go to Germany, I consulted with Jerry, half expecting him to warn me against it. I explained my plan to meet a man I'd befriended through email, and was surprised and thrilled he didn't attempt to dissuade me. He was, instead, supportive - with gentle urgings to be as prepared as possible, clear about my desires and expectations for the experience. I felt freed by his confidence in my judgment.

Jerry's advice, now that I was deeper into the relationship with Thomas, would carry just as much weight. As I dialed his number, I harbored hopes for that same sense of his blessing. This time, however, he was far more cautioning. Appealing to the biblical injunction against becoming *unequally yoked*, he assured me marrying an atheist would fit that passage's meaning. His level of concern made him uncharacteristically declarative: "You don't want to put yourself in that position."

Years before, it was at Jerry's urging I first considered higher education. The other person I now consulted for input was the president of the college I attended as a result. Dr. Black was as deeply passionate about faith as Jerry - but his was a version of Christian belief that flung the windows wide open, threw its arms around those of other faiths or none, and valued truth wherever it could be found. He embodied the notion of emerging from the corner room and exploring the house, coming into the sunshine of a more welcoming way. As a dedicated student at a smaller school, I had opportunities to interact with him personally, despite his high position. Now I was eager to hear his take on the Thomas question.

My phone conversation with Dr. Black left me spinning. Though I'd been away from college over a year, he took plenty of time to listen and truly apprehend my situation - and his advice was the opposite of Jerry's. He warmly encouraged, "If you love each other and find yourselves psychologically compatible, I think you should see where this goes. And don't try to convert him; let Christ's winsome character in you draw him... Go for it."

Well, you can guess which counsel I preferred to heed.

But I was afraid of being swayed by what I *wanted* to be true, and determined to be circumspect apart from what my in-love heart so deeply longed for.

Now I think I should've given more credence to desire itself.

In both voices I heard their engaged personal concern for me. It weighed heavily, in the end, that my history with Jerry was longer, that he'd guided me so astutely before.

After much soul-searching, I wrote Thomas to explain why I couldn't see myself bending further than I already had, despite my imperishable love for him. To my mind, not pressing for any distinct system of Christian belief struck a sort of balance between Jerry's and Dr. Black's perspectives. To Thomas it still meant I was insisting on something he couldn't give me.

Like a jump cut in a movie, my memory skips to a single scene that autumn - alone in my apartment, trying to prepare a meal, unable to concentrate. I'd just received a message concerning Thomas's upcoming visit, and I was reeling. All at once I became so engulfed in sobs I crumpled to the kitchen floor. My most dearly longed-for dream was falling apart.

The email from Thomas said, "Please don't urge me to come."

The Finale

The hardest part of writing this story involves confronting my role in how it ended.

Reflecting on any ending you didn't want stirs up tears and regrets. But this one's jagged little pill (hat tip, Alanis M.) is bound up in the choice I made over the faith difference. I'm sure this partially accounts for why it's taken years to return to the Box, unable throughout to explain or contain the story's abiding emotional intensity.

It isn't a question of not getting over it. I accepted and understood why the relationship ended. Later regrets over *how* it ended are a separate matter - I'm so sorry, Thomas!

Only in distant retrospect could I know that at the singular moment of intersection with Thomas, a critical element of the woman I was becoming was still under construction.

Now, rather than holding onto the story, it seems the story holds onto me. A fuller apprehension of all the adventure imparted - the taste of romance, of seeing the world, of being true to self at a high price - sinks in with a sweetness that hurts like hell. Why should that ever go away?

Thomas thought it best, he said, not to go through with visiting me, and with that our final reprieve was over. Although it was I who'd erected a barrier, I think we both understood the impasse arose from a common aim: to live out our convictions as authentically as we knew how. Our love was strong. Strong enough, we agreed, to set aside romance and re-embrace the writing friendship it had started from.

When I walked away from Thomas at the airport, he thought my beliefs prevented us from pursuing couplehood, a misconstrual we cleared up as soon as I got home. A few more months of loving each other by email found us in precisely that position after all.

My heart couldn't help but nurse the tiniest hope that over time something about how I'd articulated my faith would click for Thomas and make our dream possible after all. But I put the subject to rest - I didn't want him to think I was out to change him. We all know I was.

The reason I know the next scene occurred in November is, you guessed it, because of a song. *November Rain*, its lyrics and melody lines rife with aching regret and self-talking acceptance, became forever emblematic of that late autumn for me. Thomas and I were settling into an email rhythm I felt sure could last, but hardly any memories from the season's correspondence remain. A single sentence from Thomas obliterated them with its impact.

He wrote to say Gretchen was expecting his child.

I would quote his exact words for you if I could, but they're gone. I'm picturing him hunched over the keyboard in his computer room, weighing how to word this bombshell. As you'd expect, I instantly started doing the math, but I didn't need to. Thomas added they'd been intimate before my visit. And anyway (I reminded myself), we'd agreed before I went there to keep it platonic.

Since Thomas and I had broken up - a term we never used - nothing stood in the way of his committing fully to fatherhood. It just made sense Gretchen would move back in. They didn't intend to get married (he quoted a motto of hers: *Don't marry, be happy*), but rising to the life-changing occasion could, I surmised, reignite their relationship, and would of course limit his availability for correspondence.

When Thomas called off his trip, I didn't think my heart could hurt any deeper. I was wrong. I knew this turn of events with Gretchen meant a whole other dimension of ending. Maybe we would keep trying to remain friends, but hardly any door could slam harder on us ever being a couple.

It was a jolt I anguished over - yet without ill feelings toward Thomas. He'd given me no reason to doubt his candor. I knew the pregnancy was unplanned on his part; I had no way of knowing as to hers.

In the process of naming and reckoning with obstacles, during our sublime night together and later by email, not once (as I recall) did Gretchen come up. On reflection, I'm left to wonder where she was in Thomas's mind while he and I conversed in the dark about our prospects. If he was torn, I couldn't tell. I know how happy and relaxed he was that night and in pictures I took that week - and I'm reassuring myself there's no way I'd have let my heart float away without signals from him.

I'm not sure when the irony hit me that my favorite picture of Thomas and me was snapped by Gretchen.

This next detail I've never disclosed to anyone but my sister. It was such an absurd move on my part, I'm reluctant to raise it. But unless memory misleads, I'll be confronted by it soon enough in the old emails. It may reveal my thinking wasn't as sound at this crushing time as I liked to believe.

Since the pregnancy was unintended, as far as I knew, I thought Gretchen might contemplate terminating it. I couldn't see letting that happen if Thomas wanted the child; I offered to adopt the baby. I don't recall how he replied to the radical proposition, only that it was made moot by their plans to co-parent. An authentic gesture, to the best of my self-understanding and recollection, it amounted to a wisp of a wild idea and nothing more.

To cope with all this, I fell back on my spiritual life, not so much for comfort - it was too soon to expect any - but purely to get the anguish out. As most intensity of feeling does for me, this involved music. The scene I'm preparing to paint represents the last of the uber-highlights, the mental freezeframes which epitomize the epoch.

You recall, of course, the instant I recognized Thomas at the Düsseldorf airport. Passing the last night together on his sofa is the second, and the third is crying my eyes out as my plane lifted off for home.

These congealed through retellings long after we were over. Only later did I notice an unexpected symmetry. My first sight of Thomas is not paired with the last time I saw him. Rather, its counterpart is the view of Germany from the plane that took me away; I loved them both. There is a parallelism too between the quiet heaven of our final night and the cacophonous grief when my cherished dream crumbled for good - an experience I've never put into writing until now.

One November day, alone in my apartment, I was dancing to blaring music for release, crying cathartic tears. I don't recall the song or band - a memory-gap I take as a measure of the moment's intensity. Stepping and swaying, rivers cascading from eyes squeezed shut, I was wailing at God, "But I *love* him... I *love* him... I *love* him!" In a maelstrom of mourning, the bellowed I-love-hims converted, seemingly outside of my volition, into "But I love *you*... I love *you*... I love *you*!" - as I collapsed to the floor in heaving sobs.

It's the closest I've come to a mystical experience, as though the desire and heartache I felt over Thomas were in essence expressions of deep spiritual longing, an ecstatic and painful brush with the Transcendent. So I interpreted it at the time.

The Fade-out

If I'd set out to concoct a fictional drama, I doubt it would've occurred to me to make my character give up her beloved on principle first, and *then* twist the plot with a pregnancy, when romance was no longer in the cards anyway. But it sure felt dramatic as I lived it.

The drama was powerful too in what I'll call the grief scene. I never experienced anything of the kind before or since. Its salience dimmed over time though, replaced by acceptance and healing. I had drawn my line; Thomas was now on the cusp of his own new adventure, and I had to let go. The scene slipped into the past along with the whole fantastical life-chapter. I did let go.

Unlike the stark white wall of the airport parting from Thomas, my screen fades to variegated grays after Gretchen's announcement. We kept the emails going for a time; brief and sporadic messages tapered off to nothing after the baby came. Our story came to an end like an old screen powering off, the image condensing into a black speck before it disappeared.

All these years since, I still see my life after the Thomas affair in brighter colors than everything before. Our stories are shaped not only by *how* we tell them but by *when* we tell them. As we're prone to do, I supplied this one's meanings and interpretations retrospectively. You know those optical illusions in the shape of a grid, white bars against a black background? The brain fills in dots at the intersections which aren't actually there. This book and the distance of time are helping me distinguish the events from the dots I imposed to fit a pattern.

On a rare rainy day in Germany, I waited with Thomas for a train. He preferred to hang back under the shelter to avoid getting wet. I stayed out alone on the open platform, swaying to my inner energy, loving the feel of the drizzle. A song that came out a year later (*Midnight Blue*, Lou Gramm) always takes me back there, with its rhythmic vitality, consonant chords and wistful lyrics. In the midst of hopeful declarations to a driving beat, the pace slows and the instrumentation quiets for this:

> *Things could be different, but that'd be a shame cuzz*
> *I'm the one who could feel the sun right in the pouring rain...*

Yeah, those are dots on my grid.

I've always been grateful our unraveling brought no animosity. That was a natural byproduct of who we were, when we were, in circumstances as they were.

My heart got broken, but Thomas did not break it.

Our romantic adventure, beginning to end, played through without an angry word or a kiss.

And, my god, the laughter and sweetness between! You'll forgive my silly Thomas-twist on Tennyson (maybe I wrote this in an old email)... Better to have loved and lost than never to have loved a tall.

Laughing again through tears, how can I not marvel to think that if the screensavers hadn't glitched on my cheap computer, none of this would have happened?

VOLUME II
The Box

PART FOUR

An Inventory

STIR IT UP

The idea for how to write this book sprouted from the Box.
Its archaic email printouts hold the origins of my encounter with Thomas, and now that I've told you what I remember, I'm braced and ready to reread them.

Why do I say it's a huge thing I'm about to do myself? After all, I'm in little suspense about the story's ending. (People still watch *Titanic*, don't they?)

It's because I won't be able to go through those messages without feeling everything again. Just typing that sentence is making my eyes spill over. And the sweetness stings as deep as the bitterness.

OK, maybe not. A cursory glance at the Box's treasures tells me why I will keep going. The supreme delights - irrepressible grins and giggles already rising - will be well worth the rest. Besides, now I want my spotty memory's voids filled in more than ever.

My eyes land first on a non-email artifact: a card-stock mailing envelope with a German return address. It must have all really happened! Next I bend back a manila corner to peek at the tech support request that started it all and catch this: "Please respond - you're my only hope." Theatrical much?

I'm literally chortling, overflowing with amusement at these mere tastes. There's no way I'll be able to keep from throwing myself into this whole messy exploration. But that's all I can handle for the moment.

As affecting as it was to revisit photos and mementos months ago, the experience will pale in comparison to reading the emails. Our adventure was launched by the written word - it's how I first *met* Thomas. To relive those very words, well… now I'm choking up and bracing again. The sheer volume of pages, with the decibels of emotion, mean the emails will take exponentially longer to review. I'll need to pace myself.

There. I've taken a breather, and now I begin the herculean endeavor in earnest.

The Teal Folder

The files of printed emails fill the entire Box, the kind that holds ten reams of copy paper - with room for one exception. In front of them is an overstuffed pocket-style folder, dark teal in color, a forgotten repository of Thomas-related odds and ends, including the airmail envelope that got me giggling. It simply must be rifled through before I get to the emails.

Thirty seconds into the archaeological task, a memory is already corrected. Both diskettes are here, the original screensaver collection and the replacement Thomas snail-mailed. But I'd been picturing 5-¼ inch floppies rather than the 3.5" diskettes now in my hands - surely just the beginning of discoveries, corrections, reorientations.

Confirmations too. I indeed purchased Thomas's software with the credit card I later used in Germany. The January 9, 1998 receipt for $25 (plus $4 shipping, from a U.S. distributor's address) displays my full 16-digit card number and expiration date, unimaginable today.

The second diskette, in the airmailed window envelope with a typed note, has a stick-on label with a row of blank underscores for a password. The five capital letters Thomas filled in constitute the only handwriting I have of his. The computer-printed note, dated 18.02.1998 (which this inexperienced American managed to decode as February 18th), teems with Thomas-isms - purposeful misspellings, acronyms, informal hyphenations. A memo line beneath my address announces: "Snail mail a-coming." An explanation regarding expedited shipping closes with, "Less see how long this travels." It's signed, "CU, Thomas."

The eleven photos printed from Thomas's website are in the teal folder too, a little blurry but clear enough to make me smile. Well, I haven't actually stopped smiling since I began this chapter.

Remaining memorabilia crammed into the folder's pockets include Germany-related clippings from newspapers and magazines, cheat-sheets for learning German, humor pieces and comics, scribbled scraps with random thoughts and song titles, and more.

A few prize relics merit highlighting.

Cassettes and Other Witnesses

I forgot about the mix tape I snail-mailed Thomas that spring. A stapled paper bundle in the teal folder brings it back, copies of the lyrics

I typed out - with comments on each of the nine songs - and included in his package. I'm chuckling at how thorough I was: there's even a penned copy of the handwritten note I sent along.

From the note I learn there were two cassettes, the second a recording of me speaking for four minutes. I sure would like to know what I said; maybe he still has the tapes. Look at that - the first song happens to be *Midnight Blue*.

The enlightenments so far feel immensely gratifying.

But one torn scrap obscures more than it tells. Intrigued, I scrutinize it and catch myself waiting to breathe, its meaning hidden behind a memory wall. Scrawled in pencil on scratch paper are the words *kissed you*. The phrase hints at a sunken memory - so deep I'm not sure it's real - of the last night with Thomas. I'm seeing us seated on the sofa, his arm around my shoulders as we rested, occasionally readjusting positions. During one such moment in motion, I played pretend and furtively brushed my lips across his t-shirt sleeve, lightly enough for it to stay my secret.

Only a paragraph ago I was chuckling; now I'm swallowing a lump and dabbing my eyes.

I used to jot notes of things to say in my next email to Thomas; this may be one of those. Near it on the same undated scrap is: *anniversary of the night*. One year from that night we were no longer in touch, so the note must commemorate one month, likely scribbled in early September. Maybe I considered telling Thomas about my pretend kiss. Or... now I'm second-guessing... the note could mean I intended to say I would've kissed him had he asked.

Both explanations feel nice, both feel true. Deepest down, I'm...

right in the middle. And unless the jottings made it into a message, I'll never know.

Also in the folder is a handwritten card from a friend, postmarked December 3, 1998, sympathizing with my personal November rain. She wrote, "I can only imagine this is a difficult time for you…Just thinking about how things could've been brings tears to my eyes… No one can take away those special times, words and feelings shared between you. I hope these memories bring happiness - in time - that will last over a lifetime."

I didn't recall her priceless and prescient sentiments. I close my eyes and lean back in my chair to let them go deep.

Twenty-five years and counting, the enduring memories do bring happiness.

PART FIVE

The Emails Before

CAN YOU HELP ME?

T he Box wide open, I'm finally at the doorway to the world of words with Thomas. The printouts, you'll recall, are divided into months, and the folders themselves preface the story by their comparative breadths - slender at the year's start, thinning again near its end, March through August our thickest, most loquacious months.

Shuffling through the pages, I notice a forgotten flourish of meticulousness. Not content to go by the printed date-stamps, I numbered by hand, in green ink, each email message. Amused now by my cataloging overkill, I must say the green numbers do make working with my paper pearls easier. That wasn't all. On each email header, I highlighted the sender name and date in yellow. For longer missives, I penciled keywords in the white space to denote topics covered. All this careful archiving makes me think of packing things up after the death of a loved one.

Clearly I sensed the story's lasting impact well before I stashed away its remains.

Email message #1: January 13, 1998. Here it is!!

Using a help form in the software, I began:

Dear Screensaver Programmer Person: Please help me!

In my stunned decades-older hands I hold the simple note, customer to company, that kicked off the whole improbable story.

Only as I'm typing these paragraphs does it occur to me I'm composing them on January 13, 2023, twenty-five years to the day since I wrote the line just quoted. Like crossing paths with Thomas, this too is entirely by chance.

My request for assistance was informative, if a bit melodramatic:

It seems to install fine but whenever it's time for the screensaver to kick in, it does so for one second, then kicks back out. I'm using an IBM clone PC, Pentium 150, with Windows 95. Can you help me? I was really excited about these screensavers - in fact, it's the first time i [sic] ever registered a shareware program! I blew $29 and can't get it to work. Please respond - you're my only hope.

It'd been my habit to leave mid-sentence I's uncapitalized, for the quirkiness of it. (Future self-quotes in this book will follow convention.) Signed with my full name, the complaint corrects another data point from my memory-narrative: the exact nature of the screensaver problem.

It isn't hard to picture the easily amused and unflappable Thomas smirking at the overwrought request on his screen. In his user's words I hear (through my eyerolls) someone who sees herself as smart, who is quick to press for a remedy, and who doesn't mind resorting to the dramatic to get it.

Now that I've treated myself to this long awaited morsel - my first words to Thomas - the flavor is tart and satisfying.

Let's see what Thomas's first words to me taste like.

I Will Do My Very Best

My January 13th request, I notice, wasn't printed until March 13th. Rifling through upcoming folders reveals that all the emails through mid-March share the same print date. Evidently I decided at that point to preserve every bit of whatever this was becoming.

When I submitted the help form, chances seemed slim it would even reach a human. I figured if it did, my courteous urgency might increase the odds of a response.

Not only did I hear back within hours, Email #2 was a thoroughly engaged reply which began:

I will do my very best to get the program working.

I felt reassured already!

The help desk technician had copy-pasted my pleading salutation, then added his comment. He continued taking my sentences one at a time, addressing the cost concern upfront:

Nothing's lost - you can get your money back if the program doesn't work on your computer.

Next he took his hopeful user through a numbered set of suggestions, ending the page-length message:

*Thank you for your detailed problem report. I never heard of
similar problems with my screensavers. If it persists, please try
to send me more details.*

That was my payoff for including specifics.

He signed, "CU," with his first name. How meticulous, pleasant
- and accessible - this Thomas sounded. I could not have been more
impressed.

I will do my very best to get the program working. Thomas's first-ever
sentence to me plays like poetry now. In his message, I hear someone
considerate and conscientious, brainy but not arrogant, invested in
resolving the problem.

The bland back-and-forth you've just read hides a piquancy for me
that's making my eyes water, blurring my view. With both halves of our
inaugural exchange now out in the daylight after long entombment, I
sit with them a while before I go to the next message.

The third printout shows I hit Send on my reply three hours later.
This time I could address Mr. Tech Support by name:

Dear Thomas,

WOW! Thanks for your speedy and attentive answer!

I described the unsuccessful results of following his steps, with
none of the earlier frustration in my tone, appeased by his assurance
of a refund. I didn't mind working with technical details, since he was
providing such personalized attention.

A warmth spreads through me as I blink at my old sentences,
because they resurrect how I *felt* when I wrote them. They don't just
remind me, they transport me - the way hearing an old song puts you

straight back into a time and place and feeling. The sensation is more potent than I predicted.

In the presence of my 1998 words, I experience again their surprised delight. And as sweet as this tastes, a memory-shadow whispers the corollary: less pleasant emotions, farther in, will be acutely re-experienced too.

But it's early, and I'm enjoying this.

My calmer state shines in the closing:

Thanks again for responding so quickly and personally - kind of takes the wind out of some of my cyber-cynicism. I hope we can figure this out.

This time I signed "Katherine."

And we're off!

Once In A Lifetime

What profound satisfaction to read how it all started!

It was a Tuesday. Our prefatory trio of messages were exchanged within 24 hours. I couldn't have known it was already Wednesday for Thomas when my evening reply hit his inbox.

My next mouthwatering curiosity is: how did our technical correspondence transition into a personal one?

Thomas responded again within hours with steps to "perform another test." He suggested a workaround (requiring use of a password) and probed further:

Could there be a background task that starts at the same time

the screensaver shall start?... Please let me know if the behavior
changes.

Notable in retrospect are the traces of British usage and spelling.

He included two paragraphs about software enigmas he'd untangled
for other users and concluded:

Obviously, neither of these problems helps at all in your case. I
just wanted to illustrate how difficult it can be to solve software
mysteries.

Aha - so Thomas was first to toss in a conversational passage, in
only his second dispatch.

This is significant. I would've guessed I had drawn him out, since
initiating and inviting conversation come naturally to me. I notice too
how he presumed on my ability to comprehend his explanations. (I
only partially did.)

A few days later, I sent results of the requested diagnostics and
informed him the workaround had done the trick, enabling me to enjoy
the screensavers. I cheered:

You did it! Another software mystery solved?

Wait - what? It couldn't have been fixed that quickly. And then I see
what kept the exchange going. He'd succeeded in getting the screensavers
working, but not as smoothly as they were designed to. I asked whether
they'd eventually be usable without the workaround.

A tiny turning point came next - the personal greeting in Thomas's
same-day response:

Hello, Katherine!

Well, that sounded happy - and felt good. He assured me if his current attempts didn't succeed, he would update the program and "email a new file." The message walked me through yet another set of steps and concluded:

Thank you very much for the good and detailed feedback you provided (and for your patience). I'm glad we're on the right track.

I'm feeling hooked all over again. My input was clearly valuable; his spirited opening and his gratitude were my rewards. Win-win.

My message the next day mirrored his greeting and reported that his newest instructions produced no change in the underlying problem. I asked if my antivirus software could be a factor, then closed:

In any case, is this as far as we can go until you send me the upgrade file you mentioned? Thanks again for your attention to this. I've been so impressed with being able to communicate with the program's creator (as I understand it), and by your helpfulness.

Thomas replied within an hour, bottom-lining the situation:

I don't know what's causing this. No more ideas except sending a new DLL. I hope you don't mind receiving approx 60 kB by email!

How could I mind? I had no grasp of that figure and didn't know what DLL meant (the file type). He would send it on the weekend, he said, then recited a rare case where, as with mine, he was ultimately unable to unsnarl a program's malfunction. He added:

Yep - I am the creator - that's my claim to fame. Not much fame yet.
Not much money either. But then it's only a part-time job for me.

There it is - spelling out what had been implied. I remember finding Thomas's know-how and quirky way so appealing, though I'd forgotten these exact words. Now they come rushing back vividly, and I'm grinning again, wide as ever.

That was our tenth message, dated the tenth day since this started. Who knew getting technical help could be this much fun?

It's Something Unpredictable

Thomas's side hustle was my delightful diversion. This morning as I peruse newly reclaimed emails, I succumb to renewed enchantment. How can I help you taste what it's like?

Picture my pillow-propped laptop nudged out toward the knees, at the ready for tapping out thoughts, leaving lap space for the paper portal in my fingers. Nearby a heap of printouts awaits. Noting the date and sender, I begin to read, letting the words take me back into the wonder. With each successive message, little jolts of recognition alternate with sparks of discovery, propelling me to the next. Well into the reading stint, I take notice of the grinning and slow sideways head-shaking I've been doing the entire time. At these moments, I deliberately lower my mouth's corners, loosening my expression to give the happy-face muscles a rest - and consider myself almost undeserving, as eyes well up, of the amount of gladness this is giving me.

I offer this macro-portrayal, now that I've canvassed the opening messages at granular level, because it's time to raise the elevation. That is, I mean to fly you over the unfolding between Thomas and me, descending only for revelatory extracts. To do this, however, I first need to ingest every iota, every sensation, myself.

I'm going in alone.

But not all at once. I'm pulling from the Box in batches - limited groups of emails at a time - to peruse, ponder, and choose what to share with you. The correspondence spans more than a year's time; a straight read-through, without note taking or emotions, would take days.

So far I've read 25 emails, and have written about the first ten. Curiosity gets the better of me as to the proportion this represents. (Yes, I've always liked progress bars.) I paw through to locate the hand-inked numeral on the final printout - and find it unnumbered. None of the emails after my return from Germany have green numbers; I'm mulling over what to make of this.

For one, it underscores I instituted the archiving measures - numbering, key-wording, highlighting - prior to the trip to meet Thomas. It makes sense that after the trip I was too high, then too strained, then too crushed to complete them before closing up the Box.

Well then, let's see how many emails were exchanged in the six months before the July trip: 379. Eyeballing the boxed folders from above, the quantity of post-trip printouts appears to add at least 200 to that figure. Which means... I've made a fine start - with a long way to go.

Our initial exchanges show me this about myself: how bedazzled I was by the written expression of an unpretentiously smart and witty person.

As I relish this thought, I'm distracted by tiny brown spots to the upper left of the printout I'm handling - and then notice they appear on most pages. Close inspection produces an easy explanation: rust. Multi-page messages were stapled together; moisture rusted the staples, and the rust bled onto single pages too. Not long after our ending, the Box was relegated for a time to an especially dank basement. (Other possessions stored there I later found had molded.) In my need to move beyond the story's emotional wreckage, I didn't protect its tangibles very well at first. Only extreme good fortune prevented their ruin - like losing a whole library to fungus rather than flames.

Apart from rust stains, my email treasures remain intact. So far, I've retrieved them in arbitrary quantities (an entire folder too many to handle at once). When I grabbed out the first three printouts, I had no idea they were from the same day.

The batch I'm taking on next goes from Email #11 to #25, through my third week of contact with Thomas. Recollections from this early phase are with me only in shards, and soon I'll be treated to the full context of some of the sharpest.

ORDINARY WORLD

I couldn't have known all I was preserving. Over the years, I've held onto plenty that wasn't worth keeping. Yet, isn't it true in some cases that we fully appreciate the value of something we've kept only *because* we kept it? The words I saved in print built my relationship with Thomas brick by brick, message by message. Now they also allow me to re-inhabit *who I was*, to view myself from the distance of time.

The woman I was bumped into Thomas as he was. I remember us both in pieces. The emails help me reassemble them: my bond with him, my memories, my self.

The side of me Thomas saw at the outset tilted toward histrionics but regained equilibrium easily. What I saw of him first was intelligence and charm. As the screensaver fix became a prolonged affair, increasing familiarity snuck into our technical exchanges. To Thomas's stated plan to email me the updated program, I responded:

> *I think I'm honored or something. As for your fame as the creator, well, it's quite a commentary on the state of technology when an anonymous consumer can communicate directly with the programmer and solve problems. It's been pretty fun for me, and in lieu of the $ you deserve, I will personally do all I can to increase your fame quotient. By the way, I'm curious as to what your "day job" is.*

Oh look, two firsts - a personal question and an expression of enjoyment - on the first Monday in February. My next remark became the setup for a consequential revelation:

> *Since I didn't receive the file yet, I hope it means you took the day off yesterday to watch the Super Bowl. I'm writing you from a town an hour south of Green Bay, so I think you can figure out who I was cheering for.*

Thomas responded:

> *You have the honour of receiving the very latest version via email (but you are also a guinea pig). I live in Germany near Cologne and I haven't heard anything about the Super Bowl. I guess it's the football final, isn't it?*

There it is - the sterling linchpin of the story! I can still see me facing my computer slack-jawed. I've never forgotten that sensation.

This is the first marvel regenerated in print which wets my cheeks, undoubtedly not the last.

What Does That Stand For?

Learning Thomas hailed from another continent was both a surprise and an object lesson in unexamined assumptions. There'd been no reason for locations to come up - until my lighthearted absolution for his delay in emailing the file.

Thomas also addressed my curiosity about his work:

I earn my living working as a software developer. I've seen a program stating, "We don't want your money - we just want your admiration." The screensavers don't pay in terms of bucks per hour, but I also like the appreciation. I ain't complaining - I hope it didn't sound as if I was.

You can add his self-deprecating posture to the growing list of qualities I found appealing.

Thomas's idiosyncratic, unfamiliar lingo - especially the acronyms - took me to our next tangent:

I'm not quite literate in terms of email conventions. Is the CU in your sign-off as obvious as it looks? And to think I've been typing out "see you" all this time. And what does OTOH mean? In context ("OTOH I love to solve 'computer puzzles' - sometimes."), it looks like it should mean "although," but I can't quite unravel it. I guess that's why you're a computer programmer and I'm not.

I closed with a paragraph returning to the technical issues at hand. A pattern was forming in our messages, alternating casual content with problem solving.

His next message opened with a short list, including:

<g> = grin

<eg> = evil grin

OTOH = on the other hand

ROTFL = rolling on the floor laughing

CU = cu

CU L8R = ???

*RTFM = read the f*** manual (I hardly ever use that acronym)*

All these were new to me. His silliness around the CUs made me actually laugh out loud and, along with his signoff ("Hasta luego, Thomas"), conveyed a fledgling familiarity.

After two weeks of contact, all under the email string kicked off by my help request, my reply launched a fresh one. I titled Email #15, "ROTFL." How perfect that the first non-tech-support subject line would be a reference to laughter.

The emails show us becoming acquainted rather rapidly, even before we exchanged much in the way of personal information. My ROTFL message harked back to the Super Bowl revelation:

I was profoundly amused to learn you're in Germany - not sure why. I suppose because it exposed an assumption I operated on without realizing it. How can your English be so flawless if it isn't your first language, but how could English be your first language and you not be aware of the Super Bowl?...I haven't been to Germany, but one of my college instructors grew up there during Hitler's time and I still stay in touch with him.

Thomas replied:

Still in touch with Hitler? Sad chapter of German history. He

thought he was a great painter, but couldn't convince anybody.
He used the BSE technique (Blame Someone Else) and started to
blame the Jewish people for his lack of talent. Too bad he found
another field to claim his fame.

Ok, this guy was entertaining - even on a serious subject.

I'm enjoying seeing how early the banter blossomed. Well matched
as to wit and disposition, Thomas and I clearly savored the frivolity;
it's not too much to say we already *liked* each other.

Our exchanges continued during Thomas's delay in emailing the
updated program. He thanked me for my helpfulness and patience, and
reiterated his intent to get to it "ASAP" (finally an acronym I recognized).
My reply touched back on his earlier label for me:

Hey, happy to help (and even happier being honored)! I can live
with the guinea pig thing. Actually, another reason I don't mind
is I've been getting a kick out of our correspondence, and wouldn't
mind if it continued even beyond the termination of my guinea
pig status.

Wow - I didn't recall saying something like that so early. I do now.
My eyebrows spike as I say to myself, *Hmm, that's putting myself out there.*

Around the World in Eighty Seconds

Thomas had been first to veer from strictly business, on that mid-
January day. In early February, while the screensaver snag couldn't yet
be put to rest (not that I minded), I was the first to float the notion of
staying in touch after they could be.

The casual conversation took off in the meantime.

I observed the coincidence in his "Hasta luego" since I spoke

Spanish; he returned that its main use to him was for saying, "Why do something today if you can do it mañana?" He observed my surname (at the time) sounded "a li'l bit Dutch," and responded to my compliment of his English skills:

I hardly ever speak English. I am sure I have a flawless German accent when I speak. I listen to the British Forces Broadcasting Service quite often - sometimes I even understand what they are saying.

I remember finding his written accent hilarious. And to my delight, that last phrase confirms verbatim a line from the memory-narrative you've read.

Today's rereading succeeds, amazingly, in beaming me back to when this was all I knew of the programmer - a peculiar and pleasing sensation.

My next message took up the surname thread:

Yes, it's Dutch, and more than a little - it's all the way Dutch. However, it's not *my* name exactly - it's my former husband's. As the saying goes, I kept it for the sake of the children (two sons, ages 9 and 6 - the oldest wants to grow up to "make up computer games"). My surname is Danish in origin.

Wow, look at me go.

Thomas had meanwhile finished the screensaver update and, with a separate message string, announced, "I include the DLL for you." He ended a set of instructions with:

I send this message on Thursday, but it should arrive on Wednesday. Around the world in 80 seconds (or -6 hours).

The literary allusion incorporated both speed and time difference. When he clicked Send after midnight, it reached me almost instantly - early the evening before. In the 1990s, this was head-spinning.

At last I'd be able to try the new version - or maybe not? Thomas's message was actually a forward of his original announcement. At the top he inserted the text of an error message from my email provider, rejecting the file as too large, and added:

Got to figure out a different way to send the file to you...Did you ever receive an email with an attached file?

My response opens a window onto that time period, technologically speaking:

I am not on the internet; Juno is all I have for email. No, I haven't received an email with an attached file.

How odd it sounds to have email but no internet; I forgot about that phase.

What followed was yet another technical back-and-forth, over multiple messages. He tried again to send the attached file, split into two parts to evade the file size limit. This time I had difficulty with his instructions. Regretting my own limitations, I explained the steps I'd tried and where I got stuck:

I'm quite frustrated because I feel so woefully inadequate and, well, stupid, about all this. I just wish I knew more. :-(I hope I'm not being more trouble than I'm worth.

My, how self-critical, how quick to sell myself short.

I Get Knocked Down

My fleeting spell of self-doubt blindsides me now - not so much the struggle itself, but the intensity with which I expressed it to Thomas.

He treated my upset with kindness and context:

I'm afeerd your email client software is a bit of a dinosaur. There is nothing wrong with you. I shoulda been warned after Juno rejected the 1st message.

The goofy spelling and succinct consolation helped a lot.

His ensuing technical commentary contained another coding acronym I didn't recognize. But I didn't need to, to get his circular point:

To decode the two messages you have, you will need a MIME decoder. I could easily email you a MIME decoder, but you'll need a decoder to get that program.

With emailing options exhausted, Thomas offered to get me the update another way:

Email is fast and (relatively) cheap. Snail-mail is slow and expensive. I estimate I can post the diskette next Monday, so you can expect it during the next two weeks.

This was February 3rd. Exactly three weeks in - it's so satisfying to put the history together - and there they are, the words behind the airmail envelope in my teal folder.

My response began with empathy:

This has turned out to be quite a production, hasn't it? I hope what you learn from experimenting on me is worth the time and expense to you.

His ongoing customer service was not taken for granted; to this day, I'm glad I told him so. My next segue:

I gotta say this: I'm continually astonished at your familiarity with idiomatic expressions and oddities of English, especially after your claim that spoken English is difficult to understand. "Afeerd"?! I love it!

Since he was acquiring American customers, my take on his English usage was probably good to hear. A further compliment mentioned my boys:

If I burst out laughing, they want to know what's so funny. So far they know I laugh a lot at your messages.

This surely pleased him too - it's central to my keenest memories.

I'm realizing how many nuggets, carried in mind all these years, came from this foundational period. They make luminously clear it wasn't just the technical process that kept me interested. We riffed and sparked off each other's lines, and I was enthralled. Yes, that's what did it - the amalgam of smarts and laughter.

When I was a young girl, I harbored a recurring fantasy, fed by unrealistic tv shows. I'd imagine myself singing out free-heartedly, oblivious to being overheard by some talent scout who would discover me, and then I'd hit the big-time. Emailing with Thomas felt a little like that, like I was being seen the way I wanted to be seen. A stranger with expertise and sensitivity was discovering and appreciating qualities I most liked in myself. That must be why some of the smartest, funniest lines I'm reliving today are making me cry.

I didn't remember revealing the insecurities to Thomas. My response to his consoling shows me working through self-consciousness about having exposed them:

> *I'm not often that hard on myself, but as was obvious, I was quite frustrated. I sometimes flatter myself that I know a lot and then get deflated when I'm completely stymied like that. I suppose it's healthy to get a reality check once in a while. Appreciated your reassurance, BTW.*

It had taken so few words from Thomas, still a stranger, to help me regain confidence; you can see how I leapt from them to disclose even more. Was it something about me or something about Thomas that drew me to share? The answer is yes.

I mean, it was both.

Where the conversation went next I can't tell you yet. I've come to the end of the stack of emails I've been luxuriating in.

We leave this batch waiting for Thomas to snail-mail the diskette. Quite a production indeed, and we're only 25 emails in.

℣ CHAPTER 16

TAKE ON ME

When I laid out this story from memory in Volume I, you'll recall I marveled at the un-layering. The act of conjuring long held recollections brought about the fresh uncovering of buried ones.

Working through the email record, a parallel wonderment presents. With each watched-for passage I encounter in print, a new fragment springs to mind to watch for, one I hadn't previously thought of. Then there are the myriad *un*recalled pieces I meet - some with the *aha!* of recognition, others which stare blankly back at me, stubbornly refusing to return. This holds true for the momentous as well as the tangential. Unpredictability abounds.

It surprised me to learn, as you've seen, that when I began corresponding with Thomas, I wasn't yet on the internet; along with my too-basic email carrier, this explains the need for snail-mailing the diskette. I told him Juno had been "a good initiation for me into electronic communication," and that I would eventually decide to pay for home internet service.

This makes me curious whether that step became expedited because of Thomas. If so, it would've come up in our messages, so I'm adding it to a growing list of what I'll call Strands - tidbits and topics I'm on the hunt for as I work my way through.

Another Strand I'm after concerned the time difference between Wisconsin and Germany. Before then I had little cause to be aware of time zones, especially outside the U.S. A smile breaks out as I recall we had a funny exchange about it, but all that remains is a partial phrase. The current email terrain suggests both Strands must be coming up soon.

Thomas had said in early February to expect his package within two weeks. Today I retrieve a new batch of printouts from the Box, taking us from that message through the end of the month - over twenty more. At a glance, the abundance of staples stands out.

With no technical issues to occupy us in the interim, we continued to converse, recounting essentials of our current lives and backgrounds. In the process, topics of mutual interest arose and expanded, as did the lengths of the emails (hence the staples).

I'm taking a moment amid my summarizing to close my eyes and inhale deeply. Here was the genesis of our shift into the personal.

Caught up in this breakthrough, I'm well aware I haven't given you enough to go on - you'll need illustrations. Hold on, they're coming.

Thomas and I interspersed moments of hilarity with moments of poignancy - and I'm suddenly sobered by a passage I haven't come to yet. All I can summon is that it was a story from his childhood.

Shake it off, keep reading; yet another eagerly sought Strand.

Meanwhile, I notice a shift of a different sort, an internal one relative to the strata of memories. The turn to personal topics in our emails now begins to generate a greater proportion of un-layered rememberings.

While our sheer quantity of words could account for that, I think it flows more from reexperiencing the emotional bond I'd already begun to feel and tried to downplay, doubtful our link would last. I told myself to treat it lightly, enjoy it while I could - don't get too attached, even secretly. Wouldn't I feel foolish when it disappears, with nothing having come of it?

When I shelved the Box some eighteen months later, with indeed so much having come of it, I couldn't know with precision the shape of the enduring imprint on my being, or guess the number of early email highlights I would keep inside me forever.

After all, I could only carry so much.

My old pencil markings on the printouts emphasized what seemed most significant at the time. It feels good to see them match, for the most part, my perspective today.

I'm finding exceptions, though - passages that stand out now, left untagged then. I've decided to add no new markings. I'm not even removing the rusty staples to make photo-archiving the pages easier. I want to preserve these parchments, to the extent possible, in their original condition.

It's as though I'm keeping a museum of memories under glass. And I have so many exhibits yet to view.

Yesterday Was Yesterday

My reactions as I read through the emails are all over the place.

Because I live alone, I'm free to vocalize. While most of the time I'm quietly contemplative, frequently beaming or teary or both, often I gasp, laugh, speak thoughts aloud. On occasion I pump my fist and yell *Yes!* (which the cat doesn't seem to appreciate) at encountering a passage I remembered - or one I didn't.

Wending through conversations that revolved around Thomas's field of expertise produces a unique form of amusement. In a message string Thomas titled FOMM (Friday on my mind - I had to ask, one of his little guessing games), I questioned him about email servers he would recommend. He replied:

> *I think it's good to have a PPP connection to the internet. PPP is a protocol that allows you to use the Remote Access Service (or Dial-Up Networking) of Windows 95/NT to connect to the web. Currently I prefer MS Internet Explorer 4 - it includes Outlook Express (email and news client). You can get it for free from the web, but downloading several megabytes can be pretty expensive.*

That excerpt is lifted from a soliloquy three times as long, with again as many specialized acronyms. I included that much because the freeze frames of 1998 technology are a kick. Here's another:

> *There are computers where people can meet on the internet (known as IRC, Internet Relay Chat). You go into virtual rooms, and everybody in the room can see what you type in. Many acronyms come from this usage (e.g., AFK - away from keyboard). You are online while chatting, so acronyms really can save money.*

Not only was Thomas a fountain of tech info for me, I could see he enjoyed imparting it as much as I enjoyed learning it. He was on the forefront of a revolution I was barely beginning to participate in.

I learned that standard email headers were truncated versions of many more lines of inscrutable text (which he knew how to interpret) when Thomas wrote:

I found my atlas, and found Green Bay. Your messages come from 'm10.boston.juno.com' so I thought you were in Massachusetts. Missed by 8 cm (3") on my atlas.

How funny to think he'd been misled about my location too. (The explanation for Juno's Boston datum was over my head.)

Clearly we each had an eye for detail. When I asked about capitalizing "internet," Thomas answered:

An internet is a network of networks. The Internet (capitalised) is the global network.

He liked to refer to it as the World Wide Wait and explained:

You have pages of formatted text that contain links to other pages. The most important sites on the WWW are the search engines - there must be at least 200! The Internet contains vast amounts of information - much may be trash, the rest is hard to find. And it's easy to get distracted with links leading you to more (or less) related sites that contain links to other sites. That's surfing the Web - you start somewhere, click here, click there, and find pages you never even dreamed of!

It's still the best summation of web browsing I've come across.

Walk On the Ocean

Our points of connection surprised me. Thomas's messages were sprinkled with literary allusions - delighting this English major. He threw in references from American pop culture too. When he explained where he'd picked up *afeerd*, I replied:

> *Well, yes, if you're reading Dickens (one of my favorites), you'll certainly expand your idiomatic horizons. I thought it sounded like the 1800s American West. (Or you might hear it on reruns of "The Beverly Hillbillies.")*

A term in his response gives away our pre-Twitter setting:

> *We can see lots of U.S. TV series, but they're all synchronised (German actors speak German text)… It's pretty funny for me to hear Tom Selleck tweet because his German voice is much deeper!*

Now it's hard to think of tweeting apart from its social media connotation. (Twitter would be founded eight years later.)

Marbled through exchanges in this batch are quotations from Shakespeare, Oscar Wilde and others. I'd forgotten the extent to which Thomas and I met in this arena, how well rounded he came across.

Several snarky asides I also stumble upon in today's reading represent Strands I can check off my list. For instance, I knew Hitler came up again, this time as a source for my impression of German as rough-sounding. Thomas remarked:

> *Hitler was a vertically challenged pygmy - always shouting on top of his lungs! I don't think German is a harsh language (how can I know, I grew up with it?).*

You may recognize that Strand from the memory-narrative; I find another in a conversation about world news. I wrote:

I very much enjoy discussing such issues, and I consider it a privilege to do so with someone "overseas" (that would be you).

Thomas's retort:

You have a wrong perception of "overseas" - I am here and you are overseas!

He'd caught me; the reversal of perspective made me laugh.

The jesting was constant as our emails rounded a corner from business casual to downright sociable. A key turn was set in motion by a bit of boldness on my part. To show you this, a little backtracking is needed.

In the course of early February's exchanges, I noticed Thomas hadn't asked a direct question in some time. Unsure his level of interest matched mine, I backed off slightly, keeping the interaction going but with shorter messages, like this:

Hey there,
More good info on email servers - TNX. No question marks for me to respond to from your message. Heard any good jokes lately?
CU, Katherine

He answered with a few silly jokes - and no questions.

This was just before he'd finished updating the screensaver program. When he wrote to say the diskette was ready to snail-mail, he stated he didn't have my postal address; my response gave it, with not much more. I signed off with a made-up acronym (KIT, keep in touch), leaving him to guess at its meaning. Four days later, he admitted with apologies the snail mail was not yet in transit and assured me "it'll be in the post box tomorrow."

I started the clock on that date - Thursday, February 19th - eager to track the number of days it would take his parcel to reach me.

There - that covers the prelude I wanted you to have. Laying out highlights is tricky because we commonly had multiple threads going. To take one example, Thomas's responses about being overseas, the Internet, and Hitler all appeared in the same message (our 41st).

As of the day his package took to the air, it happened to be me who next introduced a fresh subject. I can scarcely convey to you my glee in rediscovering it. It began with a display of directness I wasn't prone to in person:

Not meaning to be too forward, but have you ever noticed you don't use question marks often? I notice that the couple of times you got info from me, I responded to a statement, not a question. (E.g., "I don't have your postal address.") As Seinfeld would say, "...not that there's anything wrong with that." Go ahead, ask me anything.

Thomas's reply opened with:

Hello! H'are ya?

Oh did I laugh! He hadn't ever asked, which made his greeting uproariously comical. He continued:

Your observation may be true that I sometimes use statements where a question would be more polite. And the statement "I don't have your postal address" is an appellation. How about the following: "Would you mind sending me your postal address?" I could have written: "Please send me your postal address!" (No question mark.)

I was still guffawing as Thomas continued:

Not meaning to be too forward, but have you ever noticed you don't use upper-case letters often?

He was referring to my purposely not capitalizing I's. I replied (putting to use his acronym list):

ROTFLSTCIIHO [rolling on the floor laughing, scaring the cat if I had one]! I think that's the hardest I've laughed since, well, since your last message actually. I enjoyed your levity, since I wondered if questioning your "style" would put you off. I can't help wondering if you are as affable in person as you are in cyberspace. Are you as affable in person as you are in cyberspace?

I remember feeling such warmth in this conversation, so I kept going:

I must question a vocabulary choice, however. You said the postal address statement was an appellation. I checked, and this proud English major was relieved that my definition (a name or title) turned out to be correct. Might you be thinking of "aberration," a deviation from the normal or expected? No need to thank me - it's reward enough to know my college education paid off. <g,d&r> [grin duck and run]

Since he'd mentioned politeness, I went a step further:

My thinking wasn't that you were rude; rather, I wondered if not asking questions meant you had, how shall I say it, um, a sense of yourself as already knowing most everything. Loved hearing that's not the case - your jocularity, as opposed to defensiveness, answered the question. And I was curious whether you are curious.

His response:

Re appellation: I attended a seminar called "leading thru personality" where this was discussed. It means statements that are intended or interpreted as requests. You sent me your address without me asking for it, so I have absolute control over your brain. <g>

Again Thomas had me in hysterics. He included the German term; I now think a better translation might be *appeal*, as in an implied appeal. At the time, I conceded:

Yes, I did interpret your statement as a request, so either it was an appellation or you do have absolute control over my brain. That's where I laughed the hardest, BTW.

MORE THAN THIS

If laughter was the earliest catchword for my correspondence with Thomas, the next was charm. Every aspect of Thomas's reaction to my question-marks nudge hit me as charming.

From that point, it may not surprise you, he asked a string of questions, even closing one message with, "'Nuff questions this time?" followed by a wink. I'd invited him to be inviting; he more than met the moment.

For my part, I understood complying with implicit requests said as much about me as it did about him. This development in our discourse - humorously co-observing the subtext of how we communicated - resulted from exercising an assertiveness muscle I'd lately learned to flex in other areas of my life. Thomas's ready engagement signaled I wasn't the only one finding the email socializing worthwhile.

This was among the exchanges that glided us from mere agreeable repartee toward a resonant meeting of minds and emotions. From the moment this book project first lit a twinkle in my eye, *this* is what I've wanted to see! I longed to comprehend exactly how this crossover came about. Now the fabric of what I did recall can be embroidered with the details I didn't. If someone told me this happened to them, this fulcrum is what I would most want to hear about. Now that I'm here, I am transfixed.

The progression involved lost delicacies I would've never tasted again. I remembered, for instance, Thomas's line about being overseas, but had forgotten my comeback:

Ya gotta believe me: as I wrote that sentence, I *knew* you were gonna say that!

It wasn't the only time I made that claim.

His rejoinder about my lower case i's prompted me to elaborate on the practice I'd adopted the year before:

I determined email was a poor substitute for face-to-face time with friends, and that, as my personal acknowledgement of email's limitations, I would refer to myself in my messages with the lower case instead of capital i.

Thomas's comeback:

So when you speak on the phone you use a capitalised I?

And I countered (you may be ahead of me here):

You don't have to believe me, but I *knew* you were gonna say that. :)

Both boasts underscore a shared wavelength I felt with Thomas. In the same message, I inquired:

Incidentally, do you do this kind of thing all the time - write back and forth to people you don't know, halfway around the world? Cuzz this is a first for me and I'm having a blast.

Thomas replied:

The length of our conversation makes you second to one. I regularly exchange emails with Dave from England - he helped me proofreading my fab screensavers. He's always impressed when I dig up a line from Shakespeare out of the deepest zones of my brain.

It couldn't have been long before I knocked Dave out of first place. I ended that message:

Well, I've had several interruptions, so this has taken me quite a while and I'll have to close now. One particular interruption should interest you: my snail mail came and there it was - a package from you! True story, how about that?! I'll let you know when I get around to messing with the diskette.

The airmail took only five days. I gave him this report the following afternoon:

Hey, here's the big news: By Jove, you've done it! I loaded the new program and I no longer need to use the workaround. Yippee! (I'm easily amused.) All in a day's work for a guinea pig.

The solution I sought January 13th was fully accomplished February 24th. Six weeks, 42 messages.

I didn't recall it taking that long. By then, the personal content had overtaken the technical; it makes sense that my memory prioritized the personal. Our missives had mushroomed into all kinds of themes and threads; the screensaver success became almost secondary. We didn't need to be in touch anymore. We wanted to be.

How to refer to this faraway connection? On the day the package arrived, I signed off:

A cyber pen pal?

Thomas riffed:

Cyber is a hype word - and no pen required! Cyber Keyboard Pal?

Me:

WFM (works for me)! How about "Your Cyber Friend"?

Thomas's next message opened:

Dear Cyber Friend!

Based on a phrase I'd learned from him, I signed my reply:

Your Friend OTOSOTP

On The Other Side of the Pond, I knew whatever term we used, I didn't want this to end. Sprung up out of nowhere, it felt natural, gratifying, *real* - like it just might last. That I remember.

Now We're Talking

I've always thought *if memory serves* is a nice phrase. Smoother than *if I recall correctly*, it implies that an accurate recollection, in a way, does you a good turn. I'm pondering at the moment how my memory serves me. Rather, I'm thinking of occasions when it doesn't.

Earlier I wrote there doesn't seem to be a formula as to memories called back by prompting from the emails. A February message catalyzes this train of thought. Thomas and I were discussing drawbacks of free email and costs for internet service. He provided loads of information, of course. I quoted him as part of my response:

Long time no type. I've been email challenged because of distractions from my real life, such as sick children and car trouble. Back to normal now.

"You have to make your mind up if the internet is worth $120 per year."

Exactly. That's not clear yet. But I'm looking at a job change this summer.

I didn't recall knowing of that job possibility so far in advance. Crucially, I still don't. By itself that wouldn't strike me as unusual, but it's got me asking, What have I been expecting from my own memory? If I'm unable to call to mind, with the data in my hands, this segment from my personal path, why would I expect to recall minutiae of the cyberspace crossing with Thomas's?

Apparently I've had it backwards. I keep finding lost surprises - when the real surprise is how much I *have* been able to hold inside.

These emails where Thomas and I really got going present an uneven patchwork of scraps I still can't recall sewn to pieces that do come flooding back - a sensation that is (paradoxically) impossible to put into words.

Now I remember what I said to Thomas after he'd looked up Green Bay:

I didn't know my messages say Boston. Yes, that's a few centimeters off. About the same as me putting you in France, I presume? I grew up in a town of about 50,000, settled by Germans, so there are a lot of German names, influences, and people around here. My college was founded in the 1800s by German immigrants, so the halls have names like Muehlmeier and Grosshuesch.

Thomas probed:

Could you let me know what you think about Germany? What are the latest headlines about Germany you remember? BTW: I don't have any Lederhosen, I don't like sauerkraut, and I'm vegetarian (so I don't eat wurst, eisbein or other cliche stuff). Most cliches recognised as "typical German" are rather typical Bavarian. You don't think your 'Southerners' are typical American, do you?

I found his analogy between stereotypes illuminating. In reply I spent four sizeable paragraphs describing my perceptions of Germany and where they came from, then concluded with an up-to-the-minute view:

I now think of Germany as a place that would be fascinating to visit, with a more post-modern, less inhibited population than the U.S.

The reference to visiting was entirely in the abstract. Never in a million years (speaking of cliches) did I think I'd ever go there to meet him.

Thomas thanked me for my expansive answer; his request had brought out my writerly side. In comparing notes on our respective countries, our discourse waded into social and historical issues, including fascism and freedom of speech, slavery and reparations, and the Holocaust and Hiroshima. What a stroke of fortune to enjoy this type of stimulating exchange with someone I didn't know and found so interesting.

That good fortune is multiplied now by being able, from this distance across time, to watch these conversations develop. I can make out the undercurrent that would draw Thomas and me toward even more personal topics - and I catch my jaw tensing with anticipation.

Time After Time

Before February was out, the correspondence with Thomas was influencing my everyday consciousness. Just as he'd checked his atlas for my whereabouts, I researched his:

I took a look at my globe today to try to figure out the time difference between us. Correct me if I'm wrong: if it's 7:00 p.m. in Wisconsin, it is noon in Germany, right?

A valiant attempt. We were seven hours apart alright, but I flubbed on which way; it would be 2:00 a.m. the following day in Germany.

To help me out, Thomas went into detail on relative time zones - but used terms unfamiliar to me (GMT, Zulu time). Even today his explanation takes concentration to follow. I give you my shortened paraphrase: "When it's 1 a.m. here, it's midnight in the UK, and 6 p.m. in Wisconsin. On the previous day of course!!!" His exclamation points emphasized the correcting I'd invited.

Now here's the fun part. I tried to reflect back my newly acquired knowledge - and did fine, to a point:

Wisconsin is Central Time, yes, so you're saying if it's one o'clock in the morning where you are, then it is six o'clock in the afternoon where I am, the day before. Well, goodness gracious, that means I was right about the seven-hour difference, but wrong in terms of direction. IOW [in other words], I see the sun earlier than you, not later. Time is a bizarre thing.

Thomas quoted my sun statement and said:

One sentence before, you said you understand that it is Thursday here while it's still Wednesday in Wisconsin - and now that! Wrong direction again!

Ha - there's the Strand I told you of. The only verbal sliver I carried with the memory of my laughter was, "and now that!" I was thoroughly amused by Thomas's mock exasperation; what a delight to relive it.

Next he copy-pasted the full header, explained its data and summarized:

The message arrived in my mailbox at Thu, 26 Feb 1998 22:20:56 +0100 - that's 3 to 5 minutes after you sent it. I read it one hour later.

Amazing. I asked:

You mean to tell me you're up at one in the morning writing me messages?

Thomas:

It got a li'l bit later 'n that. But 0100 is my normal bedtime.

A routine was taking hold for our emailing during the week. After spending early evenings with my boys and seeing them off to bed, my final activity before tucking myself in - the dessert I reserved for myself all day - was writing to Thomas.

He wrote me at night too, and I'd wake to his missive the following morning. One was titled, "The wee hours." Another, sent at his 3 a.m., ended, "It's dang late (or rather, dang early)." I closed my next one, "Lots to say, but my eyes are whispering, 'Close us...'" This was a cyber-friendship that suited our rhythms as well as our personalities.

I remember how Thomas's good-natured intellect had me thinking to myself, *I could be crazy about a guy like this.* I wanted to know more about him.

In our exchange about Germany, I asked:

You not only live there - it's your country of birth, right? Have you ever visited the U.S.? Of all the questions I could ask about you, one has me more curious than anything else, and I don't know why - your age. Care to address that?

Along with his affirmative response, he filled me in on his past schooling and career path. As for age, he typed his full birthdate, revealing him to be six years my junior. His next answer:

I have seen the USA though I haven't been there. (Goat Island, you understand?)

I didn't. On a family trip to Canada as a teen, he explained, he'd viewed Niagara Falls. I didn't know Goat Island, between the Canadian and American sides, is part of the state of New York. Always the clever one.

I thought again of my mistaken assumption at the start - and wondered what else we were assuming. I put the question to him:

> *I gotta say one thing about this email stuff: wouldn't it be true if one is getting to know someone strictly through electronic messages - no face-to-face, vocal inflections, not even handwriting - that one is likely to make unconscious assumptions of what this new person might be like, based on experience with the real people in his or her own life?*

The resulting discussion filled many pages.

It's evident how awestruck I was by the ability to get to know someone this way. I remarked more than once on the phenomenon of words reaching around the world in minutes. In our 46th email, I reflected yet again:

> *I like the opportunity this technology provides for a meeting of the minds, where what we say can be judged purely on what we say, you know? What a treat to do this with someone I am overseas from. ;-)*

I was filled with gratitude. That never changed.

HOLDING BACK THE YEARS

I've long been intrigued with how time shapes people. The woman in these emails, the me of 1998, stands at a far remove from the me of today, dissimilar in critical aspects. Yet, I am struck by pronounced throughlines as well. Recognizing ways I've changed is sobering; witnessing the constants invigorates.

It's a weird yet pleasing sensation, getting my head back into that time. Only months ago, I had not yet opened myself to this experience. Now I am pawing the printouts, fed by their blend of the recovered and the vanished. With all I'm gaining, I become aware of something I don't want to lose *now*: my state of awareness before opening the Box. For so long I relied on little more than spotty snippets and impressions. It's a forgetting I want to remember. I'm not sure why.

Immersed in the old pages, reacquainting with that time and self, I don't want this strange rapture to get diluted along the way. As the ancient milieu becomes familiar again, I strive to approach each email letter from the former mindset, unfiltered by the knowledge of what followed. This may be too much to ask.

Some passages I have no trouble meeting with a fresh eye - my disquisition about Thomas's country is one. Not an especially touching recitation, it's easy to take in with a pretended blank slate. Conversely - and I'm aware how intuitive this sounds - the closer I get to more meaningful and consequential conversations, the harder it is to read them uninfluenced by subsequent experience.

Such is the case with the long discourse I instigated about assumptions. Thomas responded:

> *I think people will always assume something in the absence of facts. What do I assume about you? I guess you're white and 30 +/-5. (Your name sounds Dutch and you mentioned your kids.) The assumptions may be wrong, but that wouldn't make a difference.*

Me:

> *I like how you asked yourself this question, which, yes, I would have liked to know. (Did they teach you that at your seminar? <g>)*

I brought to his attention his use of the word *assume* while he'd also listed supporting data - so not really an assumption. In my case, I persisted, it was data that had led me astray:

I assumed you were located in the U.S. because the software outfit I bought your screensavers from has a NY address. But your adeptness with the language also reinforced my assumption. Most important, I hardly realized I was making an assumption at all until it was blown apart. Do you want to know what mine are about you? I'm finding myself eager to confirm or deny yours about me. But it's not clear whether you want to know.

Thomas:

I did not ask, leaving it up to you to confirm if you want to. Go ahead and smash my illusions and assumptions!

Me:

How gracious and polite of you. One reason I'm enjoying our correspondence so much is I live in an area with few men who show either interest or respect. And of those that do, I know none with whom I share an intellectual compatibility. Not to be elitist: it's just that there has to be some common interest to get past the weather. If I were to bring up Oscar Wilde, most guys around here would tune out and be thinking about shooting the next deer whose antlers he'll use to decorate his cabin. I don't mean to put anyone down with generalizations; that's just the prevailing culture here.

Harsh. My overly jaded outlook was accentuated by having left the college community I'd felt so nourished by. I continued:

You leave me to confirm if I want to. But if you ask me, I could still refuse to answer. Anyway, it's very nice of you, but it's also kind of fun to be asked, if the curiosity is genuine.

Behind those words was a hunger for someone to take more than polite interest, to expressly draw me out, to really *want* to know me.

As a counterpart to his, I gave Thomas a life-outline:

Nothing much to smash actually - you weren't far off. I was born sixteen minutes before my identical twin. I finished high school without parents, and thought I knew so much about life (wrong), I got married. His was a parental-child mindset but I didn't recognize that then. When I showed I wasn't a child, he became abusive. Long story short (a handy acronym candidate!), the 14-year marriage ended in the legal sense six years ago. (He still hunts deer.) A year later I started college, and graduated last May. I'm still flying high about it!

Springboarding from this (much condensed) series of disclosures, I posed a set of additional questions to Thomas, the most probing yet.

As you'll see, he proved to be an attentive reader, ready to reciprocate with disclosures of his own.

Ask Me Anything

My correspondence with Thomas came to share characteristics of a rich in-person conversation. Jumping from subject to subject, taking sidetracks, working around interruptions, circling back to unfinished points. Imagine recapping a long talk you've had with a friend. How much could you replay of its themes, tidbits, turns of phrase? Which essentials would stay with you to ponder and return to next time? You might note highlights for a secondary purpose - journaling, say, or (apart from matters shared in confidence) telling a third mutual friend.

In this scenario, you are the third friend. And I'm showing you how a written conversation turned into a relationship.

By the time the impetus for our encounter was no longer at issue, Thomas and I had dubbed ourselves cyber-friends. Now we were swapping backstories and personal revelations, a layer at a time. I followed my life-synopsis with this:

Please feel free to ask me anything you want. And if I ask you anything you don't care to answer, just say so. Are your parents still alive? You didn't mention marital or dating status, or orientation - would you? I assume you are unmarried and that you may have a significant other - go ahead, smash away.

The more I learned of him, the more I wanted to know. Since we'd begun by happy accident, it wasn't hard to imagine it ending, likely by some circumstance disrupting his availability. That concern, it's clear now, informed my relationship questions, although I would've been curious either way.

Given the distance, I knew cyber-friends was all we'd ever be - but I *really* liked this guy. Best to get the whole picture, tamp down irrational imaginings.

Thomas's response accomplished exactly that. They also contain one of the most sought-after pieces of information from this entire project. He wrote:

Few questions that allow a long, long answer. Orientation? I'm an atheist, but I still pay church tax. Or did you mean orientation in a different sense? For me "appropriate sex" and "opposite sex" are synonyms. My special one (SO) moved to an apartment of

her own in December. She's been living with me for four years [...]
We'll see how our relation will carry on. I ain't married, never
was, and I don't currently date.

He'd been mostly correct about me; I pretty much nailed it for him. He even re-termed *SO*, attaching a phrase more affectionate than the common *significant other*.

In playfully addressing orientation Thomas introduced the subject of beliefs, which I hadn't asked about. Isn't it ironic (you're singing it now, aren't you?) that it came up from him first?

Equally full of portent is Thomas's account of the yet unnamed Gretchen. My jaw drops at this Strand above Strands, his level of detail catching me off guard. The ellipsis is mine, to leave private her reason for moving out; his tone hinted at annoyance.

This is an enormously consequential correction to my memory-narrative. The clear implication was their relationship hadn't necessarily ended - but at some later point, I must've mistranslated the moving out into breaking up.

Learning so soon that Thomas was involved with someone would've thwarted any ridiculous ideations on my part - just as I'd less than consciously fished for. As I stare at the rust-stained page, my old reaction replays: a faintly deflated, shoulder-shrugging oh-well.

Today though, this encounter with Gretchen is shaking me up, making me queasy. I need to sit with this, work through it, let my heartbeat slow back down. I've known all along to expect surprises; this revelation is an earthquake. I'm inclined to consider this particular trick of memory/forgetting as deeply significant.

As I told you, I've been attempting to bring my 1998 mentality to these emails. Had I been able to abide by that dictum with this 45th message, I'd be feeling only mild disillusionment at hearing about Thomas's SO. Epic fail.

Yet that somewhat unrealistic objective is helpful for gaining broader insights, and here's one now. As my sense of connection with Thomas deepened, trepidation rose, which points to a lifelong pattern. Whenever I start to feel attached to something satisfying, I anticipate its loss - and try to steel myself against how bad that will feel.

In the case of forming friendships, this manifests as an inkling that even though we seem to click, the other person will tire of me and back away without explanation. Seen in that light, an explicit appeal I made to Thomas several weeks in was unsurprising. I listed topics I hoped we could get to - and then proceeded to show my insecurity:

If you ever get sick of all this, would you tell me so, rather than to just stop emailing?

I have a natural inclination - which fights against a learned inhibition - to volunteer info. Would you please be brutally honest and tell me if you think I'm telling you more than you care to hear?

Thomas:

To be honestly brutal, uh, brutally honest: I am glad to receive your emails! I'll let you know if you ever touch a topic I do not want to discuss.

Me:

You had me there for a second.

His reassurance warmed me, as did his way of couching it in faux warning. It's a perfect example of a Strand I well remember only after seeing it again. I followed my entreaty with an observation:

The most important way that email is distinct from other communications, I think, is in the "risk" factor - or more precisely, the lack thereof. Do you know what I mean?

He didn't, quite:

Direct conversations provide feedback, so you can realize if the other person is interested. Is that what you call "risk"? To bore someone?

He was on the right track. I did mean that - and more.

Far Away and Personal

To me, there was less at stake in getting to know someone by email rather than in person. This was, it's worth reiterating, years before online dating became common - and that's not what we were doing.

To explain, I painted an imaginary scenario:

You're right that it has to do with direct feedback, and could be related to boredom. Let's say we met in person, and I judge by the interested look on your face that this could become a friendship. If at some point I delve into something that turns you off or gives you reason to not want to get together anymore, I will experience feelings of rejection.

This reads today as obvious to the point of condescension. But I was setting up a distinction:

OTOH, if you write me now and tell me you don't want to discuss such-and-such, or more likely, you don't respond to the topic, or - as I might consider cowardly (unless your computer broke down or you were in a coma) - you just stop writing altogether with no explanation, would my experience of rejection be the same? No.

Well, that was blunt - and it indicated an emerging theme. I gave this reason for the claim:

You don't know what I look like, I'm not likely to ever run into you (a real possibility in a town the size of mine), and somehow, I just haven't psychologically invested to the same degree in hopes for future communication.

That was true enough to a point. I continued:

If you decide to stop messaging, I'll feel a sense of loss - not earth-shatteringly huge, but some. There's almost zero implied commitment in this kind of conversation. The lack of risk over email means I'm not too worried about you deciding I'm not worth conversing with - I'd wish it weren't true, but life will go on. I'm talking about platonic relationships, not necessarily romantic ones.

I was sincere, yet now this smacks of protesting too much, of erecting an internal safeguard against how earnestly connected I felt.

And then his response made me feel even more drawn to him:

Falling in love always bears the risk of rejection. And friendship also bears the risk of rejection.

In contrast to my wordiness, Thomas got straight to the core. His lines topple me again like an ocean wave.

Our steady movement toward a *knowing* friendship continually interlaced joking with seriousness and progressed organically, in steps beautiful to witness anew. His personal unveilings tacitly invited me to do the same, while he urged me to speak up if anything he said made me uncomfortable. Likewise, when I posed penetrating questions, I encouraged him to let me know if he preferred not to "go there."

So far, he always did - want to go there, that is.

ϒ CHAPTER 19

I JUST WANT YOU TO
KNOW WHO I AM

Thomas and I meshed so well that I wasn't fully perceptive to the difference in our communication styles. That is, I didn't initially see it as such. It was my way to ask questions outright, his to put forward thoughts as an implicit appeal to share mine. When I did become aware of this distinction it didn't break my habit of looking for question marks as a fundamental measure of interest.

Today, with a keener comprehension of such subtleties, I'm struck by how often Thomas was the one to advance the relational momentum.

This is a major discovery.

For all my anticipations of what I might reclaim from this exercise, this eye-opener is of a kind I *didn't* contemplate. It's a whole other level of satisfying to see that Thomas took as much or more initiative as I did.

Of course, I'm leading up to a prime example. In our 47th missive, Thomas wrote:

> It would be good to know more about you...Lemme provide some "technical data" here. Once again I leave it up to you to return the information you consider appropriate.

Following his thoughtfully tacked-on reminder was this catalog:

> Blond hair, normally a beard (I don't shave very often), grey-blue eyes, 189 cm tall.
> Photos available at [his website's URL], aka the rogue gallery.
> Religion: none. Not a member of any political party.
> Member of BUND (German section of Friends of the Earth International).
> Vegetarian (another topic to get back to).

I remember being pleasantly startled by this. Interesting how he bundled the physical description with intangibles, and that he did so (contra my memory-narrative) with zero prompting from me.

I reciprocated in paragraph form:

> Like you, I'm blonde and blue-eyed (but no beard). What would five feet be in cm? Nothing else out of the ordinary. Since I'm not on the Internet at home, I can't look up your photo. Why would you have your photo on the Internet? For your business?

The questions bring home how early in the internet revolution this was.

Immediately following his list, Thomas addressed my earlier query about his parents:

My parents are divorced. My mother got married again and I had to live with a step-father and two step-brothers for seven years (until I left school) - I guess that was the most terrible time of my life. Your life wasn't easy either. This is another topic I'd like to get back to. I'll send some questions about it if you don't mind.

He was singing in my key! I was deeply moved by what he shared and by his expression of interest. Thomas wasn't given to hyperbole, so his summation of those years rang loudly.

We were turning a meaningful corner with these openings into relationships, physical appearance, and chapters from our pasts. Disposed to share from a deeper plane when I felt confident of my cyber-friend's interest, I dearly valued in return what he shared with me. Both were clearly true for Thomas as well. At the end of his message, he said:

Much more could be said, but not tonight.

It felt like he wanted me to *really* know him - so I kept asking questions. Since he'd lived with a girlfriend for years but had not married, I wanted to know:

Does this mean a) you would never consider marriage even if you found "the right one," b) that you just haven't found the right one yet, or c) something else? Will you date again if your relationship with your former roommate doesn't "carry on"?

I felt emboldened by his seeming ease with the subject. How cheeky of me to change his "special one" into a "former roommate."

If he found me brazen for doing so, he kept it to himself when he responded:

I think I'll get married if I decide to have children - I didn't make up my mind about that point yet. Celibacy is not amongst my primary goals, so I guess I'm gonna date again when I think that my relationship is over.

When?

Only now do I notice how I skated past his implied reason for dating. My reason would've been to find a soulmate.

Ray Of Light

After several weeks of emailing with Thomas, I began to talk *about* Thomas. I'd confided in my sister and closest confidants early on, but now I told others too. Among February's printouts are two "outside" messages, stored chronologically with the TH emails (as I came to call them), both addressed to friends I was in touch with from college.

My email to Sarah was in reply to hers describing a new boyfriend. I wrote:

No such action in my life, except... Well, this is sort of silly, but there's this guy I've never met that I've been emailing with, and it's been a real kick...Our messages have extra warmth and wit, and it's been getting more personal, as personal as is realistic across half the earth over email. It's all I got for male respect right now anyway.

There's that respect issue again - and the verbal screenshot takes me right back into toasty tingly feelings.

My message to Amy included a timeline and finished with:

Looking back, his reply to my Super Bowl reference was the turning point toward the personal track...Now his program works perfectly and we're still emailing.

The summation is like a plain wrapping around a priceless gift.

Both dispatches give me insight into my mentality at the time. I detect myself trying to sound breezy - enjoying it for what it's worth while it lasts and all that - while I knew deeper down how attached I was getting.

I wasn't unhappy on my own. Sure, I was open to a new relationship, but as I've described, I didn't feel a need for one.

Into that storyline stepped a surprise character.

There was such consonance between us thirty-somethings across the ocean! Thomas and I were only cyber-friends, yet we plainly took meaningful delight in our developing bond. I remember how good it felt, after giving my jaded take on "men around here," when he responded:

It seems you are far above the average doe-hunting John Deer.

The clever compliment, with its purposeful brand-name misspelling, dazzled me and pointed to the close attention he paid to my messages.

Of course, I devoured his writings just as intently. For the incidental connection to have taken off, we each had to relish both the writing and the reading - and to have hours available for them. In our unique confluence of circumstances, in that thin piece of time, we did.

When I'd asked about his travel experiences, I waxed dreamy on the subject:

I've done little traveling (but not because I haven't wished to), and
I'm convinced I will do a lot in the future when lack of money no
longer prevents it. I have a strong sense my grandiose ambitions
of seeing the world will be fulfilled someday.

These hopes were part of me before Thomas - they became more fervent because of him.

All The Small Things

What began as a blithe back-and-forth with the tech supporter before long turned into real affinity for this sweet smart man. Who knew I could feel so connected to someone without meeting them? The batch of emails I'm now finishing with has me re-relishing that growing accord. The feeling is surreal - because from this vantage point it looks inevitable.

Once again the quantity of printouts I happened to retrieve leaves us at a natural story break. Here's Thomas's closing of this batch's last message:

The time for our conversation is not limited, but the time I have
to write a response is.
Many open threads...
Thomas

My radiant recall of those three little words has never dimmed. The expectation they conveyed descended on me like a soft warm blanket.

As I prepare to fetch a new batch, phrases, feelings and themes come to me in waves - those already on our conversational table swirl with those I'm eagle-eyed to find. In one open thread, I'd queried:

Do you still see your parents? Did you have any natural siblings? Terrible is a strong word - do you want to say how it was so?

And in another, I tiptoed:

Since you mentioned the phrase, I'll ask you: would you say you have ever really "fallen in love"?

With no recall of Thomas's responses, I can hardly wait to keep reading.

There was also the matter of accessing his website to see what he looked like - plenty of cliffhangers as I leave this batch. I thought progressively submerging myself in the printouts would part clouds of memory and help me intuit what comes next. It's the opposite. While the story the emails tell is solidly, gratifyingly filled in to this point, I don't feel any less in the dark about the fine points of its unfolding from here on.

Thomas and I must've been about to delve into music, based on this set-up from me on the last day of February:

I'm as good at song quotes as I am at Shakespeare - try me.

Given the outsize role music played in our discourse, I expected its appearance before now.

I'm taken aback by something else I haven't seen yet, a Strand of self-description from Thomas. In the snippet I recall, he said he smiles a lot and referred to himself as shy.

Above all, I'm indescribably eager to reach the conversations that took us from cyber-friendship to meeting in person.

One minor mystery: since I printed all of our first two months of messages on a single mid-March day, I'm hoping the text will shed light on what prompted it. The March folder is the most voluminous in the Box; I'm taking as my next batch only the emails through printing day. Something tells me this will be plenty to deal with.

Ɣ CHAPTER 20

MAGIC POWER OF THE MUSIC

Our many open threads as the month rolled over incorporated both recent subjects and some from weeks before. "Another topic to return to later" was a frequently employed phrase. Combing through this batch, I find several notable continuities in March's first few pages.

That music subject I've been expecting? Turns out Thomas and I were a breath away from it. My eyes land instantly, as I sit down to today's reading, on the passage that kicked it off. It traces back to a Thomas quote I've already shown you - but I omitted his parenthetical:

Falling in love always bears the risk of rejection. ("Love is just a lie meant to make you cry, love hurts" - that belongs to the music topic to be discussed in the future.)

He couldn't have doubted I'd recognize the line from the ubiquitous power ballad *Love Hurts*. My response contained an aside too, naively asking if he could name the band. It was the only Nazareth song I knew (me and my Top 40 bent), and I was strutting a bit. Little did I know Thomas owned several of their albums.

Thus began a discussion about preferred genres, eclectic tastes, and the role of lyrics. It wove through other personal matters too, leading me to observe:

It seems from your quoting of songs that you use music to express things the way I do. When I think about specific music that has moved me through the years, it's as if there's a sort of soundtrack to my life. One example that reflects me right now is Phil Collins' Dance Into the Light.

A sunshiny paean to new beginnings after tough times, how exquisitely fitting that it's the first song I ever named in my emails with Thomas.

We each claimed among our collections some classical music, but both leaned heavily toward lyric driven genres. Thomas pointed to "tough lyrics" as a component of some heavy metal he liked, citing Nazareth's *I Will Not Be Led*. Until this moment I didn't know the song existed. That is, his naming of it had flown from memory; it feels entirely new.

This matters because I never forgot our talk in Cologne months later, when Thomas used a version of the line to describe his atheism. Thomas's mentions of *Love Hurts* and *I Will Not Be Led* feel as cosmically apt now as the song I'd cited. Mine expresses the elation of our beginnings; his would sum up our downfall before the year was out.

Thomas chronicled his musical interests, from childhood influences through honing his own predilections ("my taste in music is the result of a process"), listing representative songs and bands. He added:

> I am glad we have a really huge record shop in Cologne - they have catalogs with computer print-outs, 4 inches thick, with all records they have.

This must be the store we shopped at on my trip!

Interest in music animated him as much as computer science did - and as much as it did me. Matching his music profile with my own, I listed favorites from my vinyl and cassette collection and noted that "much of my listening takes place while driving" (on my car's radio or cassette deck). I described my local go-to record shop too, where I was "slowly adding to my CDs," and added this detail:

> I was even younger when I started getting hooked on Top 40 radio, maybe 10 or 11. I had a little transistor radio, and rested it on my ear at night to fall asleep to. I can still name songs I remember hearing in those moments.

Those radios measured about four inches by three; one is packed away with a few artifacts from my pre-teen years. I enjoyed telling Thomas about it; he gave me a reason for tracing my musical background in a way I hadn't before.

Musical allusions pervaded our messages from then on. As tangents within other topics, in subject lines, and often forming greetings and signoffs, Thomas and I constantly quoted song lyrics. The title Thomas gave his musical history message was "I Love Rock n' Roll" - and when I replied, I added to his subject line: "put another dime in the jukebox…"

My scouring of these old emails, as you know, isn't merely research (though it is that), but an intensely private quest to understand all that happened. The song-centered messages were lengthy, yet they're easy to summarize because the specifics aren't essential to the larger story I'm telling. Music formed one of its all-encompassing themes, and I'm sampling only a few beats to play you the cover tune.

Office Supplies

Being able to share this endeavor with you feels, so far, like springtime to my spirit. It's making me ponder again what took me so long to dig into the Box.

By the time I stashed it away in 1999, after all was said and done for Thomas and me, I'd pressed into service reams of printer paper, a dozen-plus manila folders, pencils, staples, green ink pens, yellow highlighters. Now, in 2023, I'm composing these words on a laptop, creating a digital photo-archive of the printouts, and storing project notes and documents on the cloud.

These days I use comparatively few office supplies. Keeping stocked up on them used to form an important part of stoking my writerly inclinations. I've long exhibited this quirk of buying notebooks, writing implements and other provisions - sometimes fancy ones, often when I didn't need them - and then not opening the packages for a long time. What I liked was the looking-forward, the knowing they were there.

I mostly use pencils now to make erasable notes in paper books I read, but that's about it - so I'm unlikely to ever exhaust my current supply. At least I'm no longer ignorant of my own contradictions on this.

There'll be just the right moment to break open that pristine notebook and sully its pages with thoughts in ink - but it can't be done without obliterating the comfort of knowing that special enjoyment awaits me in the future.

Something similar must be at work in the hesitation I experience each time I'm ready to retrieve the next batch of emails. Sure, bucking up emotionally plays a part, but I now think that's not all. It has to do with that looking-forward - and with wanting to remember the forgetting.

This reliving of the Thomas part of my life has been available to me all along for the moment of my choosing, printouts and profound emotions tucked away like my never-sharpened pencils and still packaged highlighters. I've kept them safe and close for when I'm ready to rip into them.

Well, now I'm in. In deep.

I've stepped beyond keeping the Box untouched for Someday, exposed myself to the sweetness and the ache, and there's no going back. Now, with the desire to summon the state of unawareness from before I began, something in me wants to compare the two conditions - a version of innocence and experience. Must the Great Reopening reformat the hard drive, thoroughly overwrite ignorance with enlightenment?

The question itself suggests what I really want, in some way, is to hold on to everything I've ever experienced. It's the same reason I react against ordinary fading too, the fuzzing out at the edges. Yet I learn over and over this cannot be prevented.

So I'm declaring as of this moment it's *the moving through* that makes the most sense. Hold off a while if you wish - then open it, use it, and go on to the next thing you need.

Now that I'm this far into my Thomas emails - two months of the six before I went to meet him - it's dawning on me that the innocence of gauzy memory may not be preservable after all. But trying to keep it has come to feel less pressing in light of the rewards of excavation.

The rediscoveries nourish me more than does the keeping them at bay.

A perfect example emerges from my question to Thomas about whether he'd ever fallen in love.

Hole Hearted

I seldom use the phrase *falling in love*. Nothing against the feel-good sentiment it connotes, I've just always favored more down-to-earth ways to express the experience. So when I asked Thomas whether he'd ever fallen in love, I used quote marks to signify not only that I was borrowing his words, but also that I was attaching the idea of "so-called" to the phrase.

Thomas had taken the initiative in using the expression - part of our discourse about rejection. And it was I (also following pattern) who went a step further by directing the question to him personally. His response began with a rhetorical question:

> Well, what does "falling" mean in this context? I have been deeply in love, was deeply disappointed. 'Twas the last time I was really crying. Haven't cried since, but I've surely felt sad, sometimes had tears in my eyes. It wasn't love at first sight. I am wondering if "falling in love" refers to instant love?

His admission felt profound, although he gave no details - instead segueing to question the concept.

My interior process, rereading that response today, repeats a hallmark experience of this project. Plumbing the obscurest recesses of mind, I was unable before to bring even a shred of his reply to the surface. But it comes gushing back, emotions and all, as I'm blinking at the words on the page, as fully as if it had never disappeared - like song lyrics I can't recite in silence, yet when the song plays I can sing along. The operation replays with every poignant extract reclaimed. Each time I am ripped apart, and then healed.

It happens again - this time accompanied by literal quivers - as I drink in words I sent in return:

No, I don't think of falling in love as synonymous with love at first sight. I think there's such a thing as attraction at first sight, but love grows from learning more about the person. And I understand the pain of disappointed love well enough to feel it again as I read those lines from you.

A rekindled tenderness holds me in place; I can't move from these lines for a while.

This little colloquy on love-falling had no direct bearing on our emerging friendship - but I recall feeling stirred by if-only's. I can't speak for Thomas.

I do know what he typed. His next message included the remark:

I think it takes about two years till you're ready to start a new relationship.

That sounded about right to me. It was too early in our story for him to know he was already on the cusp of one.

Thomas's messages gave me the sense that his thoughts, feelings and stories went unshared elsewhere. Our emailing became a singular outlet for me too - while neither of us sought or expected an intimate relationship. Thomas had been forthcoming about his girlfriend, a thread I returned to a few messages later:

> *Recently I heard this quip on tv: "Sure, everybody's lonely. It's just easier to take in a relationship." Which reminds me: you gave me your story on dating, but I didn't give you mine yet. I'm not dating anyone right now, but not because I wouldn't like to. I'm glad I had the first five years on my own to focus on my children and my goals. Now that it's been over six, though, I wouldn't mind dating if a compatible someone came along.*

I didn't bother to repeat how unlikely I thought it was.

My little household kept me busy and gratified enough not to be overly concerned with the idea. Now my new email friend and I seemed to be developing from a distance the kind of companionship I most longed for from an in-person relationship anyway. What a windfall.

ODE TO MY FAMILY

I found myself intensely interested in Thomas's family background. He'd given the basics about his siblings and parents, and in my next message I introduced mine:

Besides my twin sister (who's a single mother too and lives nearby), I have two older brothers I'm barely in contact with.

Learning about each other's families (my parents were long deceased) felt meaningful, given how early in our emailing the thread began. The dialogue took us as well into future imaginings. In response to Thomas's musing about having children someday, I forayed into fervent hopes and dreams as a mother:

The absolute best gift you can give your (potential) children is to love their mother. In my situation, the best I could do for my sons was to show them about living life with integrity and facing challenges instead of running from them. Sometimes it's staggering to think about my opportunity to influence the next generation.

I expounded on this for several paragraphs; the passage well illustrates how writing to Thomas helped me articulate my own thinking.

It must be true that our writing friendship did something similar for him. More than once he used movie references as springboards for his thoughts - as he did when the subject of connecting digitally came back around in early March. Thomas wrote:

Email is a way where you can easily acquire a new, more attractive identity. (I don't suspect you did.)

He described a German comedy about "pen mates" who fall in love; confusion and hilarity ensue over "borrowed" names and photos when they eventually meet in person. Thomas concluded his synopsis:

This is not real life, so there was a happy end.

Whoa. Did this hint at some jadedness, akin to mine when I'd generalized about guys I knew? It wasn't his usual mode, but he may have just meant to be funny.

He pivoted to explaining pay-per-minute chat rooms and "flirt services" that employ deception, presenting false identities to keep customers chatting and spending. This part came from his techie-explainer voice - which I always found appealing - and drew the contrast with our origins.

This aspect of our connection, taking one another's self-expression at face value (so to speak), went hand in hand with mutuality of interest.

We each perpetuated the correspondence in equal measure, and closeness formed from far away - a constant surprise. Years later, details dropped off, but never that delighted feeling.

If this story had been written soon after our ending, its scope would've been limited by all I hadn't yet learned and lived. Now, fresh motifs reveal themselves between the lines of ancient text. Through the lens of elapsed years, I catch on to subtleties I did not perceive then - such as Thomas's indirect initiative toward the personal - and I understand how I'd missed them before.

A little farther in, this happens again. Something I didn't see at the time leaps off the page.

Between The Lines

Had I chosen to read all the old emails before beginning to write, you would be reading a very different book. For my sake and yours, I'm digesting a little at a time. The method lends itself to experimenting with ways to present each batch's highlights and excerpts. Up to now, you've seen me pick out beads from a multi-message topic and string them together for you as a unified conversation.

With printouts I'm reviewing today, I notice how that approach could've prevented an intriguing discovery, one that hides in the subtext *within* one early March email from Thomas. Touching on a dizzying variety of open threads, among them our exchange of "personal identifiers," he noted our height differential of about a foot - an interesting but inconsequential observation. His next paragraph began:

> BTW, do you smoke? It makes no difference for a cyber-friendship,
> but it would disturb me very much in a personal relationship.

Since smoking could have no more pertinence to our writing friendship than our relative statures, it sounds like he was imagining an eventual encounter.

I like to think Thomas was already what-iffing, just as I was. If it's true what we think about comes out in what we say (Lao Tzu: "Watch your thoughts, for they become your words…"), it must sneak out in what we type. Couldn't his earlier remark about how long it takes to be ready for a new relationship fit this speculation too?

Applying the proverb to my own messages, it's easy to spot what leaks out: the nagging unease that, despite my desire (or in some twisted way because of it), the rewarding connection with Thomas might end at any time.

In a single message (our 50th), I count three manifestations. First, as part of our prolonged give-and-take about email risks, I wrote:

One risk for me is the longer this goes on, the greater my sense of loss will be if it ends.

This was a mere two days after saying I could roll with it should he lose interest. Looks like I got more honest with myself in the interim.

In an unrelated thread, I responded to Thomas's description of the "technical creativity" involved in his programming, and this oozed out:

If you ever stop writing, I'll always have the screensavers. (Sounds like a line from a B-movie!)

That turned out to be false, ironically enough. Well, technically I still have the screensavers, but only on 3.5-inch diskette, an obsolete format. I'd love to see the designs again! Had I not printed the emails,

I wouldn't have our writings either. Not such a waste of paper after all, was it?

The third emergence took a photo-negative form. After explaining a glitch that delayed me in sending the message, I wrote:

> *If you at some point don't hear from me in a long time, please assume something's wrong with the technology, or that I'm sick, or working, not that I've just quit.*

I was offering him reassurance I myself craved.

Can We Talk

It's striking to me how early this was, the verbal friendship as yet unornamented with each other's images. You'll recall Thomas had suggested I visit his website to see photos of him. In response to this online neophyte's inquiry about their purpose, he gave this explanation:

> *I am not a faceless company like Microsoft, so I decided to provide some information about me on the web; a few months ago I added some pictures.*

The admirable motive brings into relief a downside of technological development since. With the advent of invasive applications, it appears his transparency gave way to a pragmatic imperative. The photos are no longer displayed on his inactive webpage.

To view Thomas's pictures then, I located an *internet cafe*, a recent innovation. One had just opened in the city near me; the day after he emailed the URL, I dashed over there - with just enough time to get a quick look. It felt incredible being able to superimpose a real-life image onto my friend's words!

Eager to share what I looked like too, I brainstormed:

*I have a scanner; I can scan a snapshot and try to attach it to
email, or I could fax it if you want to give me a fax number.*

My glee at small finds like this doesn't lessen. I forgot about that
scanner; now the visual returns of the oblong, cumbersome device in
my kitchen, behind the computer.

Thomas replied:

I have a fax, but it is not urgent to see your picture.

I wilted a little.

Another hidden assumption laid bare. He wasn't indifferent toward
me, only to seeing what I looked like. Given the connection I felt in our
messages - and how electrifying it was to see pics of him - I expected
this interest would be mutual too.

I shook it off, stayed on topic. Scanning and faxing made me think
of landlines:

*Speaking of phones (almost): Back when you explained your
familiarity with English, you said you don't speak it often. Does
that mean if we were to talk on the phone, we would have trouble
understanding each other?*

My sideways suggestion of a phone call puts an entry on my side of
the initiative ledger; I was the first to raise it. Thomas clarified:

*My listening comprehension is not on the same level as my reading
comprehension. I'm trained in "Oxbridge English" - Americans
sound a li'l bit different. And I can't use my dictionary on the phone.*

I understood his reluctance; these objections made complete sense, which is why his next sentence flummoxed me:

If you get access to the WWW we can try to use the Internet phone. It's much cheaper than real phone.

That's hardly where I thought his explanation was leading - and it sure got my attention. Still less could I have anticipated his next move - proposing a remedy:

I have an account with CompuServe that includes five hours of free access per month. It wouldn't cost me a penny if you would use three or four hours per month...Do you think this is interesting for you?

This is an astonishing discovery! An important turning point I'd completely blanked out, it answers the question of how and when I first got onto the web at home. Expectations of such light-bulb moments drove me to this project in the first place. This one enhances the early portrait of Thomas - and explains some unrecognized notes in my teal folder: gibberish codes, passwords, a tracking of hours.

My first reaction to his Internet phone idea hits me funny now:

Sure, this might be something I'd be interested in. Sorry to say, I'm not sure I understand it all. How does this get us ahead of what we're doing now? Are you talking about being able to "converse" or type messages back and forth in real time?

Thomas enthused:

This is really speaking!

When I'd hinted earlier at a landline call, I quipped about trying to sound like a Brit, throwing in "Cheerio! Pip pip!" to help him understand me. Now I shot back:

Simply smahshing! (That's my British accent.)

Thomas noted that my having internet access would be useful to both of us for exchanging "binary files." I understood the term only well enough to feel grateful in advance.

From the beginning, Thomas showed generosity as a software creator/peddler, with the time spent on the screensaver problem and with the expense of airmailing the replacement. Now his internet sharing proposal reflected *personal* generosity - and trust. This cyber-friend of his took both as huge compliments.

The offer expanded the possibilities for interacting beyond faceless basic email. We were really getting somewhere.

PRINTERS AND PAGES

In the process of printing the emails, it was my habit to reuse paper. On discarded pages of text (inadvertent duplicates of prior messages, often), I drew a bold diagonal line across and fed them back to print on the blank reverse side.

The email containing Thomas's internet sharing offer is printed on a reused sheet. On the crossed-out side, this line of text catches my eye - a promo for Juno: *You don't need to buy Internet access to use free Internet email.* I mean, come on.

I'm easily amused by such coincidences - this one sidetracks me into repeating an important element of our story. Although internet calling was the catalyst for his proposal, Thomas and I never spoke, over landline or internet, before I went to meet him.

He made the offer in mid-March, when our happily preoccupying correspondence approached a hundred messages. As I told Thomas:

The hardest part of keeping track of our conversation, and trying to get the most out of it, is that this much written expression is time-consuming. I'm doing it when I should be working or keeping house, and you're doing it late at night when you need to sleep. If only there were more time...

How well I remember feeling profoundly *fed* by this faraway friendship - with a man I was sure I'd never meet.

A message I composed on a weekend morning wound to a close:

Gotta go - my kids have waited a long time to get a turn on the computer. Lots more to go back to, huh?...BTW: How's the weather?

These few words glowingly evoke that milieu. Thomas would not have missed the allusion to how far we'd come since our exchange about initiating conversations. By this time, it was possible for me to say:

I had so many additional thoughts churning after your last message that I wrote them down on (gasp!) paper. I still can't quite get over the idea that two people on this planet of billions can "talk" like this. Last night I went back over some of the earlier messages just to see how it came to this.

Just now I let out a *Yes!* at this indicator I'd hoped for, the contemplation that must've led to preserving the emails in print. Next I repeat quietly to myself, eyes gleaming: *How it came to this indeed.*

The old musings leave me more impatient than ever to retrieve the next batch of emails. It's my own story - yet I can't wait to find out what happened next.

I'll Take You There

The printouts teleport me to another place, time, self - at once familiar and startling. I'm away, like Narnia's wardrobe, far longer than the clock on my wall shows. Watchful for wonders, I step into this batch with a hand shading my eyes, reminded with each footfall that more has been forgotten than remembered. It could hardly be otherwise, given the profusion of words between Thomas and me; March's volume nearly overwhelms.

During the first 13 days of the month alone, we exchanged 48 emails of varying lengths. The printouts (font size 10, single-spaced) average two pages per message, and as the math shows, most days we wrote more than once.

These missives were marked by enthusiastic familiarity - a phrase which describes as well my disposition rereading them. When I began with January's messages, ribbons of recall were surrounded by white space and tentativeness. But with this batch, a settling-in takes over. It's cozy now, engaging with who we were to each other then.

Our patterns and pacing became so regular that when one of us anticipated missing a day, we warned the other in advance. Without this record, I couldn't have comprehended the constancy Thomas and I achieved.

Remember the thought exercise of recapping a one-on-one conversation for a third friend? Now let's say you two met *every day* for months - and that you saved a verbatim transcript of everything you both said. That's what I have with Thomas. Every single word.

Early March's defining moments crystallize within three prevailing topics, braided yet distinct threads that knitted the cyber-friendship. They make plain, as you'll see, why I resolved, by the middle of that extraordinary month of that extraordinary year, to immortalize our budding relational phenomenon - by printing every message for my future self.

An interesting juxtaposition presents itself at this stage. A growing number of specifics don't return to mind as easily, if at all; at the same time, the overall *texture* of connecting with Thomas feels as familiar and comfortable as a favorite sweater. I wrap myself in thoughts of the cyber-friend I cherished; *he* feels familiar as ever. Here is that knowing and being known, through nothing more than our keyboards, I've so dearly longed to see and feel again.

I'm stuck in a moment, more profoundly moved than I'd even braced for.

The emailing with Thomas offered a vehicle for expressing my truest self - and the privilege of receiving the truest of his. I suppose that's not a bad definition of friendship. The word *celebrate* comes to mind too. We were each celebrating aspects we most liked about ourselves by showing them to someone who uniquely appreciated them.

Nowhere was this more transparent, as you might expect, than in Thomas's role as a techie.

Snags and Advances

I have insisted to you I'm relaying these events as *my* story. Yet there's no denying it traces back to a single data point about a complete stranger an ocean away: Thomas's profession as a software developer.

Yes, the saga kicked off with *me* purchasing the screensavers - but it was Thomas who created, distributed and tech-supported his artistry. Eight weeks later, the cyber-friendship that came of it widened beyond typed words alone.

Of the Box's revelations so far, uncovering how Thomas was key to my inaugural home internet experience feels seismic. Seeing the pages of trouble it took makes it all the more perplexing this major plot point got memory-holed.

Landline dial-up was the only on-ramp to the information superhighway. Getting me up to speed on his CompuServe account entailed a fair amount of Thomas's effort and techsplaining. (The password he set for me: TOSOTP.) These labyrinthine passages contain amusing testaments to the era's technology - such as having to reinstall Windows 95 from fifteen diskettes.

While we went about the work, we traded high-tech reminiscences. Thomas went first:

I was 16 when I started programming - had to leave my old school then; new school had 2 computers: Apple][, with 48 kB RAM, no hard disk, and about 100 kB per diskette. I think the CPU was running at 1 MHz.

This is only marginally comprehensible to me now. I returned:

I started using computers about a year after you did, but I started on IBM, at an insurance office job. The first hard drive had, I think, 10 megabytes; it was a big deal when we upgraded to 30. I was learning straight DOS commands with their data base.

Returning to the issue at hand, at yet another snag, Thomas pointed to the sort of loop we'd encountered before:

Dang - another deadlock! I could email all the software you need - if only you had access to the 'net. But I wouldn't need to email the software if you had the 'net. Let me know if you want to surrender! If you want to keep on trying, I'll come up with a new idea.

My response co-opted an 80s song title, with optimism rooted in Thomas's previous successes:

"Never Surrender" is my middle name! Let's give it a few more rounds - I have a feeling we'll come up with something.

No surprise, he succeeded once again and I exulted:
WE HAVE LIFT-OFF! IT WORKED! I'M SHOUTING! YOU'VE DONE IT AGAIN!

I connected for 4 minutes tonight. I am now ready to take specific instructions.
Your connected friend OTOSOTP, K

Thomas's offer came with few conditions (honor the three-hour limit, keep the password private). Now he swept his figurative arm across the cyber landscape and urged:

I have no instructions - feel free to look around! You should try to visit my homepage.

That was precisely my plan. He added tips for keyword searching and a list of search engines - a Strand you saw in the memory-narrative. How peculiar that I retained that snippet but not the pivotal development it flowed from.

Whereas Juno email didn't allow attachments, we could exchange them via Thomas's shared internet account - so I was finally in a position to show him what I looked like, as I'd continued to contemplate despite his saying "it isn't urgent." On top of that, the technology was now in place for Thomas and I to have a spoken conversation in real time. Be still my heart!

Following my shouty celebrating, I reiterated my gratitude, from the bottom of that excited heart:

You are kind to trust me with this.

While I geared up to surf the web, Thomas declared he'd be searching too:

I have to use one of these search engines to find out how to phone over the web. I think there is no hurry!

There was for me.

PICTURES OF YOU

When I composed this book's opening pages, I underscored the story's setting in the early internet age, with no recall of Thomas's role in bringing about my *personal* internet age. We managed the difficulties of getting me there while juggling numerous other topics. Similarly, synchronous tasks occupy me now: resolving mysteries, resurrecting Strands, and - like a computer operation humming in the background - continually comparing memories with the data in the annals.

Occasionally, a single vignette brings together all three. Fittingly, our ever present music banter provides an example. A mention by Thomas of the band ZZ Top elicited this chime-in from me:

I always liked the name of their drummer: Dusty Rhodes.

My casual confidence was misplaced; I mangled a trivia tidbit I'd heard. You may recall my alluding to this from memory. My slight embarrassment was one reason it stayed with me - as was his gracious manner in countering the error:

As far as I know, the band consists of Billy Gibbons, Dusty Hill, and Frank Beard.
Two things are funny about the name: Dusty's brother is Rocky Hill. And Frank Beard (the drummer) is the guy without a beard.

How very satisfying to revisit the Strand in its original habitat. I see he spelled out the acronymic phrase in that instance (I Strand corrected?), but on the most meaningful aspect - Thomas's tact - I had it completely right.

The passage epitomizes the mirth minor details can bring me, with their *Oh yeah!* flashes. This batch explodes with them - on larger matters too. As of March 1st, seven weeks into our emailing, neither of us had seen an image of the other. (My stop at the internet cafe was on the 3rd.) Now I get to relive exactly how that major corner was rounded.

The quick cafe glimpse of Thomas's appearance didn't alter how I related to him, yet it was an epic marker for me internally. I remember how stirred and warmed I felt, how it enhanced my experience of him - making all this a notch more *real*.

Thomas would view my visage a week later. In his reply to my excited "lift-off" message, he raised this unprompted:

You can send me your photograph - only if you want.

I was delighted the notion hadn't left his mind! He included info about file types and scanner software, and this time the "CU" signoff

connoted more. Today I recognize his cue as more inviting than I might've then. Either way, I didn't need any more urging than that.

The prospect of a live webphone conversation was still in my thoughts too. In both cases, I notice, Thomas advanced the possibility first, then subsequently downplayed it. Both were again under discussion when I wrote:

> *Re no hurry to phone over the web... You're right, of course, but I'll admit I'm eager.*
> *Re my sending a pic... I'd like to if you're interested.*

I was angling for a more direct expression of interest; he didn't indulge me. The minute I could, I emailed him an image anyway, a tiny headshot (I'd misunderstood his file sizing guidelines):

> *Well, let's see if this works. It took a lot of experimenting.*
> *His reply:*
> *Hello! Sending the picture worked fine. Now I C U. I was surprised to see that you wear spectacles. But then, you ne'er said you didn't and I ne'er ast!*

I responded:

> *They must not be crucial to my self-image cuzz it never occurred to me to mention them.*

Thomas later added that despite having no logical basis for expectations, my appearance was about what he expected. (As I told you earlier, I remember noticing the absence of a compliment.) I remarked in return:

My expectation of what you would look like was vague and unformed, so anything would have been a surprise.

Not only could I now picture him while I emailed, I liked knowing he could picture me too.

Our next progression would intensify the connection even more.

Unreserved

When I reflect on my deepening fondness for Thomas, I think of our storytelling. The smattering of tales we traded, including deeply personal and troubling episodes from our pasts - that felt like intimacy. These sprang from our ordinary discourse. How else would they?

Thomas's earlier asides about his family made me hungry to know more. He'd shown reciprocal interest by saying he would "ask more later if you don't mind." Of course I didn't mind! And the *later* is in the group of emails I'm reviewing now.

It came back around because of a song. In an exchange about our favorites, Thomas asked if I knew Suzanne Vega's *Diner*. I replied:

Can't say I do, although I'm familiar with her. My book says the song went to #5 in 1990 so I'm wondering how I missed it - unless I just don't recognize it by the title. I remember well her hit of three years earlier, Luka.

The book in question, *The Billboard Book of Top 40 Hits* (Joel Whitburn), a tome I kept handy throughout the 1990s, was a massive paperback which fed both a penchant for reference works and my pop music passion. As I compose this paragraph in my living room, I can turn and see my old copy on the bookshelf. Now that the internet is the go-to for music trivia, the possession typifies the technology of the time as aptly as my vinyls, cassettes, and CDs do.

Although our friendship began near the close of the 1990s, a musical frame of reference Thomas and I had in common came from the radio airwaves of the 80s; it became the basis for quizzing one another and explains why I still associate so many 80s songs with my Thomas summer.

The subject matter of *Luka* apparently reminded Thomas of a question he'd intended to ask. I liked his lead-in:

> *Back to music (or maybe not): I love the song Luka...I don't know*
> *any women who "walk into the door." You mentioned your marriage*
> *was bad in the end. Maybe I shouldn't ask, but did he get violent?*

It felt good that he wanted to know. My affirmative response left out specifics but reiterated openness to sharing more, and touched on my intersection with the song:

> *I still remember hearing Luka at age 27, before I recognized the*
> *seriousness of my marriage situation. The song was properly*
> *disturbing because, as you say, women don't just walk into doors,*
> *any more than men do, and she captures an important aspect to*
> *the problem of violence in the home - the fear of telling about it*
> *(for lots of reasons). When I left my former husband, my boys*
> *were ages 18 months and 3 years.*

In his reply, Thomas revealed a little more:

> *Parents shouting at each other every night are very bad for the*
> *children (and for the parents). Some women (including my mother)*

*may think that a family with problems is still better than a single
mother.*

He continued with a detailed recollection of a violent incident, one
I empathized with from experience. I answered:

*My mother thought that too - my father was an alcoholic and at
times violent. I also used to think that single mothering might
somehow be worse for the children - no more! I couldn't be a good
example to them if I'd stayed.*

Within this short distance, we weren't talking about music anymore.

The seriousness settles on my chest, again. I pause to give attention
to it - and to that self-assurance I landed with. To think of the tiny seed
this story-sharing grew from.

Another childhood story Thomas shared sits me up straight, a
Strand I've waited to find. I told you of it earlier in the vaguest of terms -
because that's all I remembered. Now I see why it meant so much to me.

¥ CHAPTER 24

SNOW AND RAIN

In my discourse with Thomas about families, where I wrote at length of my feelings about motherhood, I mused about the influence parents have (or don't) over their children's eventual moral character. He replied:

During WWII some Germans were hiding Jewish people in their cellars. Many people go the easy way; only few fight for the right thing. Parents sure play an important role as an example.

His reference to that awful chapter of his country's history renewed my astonishment at our contact. As with my German professor Reinhard, I marveled at interacting with a person so closely linked to world-impacting events I'd learned about remotely.

Thomas kept pondering:

*I have one incident in my memory - I guess I was 13 or 14 then.
Other kids from my class tried to break windows with snowballs.
I also threw snowballs, but intentionally missed them all. One
classmate resisted to throw snowballs - now I wish I'd have done
that too!*

Over the years, whenever I've reflected on our moving email
conversations, it's this boyhood recollection I've had in mind, despite
the erasure of details. Receiving it anew is profoundly affecting - and
I hate that it got buried. If I had more sway over what memory stores
or discards, this would've stayed.

It's nearly as affecting to see how I responded:

*Your story about the snowballs is a poignant one and it moved me
very much - a wonderful illustration of your point. I'm honored,
and I'm not joking with that word here, that you feel comfortable
enough to share childhood memories like this.*

As with our Vega-inspired sharings, this was hardly everyday
discourse. To me, he'd vulnerably imparted a precious gem, and I
understood the unspoken regard that conveyed.

A more lighthearted passage joined *Luka* and the snowballs in the
same email, and it too demonstrated Thomas's unguardedness. Instead
of a flashback, though, he relayed an incident from that morning - and
I'm wild with delight to see it again. He began, "Today wasn't my day!"
and explained a public transit strike had disrupted his usual commute,
making him run late for work:

When I arrived in Cologne at the subway station, it was crowded. I decided to walk to the next station. I didn't get far when it started to rain. When I wanted to go down to the station, I made a quick turn on a metal grid right before the stairs - hmpf, it was "Slippery when wet," so "Humpty-Dumpty had a big fall." My trousers got dirty and I have some bruises on the back of my right hand. It doesn't hurt, so feel free to laugh about me - my colleagues did! The shame is worse than the pain.

He had me in stitches! You can tell he enjoyed telling me about it. I replied:

I'm sorry to hear about your drizzly day. You sure know how to make it funny though.

Thomas's recasting of his embarrassing mishap as an anecdote for my amusement projected a self-ease that drew me as potently as his moving throwbacks did - both reflected a gently, steadily deepening bond.

Before long, we would spell out what that bond was coming to mean to each of us.

I Said It First

Neither of us in our constant emailing had yet raised, as a subject in itself, our burgeoning harmony. As with every conversational milestone, the path to it branched off naturally from already open trails.

Reflecting on a prior message of mine, I wrote:

I've been second-guessing myself, because there's a paragraph (about beauty and respect) where I may have bared my soul too much for a platonic relationship. I now think I didn't connect my

thoughts clearly on the page. Behind that meandering was that
I wouldn't ask you a question I wouldn't be willing to answer
myself; I was answering mine about ever having "fallen in love,"
as you'd been candid enough to answer previously.

Ah, so I used the term *platonic* first.

Actually, I'd used it once before, theoretically and in passing, in the February exchange about rejection. But here I distinctly applied it to Thomas and me, as a given - and aptly so. As my thoughts pace around the passage, I recall how typing it out loud had the added utility of making sure Thomas knew I knew.

His response homed in on the label:

Our relation is strictly platonic - it has to be. I made my long story
short because time is short - and writing it in detail would have
been a li'l more painful...
I love our relation because we "talk" about emotions. Only platonic,
yes, but still something special. For me, but I bet also for you.

This takes my breath away! My heartbeat kicks up, eyes grow wide - then close tight to take it in. Doesn't it sound like he'd already been giving this some thought? When the right portal in our conversation opened up, he strode through it.

In acknowledging the constraint, Thomas openly voiced feelings that could not possibly have been sweeter for me to hear. Today his last three sentences sink into me, suitable for framing.

The relational delineation has always been essential to my retellings. Its email appearance a scant eight weeks into our contact comes as a shock. My response surprises me as well:

That's where I'm coming from too, and I'm glad you stated it because now I feel freer to refer to this being important to me, without worrying that you'll get the wrong idea, and freer also to not be so paranoid of saying too much.

I don't recall concluding this of my own accord, much less verbalizing it. I'm asking myself, What specifically was I basing it on - the geographical distance, his atheism, both?

Probably *not* front of mind was Thomas's Significant Other, who hadn't been mentioned since he'd described their separation - pessimistically, I thought. (He didn't invoke her in the falling-in-love thread either, I notice.) Even now, that seems a long while before; our conversations had plumbed soul-baring depths since. Actually, it was just five days - nine messages - earlier.

Seems to me I could be forgiven for absently coming to regard him as single. I can't say how he regarded himself.

Here's how I responded to Thomas about our special connection:

Get ready, I'm going to SHOUT... YOU'RE RIGHT! I continue to find your willingness to talk about life and emotions and your perceptiveness about such things refreshing. I feel respected by your openness, and you always make me laugh!

I love seeing the enthusiasm from both of us.

Satisfying as this milepost feels, I'm no surer of the exact reasoning behind Thomas's "it has to be" than I am of my own. That's not merely a device to keep you reading - I truly don't know.

From a Distance

Any reading bystander would recognize the buoyancy of new

friendship in our writing, as the affection and camaraderie between Thomas and me ripened.

Emailing made it possible to participate in each other's everyday existence from afar. How very ordinary the statement by itself sounds now, but it was truly extraordinary and scintillating then. We reveled in mingling the trivial with the profound, the meaningful with the mundane. Most of the odds and ends of daily affairs matter now only as displays of our growing familiarity. Some casual bulletins, however, carry enormous consequence in retrospect. Here's a perfect example from Thomas:

> *This year Cologne celebrates "750 years Cologne Cathedral." This simply means that they started to build the Cathedral 750 years ago. They finished the work in 1880 - only few centuries past schedule. That reminds me of software companies - including me, of course! Always too late!*

My eyes are large again, blinking as I read. When I told you about my Cathedral anniversary t-shirt, I didn't recall Thomas mentioning this.

Other passages hold added significance because of Strands they encompass, such as Thomas's reference to smiling a lot. I found it! The sliver appears later in the thread about viewing his pictures. I remarked:

> *I hope you have such warm pleasant smiles when you read my messages.*

Thomas's response:

> *I am not the ROTFL type, but I smile very often. I enjoy all your messages, even if they don't make me smile.*

It was my formulation, I see, which precipitated his; I'd forgotten as well his plainspoken compliment. I replied:

Smiling very often - that's a pretty good thing to be able to say of oneself, I think. Fortunately, I do too. And I always smile when I hear from you.

Nowhere in this passage, it turns out, does Thomas refer to being shy. Could this be an instance of recalling something that was *not* there?

Thinking of Thomas's smile draws one from me. So does another feature of our messages: the repartee that extended into our subject lines. Thomas titled his March 6th email (our 60th), "Yet another msg from Germany." Mine in return extended his subject line: "...there can never be too many." His next added to it: "...too many Germanies?" And get this: in the body of that message, Thomas leapt from his own offhand joke into a serious commentary on German politicians' nuanced uses of the terms *unification* and *reunification*.

How could this fusion of intellectual exchange, warm conversation and witty banter *not* brighten my days? Evenings too - they were consumed with the enjoyment of composing the next missive. On one occasion, Thomas mentioned staying up far past his normal bedtime, leading me to observe:

Hey, the other night you stayed up very late and I hit the hay really early, so that means we retired at about the same time even though we're 7 hours apart.

How sweet to think now of being so perpetually on each other's minds.

I wrote too of trying to keep my emailing time in balance, and said I hoped he found all of this as worthwhile as I did. Thomas replied:

Yes, I do! And I don't think I spend too much time "with you."

I melted! The validation goes straight to my heart again. So does this:

I have some work to do, so probably you'll have to wait 48 hours till you get my next message. Tomorrow I'll try to resist the temptation to do what I'd rather do - write messages to you!

What an exceptional kinship we built. I didn't know we were just getting started.

⚡ CHAPTER 25

JOURNEY

As I tease apart our correspondence - listening to my heartsong, chasing themes, Strands, dates, numbers - the content seems to expand as my emotions interact with it. It's making me think of bathtime playthings my little boys delighted in: foam capsules that expanded into surprise shapes when dropped in water. I wonder what shapes are yet to emerge here.

At the inception of this project, I yearned above all to ferret out the micro-steps that led to meeting Thomas in person. So far, so good - so rewarding. This is the seventh chapter-opening that introduces you to a fresh group of printouts, a group that holds the most astonishment for me yet. It's hard to believe I'm only in our first few months of emails.

In bringing the dormant dispatches to life, my notes track retrievals according to the old green-inked numbers. With this chapter, I begin to burrow into the messages through the end of March (#97-141). Each batch I write about is an odyssey unto itself, and I come away better oriented. Like taking a momentary breather during a hike, today I plant my walking stick in the dirt and take a good look around as a light haze lifts. The visibility is improving. I've known all along where this is headed, but not the intricacies of the way there. I can't say exactly what lies beyond the near path, or foresee the startlements of the coming batch, but I feel lucidly situated among the broad contours of the story.

Such was my settledness closing the previous chapter at the waymark of two months. That was the day I first accessed the internet from home, sent Thomas the first picture of me, and printed all 96 of our messages to that point. We were enjoying an easy accord, anchored and wrinkle-free under the label we'd lately applied to it. What profound sweetness it brings me to remember!

Reaching mid-March, I recall noting at the time, meant I could date our longevity in months rather than weeks. We were now familiar, in grainy two-dimensional terms, with one another's appearance, and had expressly co-celebrated our "special relation." All these markers felt to me like a landing, a place we might stay a while. I taste it again as I attempt to articulate it.

Now crossing into the next batch, dazed by hours of reading, I give you this preview: right when I felt the most restful and secure in our special friendship, the friendship became even more special, no doubt because of that security. It's all coming back to me.

I love this - first the surprise, then the remembering.

A radiance spreads through me, and I meditate on how to relay the unfurling. Musical allusions, affecting vignettes, hilarious wordplay, technology takes, treatises on cultures, languages and news events - most

of that will remain mine alone. The story's relational essence gives me more than enough to unpack for you.

Our connecting was a welcome ray of light through crevices in each of our lives. I was parched for non-superficial interaction with someone deeply thinking and world-aware; Thomas was (in my perception) primed to engage with one who animated him and met his utterances with enjoyment and interest.

The settled, easeful friendship we'd cultivated would soon induce me to speak up on a subject I never would've otherwise.

Maybe I'm Ambivalent, Maybe Not

Can you recall when you've posed an inviting question to a friend about their life, aware it actually arose from pondering your own? I spot a version of this in my March 14th message to Thomas:

> *Are you ready for another personal question? Are you doing what you've always wanted to do? What other dreams do you still hope for from your life?*

The earnest inquiries stemmed from mulling over my own dreams, which centered on hopes for raising healthy happy sons, and aspirations of becoming a professor at a small college.

Thomas had earlier expressed satisfaction with his profession. Now in a reply titled, "Sweet dreams are made of this…" he revealed what apparently came next in line:

> *I am not sure if I want children. I can imagine to marry a rich woman, stay home and care for the kids. I don't know what will be with my relationship to my SO. Currently it's rather platonic.*

It's a little jarring - and thought-provoking - to see him apply the term to his Special One. Here she is again.

I applaud attentive readers who guess the title of my reply: "Who am I to disagree?" From the security and caring of our platonic companionship, I ventured an opinion:

> *None of my business, but you sound a little ambivalent as to what*
> *you yourself want the relationship with your SO to be.*

As friends do, I reflected back to Thomas what I was picking up on. Had I been writing out of romantic fancies or uncertainty, there's no way I'd have gone there.

He didn't react to the remark in his next few messages. It wasn't unheard of to miss a topic, given our plethora of cross-content, but this dangling thread occasioned self-doubt. When I decided to reraise it, I parsed my thought process for him:

> *If I brought up a subject in person, I might be able to tell by the*
> *look on your face or maybe an inarticulate grunt that you don't*
> *want to go down that trail. With email, I'm seldom sure unless*
> *you address something specifically. That's fine, it's just the nature*
> *of it. If you don't go back to something, it could be a) it was fine*
> *with you but you had no additional comment, b) it bugged you*
> *but you decided not to say so, or c) it got overlooked.*

In my all-time favorite specimen of his conciseness, he replied:

> *It was never b).*

His declaration kicked up a self-reflection from me:

*I've recognized in myself a lingering level of caution in my messages
to you; I wonder if it's because I've been hurt by speaking too freely
in the past (before I "met" you).*

I cited my "going out on a limb" about his feelings toward his
girlfriend:

*It felt like I might be risking offense. And I tend to resist going back
to unanswered things for fear of sounding (in the raw vernacular)
bitchy. But rationally, I think if we consider each other friends, it
should be no big deal to address most things.*

While I was at it, I let him in on one more rumination:

*Another thing that's been on my mind is how this cyber relationship
could change if a Special Someone came into either of our lives. Of
course, that's more likely for you than for me, for reasons already
mentioned and because you already kind of have someone.*

Thomas thanked me for my long message - that always felt so good
- and addressed the SO topic directly. The explanation for his silence
was none of those I'd postulated; rather, he'd been waiting for time to
write a lengthier email.

In his elaboration I detected further conflictedness. Or rather, I
detect it now; none of this is coming back to me even after spending
time with it:

*Re my relationship with my SO... It's a crazee situation; I still
like her, but I don't miss her too much. I meet her once or twice
a week - and that's OK for me now. Time will tell if this is just a*

passing phase - or the final stage of a relationship. I think it's not impossible that the relation will go on.

Self-aware, uncertain - and seemingly unbothered by my editorializing. He welcomed and appreciated it, I suspect, as the gesture of friendship it was.

Thomas would soon find occasion to return the gesture.

The Impression That I Get

The further I get into the printouts, the more there is to see, and the less I'm showing you. One drawback to the narrowing focus is you can't appreciate the lushness of the foliage, punctuated by clearings. You miss my experience of sauntering through copious writings and stumbling upon a startling landscape - taken aback, amid everyday conversation, by a heart-stirring affirmation of closeness or a jarring bit of information.

During this stretch, rarely bereft of contact for even a day, briefer missives thoughtfully offered and elicited a quick hit of good feelings. Longer messages, for which we saved up in-depth disquisitions, we took to calling letters.

Thomas's letter explaining his contradictory SO feelings also furthered a separate discussion concerning male/female stereotypes. When my questions about hopes and dreams got him musing about stay-at-home fathering, he was tying into that topic too. Immediately following his Gretchen comments, he casually mentioned their plans to see the movie *Titanic* at the cinema that day. My response intertwined both threads:

From what I hear, get ready for some strong emotions - the classic

love story in the midst of tragedy. I've heard that women like the movie for the touchy-feely love story, and men like it for the bigger-than-life special effects - the perfect "date movie."

Then, drawing on his "it was never b" assurance, I goaded him about his clarification:

Cool! Watch me - I'm going to be less cautious now.
"I still like her, but I don't miss her too much."
Kinda supports my suggestion about ambivalence, doncha think?

I charged forward into lengthy paragraphs - it didn't feel as risky anymore. The abridged version:

Here's some more of my thinking behind the idea of SOs: it will come as no surprise to you (maybe cuzz I said it a whole bunch of times?) that my friendship with you is a satisfying thing for me...

Relying on imagination, I gamed out an unlikely scenario:

If a compatible Special Someone came along here, the emotional energy I (happily) expend in conversing with you would naturally transfer, at some point, to him. Not that I would ever want to lose touch with you - I hope that never happens - but wouldn't the level of conversation undergo an adjustment?

You probably see there my veiled concern about *his* relational circumstance. I continued:

Ok, stick with me on this... You already have an SO, though it's an uncertain sort of thing. Don't you think if you two reignited something deep and lasting that the same kind of adjustment would happen on your end?

My contemplations circled back:

When I heard you went to see Titanic, I thought that, as romantic a story as it is, perhaps whatever kept you together for four years would be rekindled. Don't get me wrong or think me (God forbid) possessive. If you found Ms. Right, I couldn't be happier for you, as I think you would be for me if I found Mr. Right.

Now I was really on a roll:

Just in case I haven't gotten personal enough... If I am ever fortunate enough to settle down with someone, he would undoubtedly have many of the qualities you have - sense of humor, easy-going personality, appreciation of music, enjoyment of language, and being a thinker who feels.

There you have it, a handy little checklist of the pleasures I didn't want to lose.

You'd be correct to recognize how I was, again, gamely putting myself out there. But I would remind you Thomas had set the tone, implied his consent, by offering musings about his SO and not objecting to my gutsy take on them.

And in his next turn, Thomas met me with equally as venturesome a spirit.

❡ CHAPTER 26

A GOOD HEART

Because so much of the discourse involving Thomas's girlfriend had vanished, revisiting its unspooling today feels especially unpredictable. Responding to my two cents about the two of them and *Titanic*, he wrote:

> *You are not possessive, but you get "scared" when I go to a movie? Jealous?...*
>
> *I'd say the risk of reignition is minimal. If that happened, I'd still have time for you (though possibly less time than I have now).*

His characterization of their status showed a subtle shift in emphasis - from "not impossible" to minimal risk. This time I kept the observation to myself.

Memories of this passage are returning piecemeal. Thomas's

challenge hit me hard - and yet felt intimate and honoring too. (With someone you don't care about, you wouldn't bother.) I felt defensive at first, but I thought it best to resist the impulse to explain, to not dismiss the idea too quickly in case he was onto something I'd missed in myself. My levelheaded reply after taking time to process betrayed no unease:

Interesting... Thanks for asking more about this. I may have miscommunicated something on this point. My true feeling about you two going to the movie was simply curiosity as to whether it would bring you closer together again, which I didn't see as a negative thing. There was nothing scary about it.

I recall being completely candid, with all the self-awareness I was then capable of. Now though, I can acknowledge overplaying it, out to convince myself as much as him. I continued:

There's no issue of jealousy either, which I meant to convey by saying I'd be happy for you. How can there be jealousy in a friendship where each hopes for the best for the other? It wouldn't be friendship if it weren't freedom-giving. (If I could italicize those last two sentences, I would.)

The parenthetical points to early email's formatting limits. The sentiments I meant to emphasize are ones I've never wavered on.

You and I know it wouldn't have been painless for me had Thomas declared their rekindling. It would've undoubtedly resulted in less access to those qualities of his I relished. I never forgot his response to that list:

Thanks for naming some of my virtues - you ain't seen much of my vices yet.

Confessing to his negative side: not a response I anticipated. If he meant to temper my ardor, he failed. The taking stock of himself only attracted me more, because I too strove to face all sides of myself squarely.

In the circumstance, that meant admitting my heart's stirrings to myself, while trying to stay cool-headed, realistic - and freeing toward my friend.

This I well remember. Much else, I don't. I'm not thrown by misrecalling the name of a family pet or the local computer techie (both corrected in this batch), but I'm endlessly confounded that such consequential developments between Thomas and me became obscured.

True, they were embedded in so very many words, momentous and moving to me today as they were then. Among these pages is this lyric I quoted: *Invisible airwaves crackle with life / Emotional feedback on a timeless wavelength* (Rush's *The Spirit of Radio*). The 1980s lines could describe Thomas and me and email.

Our digital connecting comprised a relational adventure all its own, long before we saw each other's eyes. Numerous pivotal passages in March's emails exemplify this. In Thomas's "crazee situation" message (he liked to lift silly spellings from rock lyrics), he quoted a Feargal Sharkey line (*A good heart these days is hard to find*) and added:

Whenever emotions are involved, there is a risk of getting hurt.

Truer words were never emailed.

Voices Carry

The ministrations paid to the printouts as I filed them fell short of the flawlessness I aimed for. On first surveying the current batch, I notice a skip in the green numbers; Email #110 appears to be missing.

With multiple same-day messages, I had to decide whether to give each its own green numeral or staple them under a single number. Careful scrutiny reveals the oversight which solves the mystery. Stapled behind E109 is the 110th email, left unnumbered; it's clear from the content nothing is lost.

The mild alarm short-lived, I pause to contemplate the dramatic plot twist a dropped piece of correspondence could've created. As it is, I'm finding plenty of drama in what's *not* missing. Without warning, tears of longing make their way down my cheeks. How I wish I could talk all this over with Thomas right this minute.

I can't. My discoveries of his emailed vacillations about Gretchen are left to me to bat around by myself.

That we discussed them at all is a gripping revelation. Past retellings spotlighted the spectacle of bonding with Thomas over invisible airwaves; this facet of his backstory fell away, and I never even noticed.

The answer I gave Thomas about jealousy lands as (mostly) persuasive. He countered:

No miscommunication. I would be happy for you if you found Mr. Right - I wouldn't be happy for me if you had to reduce the attention you can give me. Jealousy is too big a word to describe that.

Wow. I wasn't used to someone fretting over not getting enough of me. The flow to Thomas's thoughts there is notable. He imagined future disappointment, as I had - then backtracked on the term he himself had applied.

I reassured:

I was really only thinking out loud with you - didn't mean to say

anything for sure. How could we know? For one thing, it's quite
unlikely I would meet anyone else, much less someone like you.
Please don't worry - I can't imagine stopping our conversation!

I meant it with all my being.

That's the last of that thread, through March anyway. I can't help but
notice a distinction I may not have caught then. Thomas maintained,
were there an SO rekindling, he would still have *time* for our emailing.
But when I posited an SO for either of us, I had stressed *emotional*
bandwidth. Just me overanalyzing again.

I recognized that my gratifying cyber-friendship with Thomas
touched off longings for deep compatibility with someone "in real life."
My finding an in-person sweetheart, I presumed, could diminish the
bond we were cultivating. From what I can tell, Thomas thought he
could have both.

Free to be less cautious, I wanted to know something else from him.
A pithy recap prepared the way:

When this first started, I was amazed how much I could learn about
a person from nothing more than words on a screen. Then, the more
I learned, the more I looked forward to a visual representation to
attach to the TH file in my mind. Well, seeing the pictures made
me eager to hear your voice…

The phoning idea hadn't materialized - but here comes the big finish:

And seeing your pictures only increases the (however unrealistic)
interest in meeting you in person. Not saying that will ever
necessarily be a goal, but I'm just sorta wondering if there's a

*comparable experience on your end, or if OTOH you feel satisfied
by just the typed exchanges.*

Eureka! I spring forward in my seat, eyes bugging out. The subject
was officially broached.

I had absolutely no clue how Thomas would respond.

I Knew I Loved You Before I Met You

In movies and books, critical moments are often highlighted by
dialogue. The tale I'm telling is *all* dialogue. That is, until my plane
landed in Germany, every step of the adventure unfolded through
written exchanges alone. That's why I'm expending so many words on
our words. There's no other path through the story.

My personal excursion publicly exhibits an anatomy of a *relationship*,
born of a fluke intersection. As soon as Thomas and I had set the platonic
parameter, our exchanges started to sound less so. It liberated us to
write less reservedly of intensifying feelings, and the avenue toward
them wound, once again, through story-sharing.

I recounted the only romantic experience I'd had since the divorce;
it ended with my heart broken. Among the harsh lessons learned, I said,
was to always watch for whether the other person mutually values the
relationship:

*Otherwise I'm afraid I'll find out one day that I sort of blew things
out of proportion in my own mind.*

Thomas relayed a lesson too, taken from youthful experience. On
two occasions, feeling a connection with a woman he'd just met, they
made a plan to meet again. In both cases, the woman didn't show:

You surely don't fall in love after just a few hours, but I felt very disappointed; I had some emotions involved. The second time I was not as disappointed because I didn't expect nuffin.

I responded:

I think it's a profound challenge to adjust expectations without becoming numb or bitter; part of the trick seems to be having a clear self-identity, so as to balance one's realism and idealism.

Thomas agreed, adding:

You still have to trust people after your trust was disappointed - but you become more cautious before you trust.

You can tell we were communing about *ourselves*, but not exactly talking about *us*. That didn't last long.

It was apropos of my learned lesson that I'd written the recap for Thomas and sought his perspective in return. In asking about his inner experience relative to mine, I made no suggestion we'd ever meet, and didn't presume he would want to. That part was sheer fantasy, voiced only in the cause of gauging mutuality.

A familiar dynamic to the interplay between Thomas and me comes onstage again here. When I would take a delicate step of vulnerability, he'd come back with more directness and disclosure. This time he kicked it up a notch.

His next subject line was "I love playing with fire." After identifying it as a song title by the Runaways, he leapt straight to this:

I like the idea that we could fall in love if we should meet.

My shock drew in so much air, I didn't breathe for a second or two.

Staring at it now, I'm halted, barely knowing what to say. (I pause to jot in my notes: "officially in gasping-and-tears territory.") Breathing out, I keep reading Thomas's words:

I surely would like to meet you in person. But then? We could find out we bore each other within hours. We could find we love each other, but still have to split after holiday. Or we could find we should stay good friends and enjoy it all. Numbers 1 and 2 are the risks involved here.

Always the realist, this Thomas. Yet he was farther in than I'd known, farther even than I was. He continued:

I could try to win a green card in the lottery (there really is a lottery), sell everything and emigrate to the USA. "Que será será." "Ne'er say ne'er." We have to wait and see.

I'm still reeling. Meeting had never even been hinted at until I tiptoed up to it abstractly. My contemplations were wildly imaginary; his sounded a hair less so.

Thomas next gave a recap to match mine:

It started as a technical support problem. Eventually we found out we were two lonely people that met like ships passing by on the ocean - um, that's a different movie.

Eventually we found out we were two hearts feeling as one - well, not azackly...

It's endearing to see him indulge his silly side the closer he got to his serious point:

My view: I don't luv you - and you don't luv me. But by and by we found out more about each other and we both think more could evolve if we met in person (and we agreed our relation has to be platonic). I am not too keen to hear your voice on the phone (coz I'm afraid I won't understand much). I enjoy the typed exchanges very much (kinda sorta feel satisfied). But I also would like to meet you in person.

To his closing pair of sentences I replied:

Ditto to both sentiments. :-)

If I were forced to choose a single exchange to keep from the emails so far, it'd be the one with this sweet summation. It condenses Thomas's playfulness, realism and plainspokenness as perfectly as it encapsulates that moment in time and what we were doing with it.

In his words I hear a hint of self-talk, not unlike my own. I was trying to keep my heart in check with the exercise of reason; sounds like he was too.

ϒ CHAPTER 27

LOVE IS NOT LOVE...

The pair of synopses Thomas and I composed in March, themselves a treasure, sketch our story through the tenth week. The connection we felt engendered a sort of dabbling in the notion of love - something we could conceive of falling into if we were to meet.

Thomas titled one message, "Love is not love that alters when it alteration finds." As a literature major, it's funny I didn't recognize the Shakespeare line at first. I didn't know the Runaways song about playing with fire either. In both subject lines, you can see the toying-with Thomas was doing. No wonder I felt so drawn in.

Earlier, to Thomas's modest rejoinder about virtues and vices, I asserted:

Nope, I ain't seen your vices. But I don't hold any illusions that they aren't there.

I considered myself as much a realist as I took him to be. It was all the more reason his musings about love and meeting took my breath away. My initial reply to them was wordless - just a smiley with an exclamation point. How explosively enchanting to imagine!

My head drops back now against the chair, watery eyes squeezed tight, as I let myself reprise the giddiness.

Just like that, we two down-to-earth folks succumbed to daydreaming - while logically laying out imagined outcomes. When I recovered from the near-swoon, I responded more wordfully:

Once again, you pleasantly surprise me. I really could not predict your answer re pics and meeting. Oh, you're right, of course. Though #1 [boring each other] is not impossible, I honestly just don't think it would happen - and it would be a bigger disappointment than #2 [in love but apart]. I don't think #3 [just being friends] would be a bad thing either.

I gently pushed back on his emigrating ideation:

Come on now - you wouldn't do anything that permanent, just in case of #1. ;-)
But I like the idea of you coming here. Yes, we have to wait and see.

The breadth between my heady inner reaction and the measured tone of my emailed response is almost comical.

In his next message Thomas said:

I guess we won't meet this year - and before we meet, we shall discuss our expectations.

He was treating this as possible! With language more doubtful than his, I replied:

Maybe if we ever plan to meet, we ought to describe our vices along with our expectations.

The exchange raises two imponderables I'm pondering anyway. What most factored into Thomas's guess about not meeting that year? And, what most contributed to my being iffier than he was about meeting at all? I may never know.

To Thomas's mini-chronicle, I responded:

I liked your summation. I'm thankful for what I do have going for me in my situation, but the truth is that loneliness is a part of my life. And yes, I think there are times when our hearts feel pretty similarly.

It feels big that I spoke of loneliness plainly. I also took on his paragraph about love:

Thank you for giving me your view. I enjoy your plainspokenness. You know, the tricky part is, of course, defining our terms. Can a platonic relationship have love? A certain kind, right? Given this is "only" a cyber-friendship, I will admit to... hmm, what's the best word?... affectionate feelings, within the understandings we have established.

I loved him. Whatever qualifiers I needed to couch it in, what I was feeling was love.

At the beginning of this set of chapters, I told you of my astonishment. See what I mean? The scope of relational flourishing between Thomas and me within those two weeks alone is staggering.

This, like many of the Box's rewards, is unexpected - yet these are exactly the kinds of riches I knew must be here. In extricating them, I get to be both reminded *and* surprised. I'm all stirred up - and I'm not even done with this batch yet.

Always On My Mind

I've been trying to think of the best figure of speech for this watershed phase, and I keep coming back to *breaking it all open*. In early March, the friendship enlivening my days looked settled and stable. Two weeks later, it felt deeper, higher, in motion.

With the conversational turn toward inklings beyond friendship, I have to wonder what Thomas *really* thought and felt, given the discordant data of his other relationship. Did his contemplations about us amount to mischievous wishful thinking? Wishful for what exactly?

Such questioning likely informed my tenuous response about meeting. I needed to maintain perspective as to the colossal gulf between what I longed for and what I considered possible. Those musings I kept to myself when I replied:

That's what I'd already concluded too, that expectations would be laid out ahead of time. A year is not very long, but it can seem long in anticipation of something.

If that sounds familiar, it's because I made a similar claim - of my conclusion matching his - back when Thomas insisted the relationship had to be platonic.

A few messages after this, I offered a less-than-serious brainstorm:

When I studied Spanish, a requirement for teaching was spending some weeks in a Spanish-speaking country, your "immersion experience." See, you tell your boss how advantageous good English is for you as a techie, tell him you could improve your listening comprehension with a trip to the U.S., and then he pays for you to come here!

Thomas wasn't any more serious when he replied:

Thass it: the two of us meeting in Spain!

Such fun to dream! I came back with:

LOL. Well, wouldn't that be interesting! I sure hope the chances of you coming here in the not too awfully distant future are higher than the chances of me going to Spain very soon.

Now I too was speaking as though meeting were possible.

While we entertained such entertaining notions, we sought to define our relationship. To my confession of affectionate feelings, Thomas responded:

Our relation is something special for me. You make me check my mailbox quite often. Love has many different forms, but love is also an overused word. I'd say we're developing an intimate friendship (intimate in the platonic way).

Thomas's repeated qualifier, I now recognize, was a self-warning and a tell that his feelings ran deep. Mine sure did.

I've gone a few pages without having to pause and gather myself. I need to now. His next sentence closed that message:

No time to get into the "less cautious" stuff now.

I'd say he already had - and I couldn't wait to respond. An hour later, I wrote:

It warms my heart to hear you say so - and what a sweet thing for an email friend to say.

For you to get the impact of his mailbox remark, with its understated desire, it helps to know this was before auto-notifications. Users had to dial in without knowing whether messages awaited them - making this both a profound compliment and a beautiful emblem of this stage.

We were *involved* with each other.

A kind of solemnity descends as I consider the casual profundity of our words, how earnestly we meant them, and where they took us.

On one occasion, concerned he may have unintentionally neglected to address something I'd hoped he would, Thomas wrote:

Much more could be written in response… I hope I don't disappoint you.

To this I said only:

You never disappoint me.

He persisted:

I hope I will never!

It wrinkles the expression on my face to see his vehemence. I reassured once more, adding a gentle touch:

You're sweet, and I hope the same thing from this end. Notice I didn't say "you'll never," in the future tense.

Now I'm swallowing hard. I never doubted his words, even with all that followed. To this day, I hope he knows I never meant to disappoint him either.

Forests and Trees

That was one of those stunning clearings amid the lushness of other threads.

As for those side paths, I can't keep from touching on a select few - starting with another reference to German history. The Berlin Wall fell when Thomas was in his 20s. He wrote:

My memories begin in the 1970s, so there had always been two German states for me. The opening of the Wall and the German unification came absolutely unexpected to me. I turned on the TV and saw all these people pouring out of the East into the West!!!

I remembered that scene on TV too - from a bit farther way - and was awed to read his personal reminiscence of the epochal event.

We swapped more photos - of my sons, and some of ourselves as children - prompting more memory-sharing. This patch is dense with Strands and foreshadowings, such as this from Thomas:

Did I ever mention that I have no driver's license? I can do fine

w/o it. I think most Americans cannot imagine to live w/o car -
except if they live or work in the big cities.

Little could I imagine the factoid would become relevant to me.

Another bit of unwitting pre-relevance followed Thomas's mention that university attendance is free in Germany. I jested:

Maybe I should move to Germany to get my Master's and Ph.D.!

Not in my most ludicrous flights of fancy did I see myself actually considering, mere months later, what living abroad might be like.

A foreshadowing from nature carried less relational portent. I explained to Thomas why I was sending a message in the middle of the night:

We had a big thunderstorm, but I was sound asleep when my
doorbell rang at 3:15 - my downstairs neighbor said the parking
lot was flooding and I might wanna move my car to higher ground,
which I did. I'm back inside now…I'll be "wading" for your next
message.

I didn't recall this prequel to the months-later catastrophic flooding and, being hyper-aware about memory and its lapses, it took a moment to sort out my confusion.

One more reanimated scene is worth highlighting. After accessing Thomas's internet account for two weeks, I provided a report near the month's end to help him track the CompuServe hours used. It opened with yet another slice of life:

Some business stuff… Got up real early to drink hazelnut coffee

and surf the net at first daylight - what a treat! I left 5 or 6 minutes
unused, trying to err on the side of caution.

I went on to describe the Shakespeare and Tennyson websites I visited. It refreshes me again to think of Thomas's thoughtfulness with this gift.

There would be more precious gifts to follow.

Can't Keep It In

It's difficult to avoid repetition, describing for you this process of retrieval and illumination. For me, though, each group of emails is a fresh raw read, a confrontation with what I forgot, a confrontation with what I remembered - the current batch more than ever.

Deeply wistful amazement at what the Box has shown me so far is matched by wonder about what lies ahead. Only the sharpest flavors are still with me (have I said that before?), and because of what's gone, I get to retaste getting to know Thomas, message by message.

Preferences he'd mentioned earlier, such as his vegetarianism, I now asked more about. Here's how I circled back to his atheism:

A while back you closed with "No time to talk philosophies tonight
:-(." Well, I found that intriguing! You've said you're an atheist.
I'd like to hear how you arrived at that. I don't mind explaining
my positions, but I'd like to confirm your interest first. I realize
it's a biggie; are you interested in delving into this? Or is it too big
for our time constraints?

Big alright. You can call this another cliffhanger; there's no response in this batch.

Thomas's nonbelief was on my mind when I emailed this to my sister:

I still have a constant awareness this could end any day (though that seems less likely as we go along). I'm not building my life around it or compromising my faith, but I'm thankful for it, and I pray for TH. Bottom line: I'm involved with an atheist.

I gave her my prognostication, ending with a grin:

Realistic scenario: the issue of faith ends up dividing us (though I still think we'd stay friends). Worst scenario: he stops writing or changes to a less pleasant tone for no reason. Rosiest scenario: when I finally explain my faith, he finds it himself (and he moves here and we get married! <g>).

I'm letting out a slow sober exhale at this prescient still-life of my March 23rd, 1998 thinking.

Deb's is one of two outside printouts in this batch; the other was sent (a week earlier) to a literature prof I'd stayed in touch with. Segueing from a mention of the German professor, I wrote this breezier overview:

Speaking of Germans, I have a new cyber-friend from Germany. I wrote to an email address for Help listed inside a screensaver program I was having trouble with, and got a reply from "Thomas." He enjoys humor like I do; we quipped a lot, and it just went on from there... We're up to a hundred messages or so since January, and have exchanged pictures. It's been especially fun, and safer than usual, because it happened purely by chance, and we've established that it's platonic, yet special.

I'm so glad I kept these testaments to how I explained Thomas to others. This one counts all the more because the recipient was the professor responsible for my setting up email - mere months before my first message to Thomas.

The email to Deb stands out for how it confirms I'd back-burnered the girlfriend wrinkle by then; those ideations were hardly platonic. This time it's Gretchen's *absence* from the verbiage making me feel queasy and alarmed. Sure looks like I was sliding toward something I swore I'd never do: become part of a complicated relational scenario.

SUN AND SHADOWS

I like to survey the adventure in stages. The stretch from Tech Support Contact to Cyber-Friends measured six weeks. From Cyber-Friends to Meeting Someday took three. How long before there was talk of Me Going There, I wonder?

In our 131st message I wrote:

I had another thought about time difference today - something I experience that you don't: in the early evening when I check my messages and haven't gotten one from you yet, I have reason to believe you are probably writing to me at the very moment I'm thinking about you. But when I'm writing to you, you're usually already zonked.

It was as though we were doing life apart, together.

Even an inconsequential weather reference became a reflection I drew Thomas into, as with this from my March 26th email:

We had sun today and 78 degrees F. It felt wonderful, since we were only in the 40s yesterday. Kinda matches the sunny season in my life right now: I've got a rewarding job, a nice place to live, healthy kids, and I'm enjoying a new friend - wow!

I was *that* happy before the prospect of traveling to meet Thomas ever came up.

As the calendar flipped to April, it still hadn't. I embark on this batch (the first folder I'm taking all at once) treating expectations lightly, given the surprises so far. I'm floored at how deep and far Thomas and I went in March, the true wellspring of our special relationship.

The surprise of April is that we came to a plateau - different from early March's comfortable stability. As I listen to our voices, I no longer hear that sense of security in mine.

With this and every batch, by the way, it isn't until the second reading that I zero in on what settles, rises, sparks. First I just listen. A favorite sensation is when I hear in my old words a woman *I* would enjoy meeting. But in the 101 pages of this batch's 44 printouts, a less likable side of myself murmurs now and again through revived insecurities.

Thomas's message on the first day of April began:

Good morning!!!

That triple exclamation point leapt out; I delighted in it. He was, I think, as keenly aware of such niceties as I was.

Subject lines, greetings, signoffs: all were vehicles for wit or affection or both. You see the corollary, don't you? Occasions when they weren't stood out by contrast. These and other lenses show how the intensity of our relating - both in frequency and content - began to give way to demands of daily living.

Well, in the interest of accuracy: the slowdown came from Thomas's side. His email the following day opened with no greeting. It wasn't unusual for him to skip them in strictly tech-oriented messages - but this wasn't one of those. Rather, he was pressed for time:

This has to be a ten-minute message. Got up 1 hour early to send some messages. Not much time left. Thank you for the pics.

He signed with his go-to "CU, Thomas."

Before you allege I'm being too nitpicky - a charge I freely confess to - remember, as a new medium, a non-business email was seen as an electronic version of a handwritten note. I would never send a paper note without a salutation. Thomas's tone was changing, and I feel discomfort now over how I coped with that.

His rushed email above answered a newsy one from me, which I'd closed:

Well, that's about it for now, except for this: if there's anything you've learned about me over the past few months, you sure know I wouldn't want to find myself into this more than you are, which means I'm getting all risky again when I say... You mentioned not meeting this year, and lately I'm finding that really hard to wait for. Consider yourself invited here. There, I've said it, whew.

It was thoughtful of him, I recognized, to reply even briefly; he left the invitation unremarked upon, probably out of time pressure. My stating it so plainly was a step beyond our previous imagining and joking.

I kept my next response short as well, and then two days passed with no message from him. That hadn't happened (without advance warning) in weeks. On the 4th, I emailed again, with a blank subject line:

Dear TH,

You OK?

Katherine

I wrote to express kind concern as well as to satisfy my curiosity. Thomas's response made me glad I had.

Dire Straits, So Far Away

My nudge was rewarded without delay. The next morning, a Sunday, Thomas replied (omitting a greeting):

I'm OK, but in a dire strait - timewise and sleepwise. Thought I would have been able to write both Friday night and Saturday afternoon, but was too tired. I'll try to write more today but can't promise.

Signed with the standard CU, the sparing sentences got across how overstretched he was, which I hadn't been aware of. Relieved nothing else was wrong, I continued to send chatty messages.

When he found time to write more fully several days later, I responded:

I enjoyed so very much getting a longer message from you again! I hope this means your work burdens are easing somewhat. :-) I'm looking forward to writing a detailed reply along with some of my own news. (Are you interested in that kind of stuff - things that happened during my day? Or is that just boring? And as always, be honestly brutal.)

It's not hard to catch my former tentativeness rearing up, a departure from the certitude that Thomas looked forward to hearing my goings-on as much as I did to his.

Still, it was backgrounded against the unreserved nature on display when I resumed our beliefs thread:

Have you always considered yourself an atheist? Because I'm interested in you, I'm interested in what you believe. Lemme say this for starters about myself... After a long, intensely intellectual as well as spiritual search (which is never over) that has led me to the edge of atheism at times, I've arrived at a place of faith, for several specific reasons.

This forgotten distillation leaves me dumbstruck, chiefly because of its later significance. I added:

But I think I'm not typical as far as what that means to me, and I consider myself accepting of other people's beliefs. One thing I think matters a lot is the integrity of one's search and the ability to give reasons for what one believes. I don't hold my beliefs because they make me feel all warm and fuzzy: rather, they challenge me.

In his reply, Thomas cited inconsistencies and hypocrisy he observed in the German church, then mused:

You asked me why I am an atheist. Well, I dunno. But I'm dang sure that if there is a god, then he is not like the church is telling us! I rather believe in science. Big bang is a nice theory, but from

*where came all the matter that exploded in the big bang? If there's
a god, where did HE come from?*

This catches my attention as I type: there is latitude in both our
recitals, room to maneuver toward common ground. Months later we
would try mightily to do just that.

Indeed, my reply expressed agreement about hypocrisy ("God's
often not well represented") and about believing in science despite its
mysteries:

> *But I don't see science as incompatible with the existence of
> God. And hypocrisy can be found among adherents to any belief
> system: I hate it! If I had to base my faith on some "believers"
> I've crossed paths with, I might be an atheist. I'm not saying that
> lightly. Fortunately, I've met a precious few gems of genuineness
> and humility.*

I closed:

> *I love discussing things important to you and to me; this is a topic
> (like the male/female one) that may be nearly inexhaustible. So
> I'll stop now, but hey, ask me anything. :-)*

That was the last of that topic in April, possibly the last before
Thomas and I conversed about it on a bright summer day, strolling
side by side along a Cologne street.

I'm stunned to find we emailed about the god question to such an
extent - and doubly stunned at the parallel with the girlfriend question.
Both would become essential hinge points of our story, but neither's
earliest email appearances stayed with me into the ensuing years. Could
they have fuzzed out for some similar reason?

In the exchanges with Thomas about religion and atheism, my voice carried a hard-won confidence. The young girl who'd been cautioned against speaking her mind too freely yielded to the woman who had studied her way to clarity about what she thought and believed and why. I was in my element writing to Thomas, and I loved our discourse about big ideas. Yet I recognized my time and drive for connecting on that level was now in greater supply than his.

When Thomas's email pace let up, for perfectly understandable reasons, I continued to email not just messages but letters, while my old reluctance about coming on too strong hovered. (It has never completely gone away.)

By *coming on too strong*, I mean excessive self-expression that saps the interest of another. In my cyber-friendship with Thomas, it would've meant writing more words than he cared to engage with. I'm not sure that was the case in April, but I worried about it. In light of the leveling off, I worked hard to hold on loosely. I'd had plenty of experience with having to let go of something - of someone - precious.

On a weekend when my boys were away, I acknowledged our shifting rhythms:

> *I'm writing a rather long message, even though there are threads we haven't finished. Seems to be the pattern of things for us, since time and energy to write are largely controlled by outside influences from real life. I have time today, so I'm going to take advantage of it. And you may have things to say too, but don't have the time.*

It felt important to remind him I understood the demands on his hours.

Given Thomas's circumstances, I came to realize it might be kinder to match his stride, more or less. I reasoned he probably still enjoyed what I wrote, but that the reading itself could add to his load. Of course, I had plenty going on too, but writing as a pursuit energized rather than drained me; it's doubtful that was true to the same degree for Thomas.

The conundrum amplified an inner tug between self-assurance and self-doubt - and challenged me to trust what I'd already experienced of Thomas's nature.

☿ CHAPTER 29

MEET ME HALFWAY

April's downshift is visible in the physical properties of the printouts. A higher proportion of single-page messages and a lack of penciled keywords reflect the decline in conversations of substance. There were fewer laugh lines too, as Thomas's busyness seemed to detract from both his frivolity and his reflectiveness. Still, it was evident he didn't wish to give up our connection altogether.

He slowed and shortened; I didn't. Well, not much. I did adapt, not wishing to contribute to wearing him out. Sometimes I wrote fewer paragraphs or responded less quickly; I avoided posing questions and toned down exuberant greetings and signoffs when he did. It was good practice, I see now, in the art of being receptive to another's cues without forfeiting too much of oneself.

One of Thomas's brief emails riffed on a popular witticism:

I wonder if I could write a shorter message if I had more time
<sigh>. Well, don't expect many messages from me this week.

The heads-up was considerate. After voicing hopes to write on the weekend, this time he spelled out his usual acronym:

See you!
Yours Truly,
Sleeping Tom

I can almost see it occur to him, fingers tapping, to offset his terseness with a cutesy close; the softening warmed my heart. Thomas had a way of saying a lot with a little - and with me, a little went a long way. It helped convince me it wasn't the interest itself that had become lopsided.

He toasted his weekend message as his longest of that month. Comprised of quick takes, methodically (like a programmer) dipping in to acknowledge my themes, Thomas managed to hit the main points, but with less emotional engagement. He had time for doing *topics*, but not for doing *us*.

I took to fishing for assurances of interest before raising serious topics or sending articles and humor pieces, and reminded him:

I'm extremely interested in discussing ideas back and forth, not
just me dumping out lots of my stuff.

The same went for sending pictures. In one instance, my boys happened to pull out old photo albums, and I came across two snapshots I thought might interest him:

*I thought about sending them, but that felt forward or egocentric
or something, so let me know if you care to see them. Some people
are more into pictures than others, after all.*

His reply was interesting:

I don't mind if you send me pictures (I mean I really like to see 'em!).

It's as though he'd caught himself sounding unenthusiastic - then
left in both clauses anyway.

Since Thomas was posting up-to-date photos of himself at his
website, I wanted him to have more recent shots of me. I sent two with
this introduction:

*It still feels a little weird to just foist these on you, but I'm trusting
your earlier comment still stands. The only "current" pictures you
have of me are almost a year old and they are not good ones.*

He didn't comment on the photos - but that wasn't my reason for
sending them.

Similarly, there wasn't time for dialoguing about my written
contemplations, so I was heartened when Thomas closed a message with:

*Gonna respond to your "heavy stuff" in one of my forthcoming
messages.*

I looked forward to it, I said (exact words: "Oh goody!"), and
continued to encourage him amid his overwork:

*Hang in there, and don't hesitate to send record-breakingly short
ones if you happen to be in the vicinity of your computer anyway.*

Even the briefest messages meant a lot, I wanted him to know. This was genuine, of course, but it also hits me now, less positively, as what my old counselor would've called *pulling on* him.

I can tell you I would handle the correspondence differently now. Given the time burdens Thomas repeatedly voiced, which I claimed to empathize with, I would curtail my volume further, loosen my grip. Rather than nudging about unaddressed threads, I'd let them slide if he didn't bite.

My expressiveness and follow-ups hadn't presented a problem before his busyness picked up. After all, our tone and pace up to then had developed collaboratively. I liked to think I wrote as much for his enjoyment as for mine. Just as he got a kick out of telling me about his Friends of the Earth convention, I enjoyed describing my son's raucous seventh birthday party.

I opened our 165th message:

Sorry you're feeling behind again, and hope you feel freer soon. :-) Thought I'd send you one with lots of tidbits, but no questions, so that you have some (hopefully) enjoyable reading, but nothing to respond to, unless you want to later.

That sounds nice of me. I don't know whether the message was welcomed as the respite from work I intended, or if it amounted to one more task on his to-do list. He didn't say.

What I Like About You

Neither Thomas's increased workload nor my insecurities hampered us for long. Eventually he found a window of time to catch up:

Checked dozens of old messages…Found no threads I want to

comment on now. So please let me know if you expect a response to one of the old messages.

My run-on response sounds like it was teed up before he asked:

Well, that must have been tiring. One major thread I was expecting a response on was the "heavy stuff" from Easter weekend, because you wrote back immediately to say you would, and I wondered if that was because you had a reaction to my being afraid of loss if something happened to you.

I wasn't done:

Along with that, did you have any reaction to the song lyrics in that one? Oh, yeah - and did you get the most recent pictures? Two minor threads: I just wondered if you found anything funny in the church bulletin excerpts and/or the computer gender lists. And lastly, if time should ever permit it, I wouldn't mind talking some more about philosophies and faith, if you're interested.

The way my answer snowballed has my eyes rolling.

Clearly I didn't quite grasp the alteration to his availability, or I'd have known he didn't have the bandwidth for all this - though it's easier to see in retrospect. And because I was still expecting too much, I wasn't freeing him like I thought I was, like I would now.

This realization taps into an unpleasant feeling. I was fully prepared, going into the Box, for spirited glee and heartrending regret, but I didn't expect to dislike my old self in this way. (I thought it was too early in the story for that.)

Fortunately, the discomfort is eclipsed by enjoying our co-celebrating in other passages. Its most constant expression came from our mutual delight in music and wordplay; these were in our conversational DNA.

One April exchange centered on 80s duo Milli Vanilli, their connection with Germany, and their fall from grace. In another, I used a song by a favorite artist of his to circle back to our long closed discussion of relational dynamics:

> *Heard Joan Jett in my car tonight. (By the way, the guy in the song smiles at her first, then she gets up to ask him his name. Who initiated? :-))*

I remember feeling pleased with my rhetorical question.

Another thing Thomas always made time for was technical help. If I so much as hinted at a computer difficulty, he never failed to offer assistance, often spelling out detailed steps to try. Of course, this is where he was in *his* element.

Once, when my email service was cutting out intermittently, I wrote:

> *A super quickie just to tell you that Juno is being unreliable today. So please let me know if you don't get this. ;-)*

On a separate issue, in the middle of a series of steps, he said to expect a Windows alert:

> *Ignore this warning and trust me.*

I replied:

> *Almost completely! ;-) (It's me I don't trust.)*

It's funny I bothered with the word *almost*.

The banter with language persisted too. I took delight in acquiring

German phrases from him, and occasionally pointed out minor errors in his English. When I told him I'd appeared on local cable tv as part of my job, he joked:

Will your TV appearance be a first step towards a new career in the city of angles?

Pretty sure the misspelling was unintentional, I veiled my correction:

Well, one never knows of course! Such a city would have lots of geometric structures, I suppose. And does this mean that a square is made of four right angels? ;-)

He replied:

You got me!

He saw his chance to retaliate when I mentioned a *Time* magazine letter to the editor from a reader in Cologne, and asked whether the first name was male or female. He said, "Yes."

I mirrored:

LOL - ya got me!

The territory was changing with his busyness, but our lightness hadn't left.

THAT'S JUST THE WAY IT IS

These April emails bring a fresh paradox: they show less relational movement, yet I have more to say about it.

In one of the few deeply connecting passages, I told Thomas how hearing emotional songs that day led to "heavy thoughts" like this:

It's possible to be close emotionally to someone far away, and it's also possible to be far away emotionally from someone who is physically right next to you. I've been in both situations, and I say the former is infinitely better even if it's hard.

He addressed this ten days later:

It sounds more obvious when rephrased: better to have no relation than a bad one, and better to have a good but remote relation than none.

Once again, our generalities obviously applied to ourselves. I remember wishing he would be more direct.

He also went back to my worry about losing touch:

Friendships sometimes end when people's situations change. But we've met in cyberspace. I'm a computer addict for 16 years now, and it's not likely to change. We will see how long our cyber-friendship is gonna last. Currently I can see no reason why it should end.

OK, so he did get direct; it was kind of him to reassure me. I would've liked him to say he *wanted* it to last, but it was implied - a matter of style.

I responded to Thomas's forecast:

Indeed, cyberspace has been kind to us in this. And I know it goes without saying that I'm glad we met and that I hope it lasts a very long time - it's so bizarre not only that we got connected at all but that we feel a connection in other ways as well.

My more emphatic style stands out by contrast.

When I wasn't tentatively adapting to Thomas's cadences, my directness came out big-time. At mid-month, there was another silent spell without notice. After four days, I sent these two sentences all by themselves:

Thought I'd say hello. Hope all is well with you.

That's not the direct part yet. In fact, I deliberately avoided posing my well wishes as a question. His reply - in which he explained being swamped by a large project with a looming deadline - prompted me to bare my soul:

> *Hearing from you really matters to me. But I'm afraid of you*
> *thinking I'm too attached or something. No matter how I try, I*
> *can't seem to silence the voice inside that keeps saying, "Katherine,*
> *in your life, you've lost a lot of people who were special to you;*
> *it's only a matter of time before you lose this one too." I always*
> *have the feeling anything could change at any time, so maybe that*
> *means there's no real benefit to guarding my feelings.*

Once I got going, there was no point holding back:

> *I hope you don't misunderstand or think I'm crazy. The timing of*
> *your project was interesting because I'd just poured my heart out*
> *last weekend about not hearing from an old friend. And it's ok,*
> *I understand and everything. I learned something about myself*
> *though - that I'm past the point of it just being casually nice to*
> *hear from you. If you're not, that's ok. And another thing: I want*
> *to meet you so badly I can hardly stand it sometimes, but I know*
> *I have little choice in the matter. How's that for unguarded?*

No matter how many times I go back over them, I can't read those sentences without full-on weeping. I wouldn't have been that vulnerable with just anyone, or at just any juncture with Thomas. Our mutually frank exchanges the month before paved the way.

The midweek message reached him during his office workday; he replied that evening, noting he had to be brief. The immediacy of the response conveyed caring - while he didn't compromise on his realism:

It's dang sure that we won't meet this year. And maybe we will never meet. In the good old times I took the time every day to write to you.

I knew plenty well we might never meet, but it did something for me to express how much I wished for it. I understood too that the frenzy of our initial correspondence couldn't last. It's funny to hear him refer to our "good old times"; barely three months earlier we were unaware of each other's existence. It's even funnier to see how certain - and wrong - he was about not meeting that year.

His hurried reserve gave way to a bit of warmth as he wrapped up:

Well, my dear friend: I don't think you're crazy.

Suddenly I'm aware of my thumping heart and flowing tears. I responded:

About not meeting this year... Yeah, I know. I appreciate your candor, even though I wish it were different. About maybe never meeting... Ouch. This one's much harder to swallow. Say it ain't so. I know - you can't say that. I used to wonder in the good old times how long we could sustain that pace. How I loved it! And I'd still like to think a time like that could come around again somehow.

If I fretted that his *maybe never* suggested waning interest, it was fleeting. That was just Thomas being real. I supposed too that his pessimism was darkened by how preoccupying his work had become. Maybe it wouldn't always be that way.

As if I'd learned my lesson, I wrote:

Lots more on my mind but I'll wait until we can talk back and forth about it.

My implication that we weren't having conversations anymore could have stung, given his prior concern over disappointing me. Or perhaps it came as a comfort, proof I was acclimating to reality.

More Than Words

You and I have reached a milepost of our own. We're halfway through the months of messages Thomas and I exchanged before I went to meet him. When I first opened the slimmer April folder, its neatly compressed printouts made me think of a book never leafed through. Now the pages are roughed up, fluttering with vitality.

They contain no shortage of foreshadowings; tiers of them show up in Thomas's vignette about a kitchen plumbing snafu:

We had water in the cellar, a really big mess. Now that we have a new sink, the problem is solved. My place is safe, but Cologne has been flooded several times when the Rhine was high.

We? I wonder how I contextualized that. Maybe after four years of sharing the home he owned, the verbal habit lingered after his girlfriend left. Looks like he broke it by the third sentence.

Thomas's flooding reference both foreshadows and post-shadows deluges in my neighborhood. I said in my reply that I'd like to see what his place looked like and asked him to send pictures. (He didn't.) You already know I would soon see his place for myself.

For what it's worth, I acknowledge that with a memory-layered project like this, by kneading the raw material enough I can find foreshadowing in everything. And when I'm not seeing in layers, I'm hearing voices.

When I read Thomas's emails now, I hear them in his familiar lilt - but of course, I couldn't the first time I saw them. It's got me thinking about how we hear another's voice through their writing, someone we've never heard speak. Back then, when Thomas's words sounded terse or harried, they played in my mind in an imagined voice with the most positive intonation I could give them.

Reading my own messages, I hear and feel the state of mind behind my words - usually excited, at times entreating or angsty. If they'd been uttered orally, he would've heard me choking up. I remember hoping he would hear the inflection I imbued them with as I typed.

When we speak, or write, our voice into another's being, and receive theirs, what we want from the exchange is both self-oriented and other-oriented, ideally in equal measure. From the start with Thomas, I liked how our connecting made me *feel*, and hoped the same was true for him. Amid April's syncopations, this felt marginally more difficult to achieve - or at least to know from my end whether I'd achieved it.

The overstuffed May folder at my side, waiting to be soul-searched, suggests Thomas and I regained our rhythmic flow not much later.

Back at the end of March, no matter how ardently I wished for it, I couldn't conceive of ever getting to meet Thomas. By the end of April, although it was not one iota more likely, I could hardly stand the thought of *not* meeting him.

Ɏ CHAPTER 31

WHEN MAY IS RUSHING OVER YOU

I did meet Thomas in person.

This is the central fact of the entire account.

Everything before and after it sets forth why it's an incredible sentence for me to type. But we're not quite to that point in the email record. I'm still scratching away to unearth just how it came about, nails wearing down with the digging. And as memory's gaps gradually fill in, I'm watching a sort of topography take form.

Within May's bulging folder, we will reach a highland. I know this because of what I told you from memory about making a momentous decision Memorial Day weekend. With that attraction on the horizon, and the slew of emails to traverse before we get there, I feel nearly overwhelmed. I'm bringing this upon myself though, too impatient to take portions of the folder's 80 printouts and treat them in smaller batches. No, this time I have before me all 215 pages of May's bounty (more than twice April's) in one bundle. By the time the sunlight touches the final leaf, I will know something magnificent I do not know now.

I remember the *fact* of making plans to visit Thomas, but with no accompanying recollection of how the idea materialized in our email conversation, not even in snippets or Strands. Tantalizingly close to finding out, I settle into position, flanked by laptop to one side, mug of coffee on the other. The unruly folder balances on my knees - and before I've even lifted the manila flap, warm slow tears once more dampen my smiling cheeks.

Our return to tempo is clear within a few printouts, Thomas's regained breathing room discernible from his subject lines alone. Rather than merely hitting Reply to my titles, he was back to creating his own. Picking up on his relaxation, I wrote:

Seems to me we're about ready for a new thread (or for going back to an old one), unless you're expecting a busy week. Got anything you want to start on?

He titled his reply, "A new thread starts here" and after a perky greeting ("Hi!") proclaimed Germany's football champion for the season. The details he recited signaled newfound leisure too. For his American friend's benefit, he specified:

Football means soccer, of course.

The winning football club (Kaiserslautern) was based in the city whose university Thomas had attended, and only now do I notice the parallel with my cheering on the Green Bay Packers.

You've seen how I love to extract trifles as well as thunderbolts - there are scores of tidbits and torrents to distill from May. The process ought to be getting smoother, now that I've been at this a while. Although it has become easier to decide what to share with you, with the mushrooming of dialogue comes an added intensity to the culling and digesting this takes for me first. At times I get so carried away I almost feel able, for a split second, to not know how the story comes out.

A variation of this operates more broadly as the saga unfolds - a melding of coming-to-know with already-knowing. I get to be a storyteller whose story is being told to me.

I'm about to be told how the wispy idea of someday meeting my cyber-friend in person morphed into a solid plan. What were the conversations which took Thomas and me, over these many pages, to that highland in the distance?

I am at long last ready to find out.

Never Say Never

A sequence of crossed thresholds: that's how I'm experiencing this telling. I suppose that could describe all stories, all lives. As Thomas and I entered our fourth month of emailing, a naturalness returned to my demeanor, blotting out the unease that had surfaced during his extra-busy weeks.

I closed an early May message:

One more itty bitty thing: I was thinking the other day of what you said about possibly never meeting, and I thought of just one more

response to that, and it's in your own words (from the first time
we talked about it): "Ne'er say ne'er, we have to wait and see..."

The quoted line went back six full weeks - a long way in our time scheme. I considered the subject settled, had no designs on reopening it, and got a kick out of throwing his own words back at him.

My breezy manner brings a moment of hesitation... Did I overplay the disquiet I saw behind some of my April emails? I doubt it. In any case, I'm uninclined (indeed, I refuse) to revise those chapters accordingly. As you know, I've framed this project as a commitment to bring you with me through such fluctuations, rather than "correcting" myself. After all, although we mold for ourselves what old episodes mean, there's only so much revising of the past we can do in real life.

My very next message shows me another bit I won't amend. Alongside Thomas's Kaiserslautern paragraphs, he'd remarked he didn't otherwise care much about football. I replied:

That's how I am about American football - except when the
team from Green Bay is winning. They won the Super Bowl in
January 1997, and made it back in 1998, but lost. That's the game
I mentioned before I knew you were in Germany.

Reminders of how I learned Thomas's location are always a treat; I highlight this one to poke fun at myself over a contradiction. Mere pages ago, I told you the parallel between his nearby sports team and mine had only just occurred to me. Wrong again, all part of the process.

This batch teems with delightful morsels. Penciled keywords - you know, the ones that disappeared from April's printouts - are still absent on May's, despite our extended colloquies. I do, however, find penciled notes where I didn't expect them: on the inside flap of the manila folder, a careful log of time spent on the web using Thomas's account.

Maybe tracking those hours prompted me to ask, out of curiosity and renewed ease, about another settled matter:

Re your webphone idea... We'd discussed system requirements and times of day, and you said you'd do a web search about it. Ten days later, you said you weren't keen on it because you might not understand much, which I understood. Was there something specific in between that changed your mind?

His response was unexpected:

I didn't change my mind about the webphone - it's something I'd like to try eventually. We have to find and download software, set everything up, and log into a "meeting point" on the web at the same time in order to start speaking. I'm still past schedule with some programming I have to do. Just finished 8 orders, and it's past midnight again.

Glad I asked! He sounded busy but not frazzled. I replied:

I'm pleasantly surprised - guess you caught me in another errant assumption.

The assumption wasn't unreasonable, given his earlier waffling. I well recall my excitement at his being open to it after all.

In this thread, I also presented a separate scheme to Thomas, with the same objective of hearing each other speak - though not in real time. Before webphoning ever came back around, I charged ahead with my new idea.

Can You Hear Me Now?

For arrangements to talk live over the web, I was entirely dependent on Thomas the techie. But for what I had in mind, I was less so:

I have an alternative proposal. It requires a leap backward in technology, but it's a way we could hear each other's voices without having to worry in real time about being understood. We could snail-mail cassette tapes - I used to do this with friends years ago.

His being out front technologically could've made it unworkable, so I probed:

Do you even have a cassette player that has recording capability?
I do, and it would also enable me to send you a song or two to get your opinion on. Just an idea.

It's comical to me that I was asking Mr. Cutting Edge to resort to older equipment for this. Again, he pleasantly surprised me:

We surely could do that. But before I can record CD music for you, I'll have to get some of my ancient technology repaired (or try to repair it myself).

At his mercy only for his half of my idea, one week later I wrote:

BTW: a snail mail package is going out to you tomorrow.

Just shy of three months after Thomas had airmailed me a package, I returned the favor. These were the cassettes documented in the teal folder. From my May email I learn that whatever I said on the speaking tape, I repeated it in Spanish.

Days later, he wrote:

Your cassettes arrived. Took the time right now to listen to your voice recording. I think you have a pleasant voice. And I think I understood every word you said.

The compliment elated me and, as I noted to Thomas, the $3.84 airmail cost was money well spent. I remember how this incremental step *mattered*. What a sublime find his response is! It shimmers, held between thumb and forefinger up to the light of all that came later.

In May Thomas also had the mental space again to comment thoughtfully on my topics and to raise new ones. We were back to *conversing*. One discussion he kicked off centered on the issue of assisted suicide. He concluded his introduction:

What do you think? Some heavy stuff. I hope I don't mess up your morning with it.

Far from it, I told him. His invitation invigorated me. The theme generated expansive paragraphs from both of us, its crescendo a gripping personal experience he shared in detail - one I'd forgotten about entirely.

MYSTERIOUS WAYS

It was heartening to see Thomas back in a frame of mind conducive to in-depth exploration - for his sake and mine. Our discourse on assisted suicide was particularly engaging, in that our viewpoints differed somewhat, yet in the course of explaining our reasoning, we found ourselves more aligned than first appeared. It was in this context that Thomas described a brush with mortality:

I once experienced a collision between a car and a train - I was in the first car of the train. It was dark outside. Suddenly there was a big noise and showers of sparks were flying outside the window. The train was trembling. After the train came to a halt, I said to another passenger: "So that's how it feels when a train gets derailed." I really thought some playing children had placed a stone on the rail or so.

I was riveted. He continued:

I opened a window, looked out and saw the driver of the train open a door and examine the situation with a flashlight - only then I realized the train had collided with a car. He said the car had been waiting next to the rails, but made a jump ahead moments before the train arrived. Newspaper said next day this man had been left by his wife. I think only one axle was derailed. If two axles were derailed, well, maybe I wouldn't be here.

That last remark elicited this from me:

That's a heart-stopping thought!! Which is strange if you think about it, cuzz if that had happened, it wouldn't have affected me - I would've never known what I'd have missed (unless the accident would've happened since last January). Time is a strange thing. It's sure heart-stopping to think of that as a present possibility.

Again I couldn't move on without revealing, in so many words, that I feared losing him.

His train wreck passage epitomizes the kind of stories I relished hearing from my favorite "foreigner." May's emails offered numerous windows into Thomas's life, such as how he came to do beta testing for Microsoft, and the backstory to developing his screensaver collection. These are absolute delights to relearn now.

Because I imparted so much about myself, I'm being reacquainted with episodes from my own past as well, with eye-opening details I never would've reclaimed. The stories going into depth about leaving

my marriage and choosing my educational direction, I notice, showed the same kind of moxie it would take to meet Thomas in person.

In Any Key

When someone you love is far from you, hearing of their goings-on and telling them yours lifts you both. Although I'd never been with this friend who became so dear so quickly, the everydayness of our May sharing resonates as if Thomas were someone I'd known personally who moved away.

Sketching present and past experiences, debating social issues, comparing notes on favorite authors: *this* is the meatiness I remember from this stretch.

Alongside frequent lyric quizzes, Thomas and I swapped occasional literary quotes. A protracted repartee about one author got launched in the thick of a dry technical thread. Thomas elaborated on a common computer instruction:

> *BTW: The Shift, Ctrl, and Alt keys normally don't work if you're asked to hit *any* key. [This is no longer true.] All keys are equal, but some keys are more "any" than others.*

Because I didn't credit him with the allusion at first, I'm embarrassed by my reply:

> *Haha. Are you familiar with George Orwell? (British author, 1940s: 1984, Animal Farm, and some outstanding essays.) In Animal Farm, the main character (a pig), says, "All pigs are equal, but some pigs are more equal than others."*

His response:

Yep. I have about a dozen Orwell books (most of them only in German, but 1984 and Animal Farm also in English).

I was impressed:

Wow!! I have both of those, but not in German. ;-)

I'm utterly charmed to see how the subject came about. His clever literary twist in such a dissimilar context wasn't the only time the technical domain provided humor. In a message I titled, "Are you ill Orwell?," I told him of an MS-DOS novelty some readers may remember:

I used to have a little program called "Drain," which was fun to show unsuspecting computer neophytes. The screen tells you it's about to remove excess water from your CPU, and then you hear the sound of draining water.

Another aural reference came with Thomas's help on a modem issue. He wasn't trying to be funny but I'm chuckling now:

You should hear a signal when the modem goes "off hook," hear a melody while it dials the number (unless you use pulse dialing), hear the modem on the other end and your modem while they squeak for several seconds. If not, there's a problem with the number you are calling (or with the way your modem dials).

How such an unadorned set of sentences takes me back! His rendition of the process (the *beeping and blurping* from my memory-narrative) furnishes a technological reminiscence inseparable from the fondness for Thomas it renews.

I was intrigued, though mystified, by the technology that brought us together; Thomas actually *understood* it. We converged on being into details. May saw us spend whole paragraphs on the minutiae of time stamps, comparing how long it took messages to reach each other at different times of day. With similar exactitude, we delved into nuances of English, German, and tech-speak vocabulary. Our shared wavelength was such a gift.

A further gift I receive today comes by way of forgotten vignettes involving my sons. I repeat the boyhood scenes to Sam and Ben and we talk about which memories they still carry. One of these old micro-moments is making me laugh my way to tears all over again.

Lightness and Laughter

Each story has its own pacing. Whereas the author of fiction dictates their contrivance's movement, this chronicle keeps faith with the timing of actual events in the email record. And yet, I'm afforded leeway in choosing when to give in to its natural momentum, when to resist and linger. With this paragraph, I'm decelerating - exactly because I feel so propelled toward the part about meeting Thomas. The forward energy derives not just from the old storyline, but from my current experience of it.

You see, I've now read far enough in the Box to understand how the trip came about. I finally know how it happened, but haven't told you yet - and I can hardly wait. Casting eager eyes ahead, I gesture impatiently toward the landscape I'll soon describe, in pages I'll soon write. But I have terrain to cover first, charms to dangle for you on the way there.

The essential cord of my email bonding with Thomas is ornamented with a variety of trinkets. Those having to do with my little boys sparkle brightest. On May 17th (in our 229th message), I wrote:

A few weeks ago, Sam noticed me doubling over with loud guffaws and squeals of laughter and, of course, wanted to know what was so funny. I was reading your responses to "20 Ways to Annoy People," so I told him about that list.

Today it'd be called a listicle. Little did I know it had stayed with my 9-year old:

Two days ago, he was very angry at me because I got sick of him begging for something I'd already said no to. So whenever he brought up the same request, I just looked at him without answering. Then in an angry pout he said, "Well THAT'S something you should add to your annoying list!" He stormed off and I couldn't help laughing.

It multiplies my amusement to read the snippet to my now 35-year-old; he doesn't recall it. But he hasn't forgotten seeing his mom so happy about her cyber-friend.

Making me laugh was one of my friend's superpowers; another was putting himself in my technologically limited place - the first trait I'd observed as his customer. When we cyber-met, I thought I was doing pretty well tech-wise just to be emailing from a home PC. Many emails from May's batch were (as usual) elongated by problem-solving passages targeting my computer issues, with his patient "if this / try that" steps. While he empathized with me, I put myself in his position:

Must be a powerful feeling to be good at troubleshooting. It sure feels powerless not to be.

In one instance, I was sure my amateur user skills were insufficient for a course of action he recommended. I lamented:

You have too much confidence in me.

Thomas pushed back with a light touch:

Won't take no as an answer from a techie woman that's smart enough to run programs in DOS boxes and download the appropriate display driver. We'll try it together.

I utter an audible "aww" - as I did back then.

To show you where this thread took us, I need to insert a tangent. Months before, Thomas had asked whether I used the nickname *Kathy*, and volunteered:

I don't like to be called Tom. Don't call me Thommy. TH is OK.

I responded:

I lived my whole early life as Kathy. In my 20s, I started using my longer given name. I like it and I think it reflects me better. Tell you what, if you don't call me Kathy, I won't call you Thommy.

TH was now helping with a PC I'd purchased a month later - from a local techie who built it with more affordable off-brand components. When it began having problems, the builder stopped returning my calls; I referred to him as "Jack, the disappearing techie." It was the modem giving me difficulties when I complained:

You'd think there'd be a way to get at the initialization string in Juno or CompuServe, but this is all over my head.

Thomas probed:

But didn't you set up your modem as one of the standard types that come pre-configured with Windows?

I snarked:

Good question - I have no idea. Let me know if you get a hold of Jack.

Matching my attitude, Thomas parried:

Why Jack? Kathy installed the dial-up network, so I asked Kathy about it.

Not about to let that slide, and all in good fun, I explained:

W-e-e-l-l-l, I *do* remember that Kathy "installed the dial-up network," but that's not what Thommy said above. Thommy said "...set up your modem..." Kathy thought Jack did the modem set-up, cuzz Kathy doesn't understand the difference between these two actions. Besides, Kathy only installed the dial-up network with LOTS of help from Thommy, so Thommy is the person Kathy should ask. :-)

Thomas bowed in emphatically punctuated defeat:

LOL!!!

It was hard to imagine a better feeling than making Thomas laugh! Since I'd recently learned the German word for day, I replied:

:-) ...makes my Tag!

I love seeing the spiritedness in how we interacted on the page - well, on our monitors.

Don't these two sound like they enjoy each other?

⟨ CHAPTER 33

RETROSPECTIVE

I t was a rapturous time, and I reveled in it. Frequently, as with this
May paragraph, I let Thomas in on my reflections:

*Got distracted today looking at msgs from mid-March. I laughed,
I cried, and then I laughed almost until I cried, and I only read
ten days worth! Although it's only email and there's plenty we
may not know about each other, it really is amazing how much
we *do* know - we've covered an awful lot of history in four
months. Sometimes when I'm writing something silly, I think you
can almost see me smirking.*

On another occasion, I'd been hunting down some specific tidbit
from our early contact, and remarked:

I laughed at myself when I reread some stuff I said about risk, like the paragraph where I said it wouldn't be that big a deal if you stopped writing. Guess it sorta wasn't at the time - that was pretty long ago (in the email realm). Remember all that stuff about who sees the sun first? How about this: you see the sun seven hours before me, but I experience life six and a half years ahead of you.

I'm picturing Thomas rereading those words today and chuckling too - I long for that. (Insert smile/tear emoji.)

Again contemplating the email medium, I wrote:

Other than the speed of correspondence, it's not that different from plain old letter writing. We've been at this long enough to have learned a lot about how we each tend to communicate. E.g., I've gotten better at knowing when your questions are rhetorical, or when you're misspelling on purpose. I imagine you know better where I'm coming from than you used to. I like the idea of getting better at this. Would you concur?

My judgment:

Whereas the speed of email makes it more like a conversation than paper letters, the lack of direct feedback makes it more like paper letters than a conversation. You could simply say there's some trust involved.

It's plain to see how my trust in Thomas and in myself had grown. Elsewhere I turned the review of past messages into self-critique:

I notice I tend to be reflective and analytical in the moment, too much for some people's tastes, I know. Saw a lot of that in my old comments. I still sometimes wonder when I'm writing long musings (like this!!) whether you're bored, cuzz I still can't see the look on your face. But what's changed is, I'm not worried about it like I used to be.

It was pleasing progress, comfort outweighing doubt. I explained further:

Somewhere along the way I got comfortable with being myself and telling you what I wanna tell you, and if you don't like it, you'll have to tell me. I'm always attracted to others who I sense are comfortable with who they are. Anyway, if I write too much let me know.

Familiar plea, different energy. I'm finding this woman more likable again.

Thomas responded:

No, you don't bore me at all. I'm just kinda sorta a bit uncomfortable because I recently haven't had the time to send you long messages in return.

And I said:

I'm *really* glad you told me, cuzz I hadn't thought of it quite that way. That's thoughtful of you.

Of course, I was heartened to read his first sentence - but the disclosure that followed warmed me even more, because he took me a step further into his experience. It always meant so much to be welcomed there, as I welcomed him into mine.

My self-reflections show how I used messages to my faraway friend as a sort of diary I freely gave him the key to. It says something beautiful about a person when their effect on you is to make you want to share yourself with them.

It wasn't quite as common for Thomas to spell out his sentiments, so it stood out when his subtext revealed them. He closed one message:

I'm at home today (and have no time), but you know I am easily distracted...That was enough distraction for this morning. Maybe I'll write more tonight.

How warm and sweet this feels, again. I returned:

Uh huh - it's one of the things I like about you - especially if I'm the distraction.

He ended a message a few days later:

Now I want to do some serious programming...unless I find something to distract me.

We had such fun with callback lines. My next message was titled, "something distracting..." and I signed off three pages later with:

Enough distraction?

We kept on - but you get the idea.

Before long, I would present Thomas with his biggest distraction yet.

Invisible Touch

A favorite early conversation with Thomas, you'll recall, had to do with question marks. I barely knew him when I called him out for not using them much. Over relational mountains we'd climbed since,

I myself came to use them sparingly when I knew he was short on time. And if he missed a question important enough, my once timid reminders now took the form of harmless ribbing:

I see you made no attempt to answer my Orwell question - I shall be forced to assume that I've stumped you this time. :-)

Or this, after his (rare) failure to answer a technical question led to a logical misstep on my part:

What you see above is what happens when you don't answer my questions! Admit it, it was funny, and that's the important thing... :-)

I'd figured out it wasn't needy of me to simply nudge for a response; Thomas granted as much with his apologies. Once, when he hadn't acknowledged an image attachment, my prompt weeks later garnered this from him:

I got the latest pictures on April 9. Everything's fine - sorry I didn't tell ya! The messages with pictures are easily overlooked by me cos they don't show under your name.

The helpful explanation was comical in its own way. I could only send image files to Thomas via his CompuServe account; it hadn't occurred to me his inbox would display those messages with his name as both sender and receiver.

With renewed elbow room for random questions and fresh topics, I tossed in curiosities such as whether he had pets. He replied with a grin:

I live alone - no pets around. Watering some flowers is the maximum responsibility I can stand at this time. <g>

My rejoinder:

I have children, but I don't do flowers - too much responsibility. <g>

As Mother's Day approached, I wrote:

The holiday is always a little bittersweet, if you know what I mean. Is this celebrated in Germany?

His sardonic reply:

Yeah, it's also celebrated here (since we also have Fleurop).

I gathered Fleurop was a European version of FTD, the flower delivery service familiar to me. On the Sunday morning in question, I asked whether he'd be seeing his mother, and his response suggested bittersweetness for him too:

I'm sorry I have to say it, but I hope I won't see my mother today - my mood is better if I don't.

It's an exchange I'd forgotten about, prefiguring what I later observed between them. Thomas's mother came up in another unrecalled passage, one that also referenced his girlfriend - by name for the first time:

Gretchen is in the hospital. My mother is on holiday. So I have to water flowers in three places, not just one. <heavy sigh>

I sympathized:

I'm so sorry to hear that. I hope she is better soon! You poor dear. <g> I'm sure the thirsty little blossoms really appreciate it. :-)

Not much later, it was me who benefitted from his sympathy. In a message titled, "a quickie from a sickie," I gave Thomas this brief report:

Thought I'd drop a quick one before I shut down early. Apparently I caught the sickness Sam had a few days ago. Woke up ok but started to feel yucky after I wrote you this morning. Been in bed ever since. The figure of speech for this around here is, I feel like I got hit by a truck.

In my favorite response from my favorite problem solver, Thomas wrote:

Can't solve that problem for you, so I can only offer my compassion...
<g>
Pity pity pity pity. Poor Katherine! Oh, poor dear...

I was so touched and cheered:

Perfect! If laughter were all it took to heal me, I'd be all better now. :-) Tnx for the compassion.

While I was still sick, Thomas's mention of Germany's unseasonably warm weather led to banter about degrees Celsius vs Fahrenheit. He sent the conversion formula, and I quipped:

You would give homework to a sick woman? That's not very compassionate... <g>
Time to rest again. It really did make me feel better to hear from you.

Our sweetness around the minor illness felt especially bonding. I let him know of my improvement a day or two later:

I'm now ambulatory and starting to feel better! (Must have been the laughter :-))

I love the braiding in this thread of hilarity and tenderness - for us, virtually the same thing.

My vision, a few pages ago, of Thomas rereading and chuckling at our words comes back with an added detail now: at the funniest parts, I see a tear in his eye.

Hold On, Things Could Go Your Way

Enough of dangling charms and delay. Parked in my writing chair, in still-dark morning hours, I'm set to deconstruct for you the emails that got me across the ocean to meet Thomas. In the silence, I reflect on making it this far into the Box, on arriving at this precipice - and erupt into raucous laughter.

As it happened, until May it hadn't occurred to me to question the pronunciation of his first name. He'd pointed out the silent 'h' but neglected to mention that in German the first syllable rhymes with Rome. Once I began dabbling with the language, I became curious about the name as he would speak it; I wanted to *hear* it. I turned to a local resource, and on May 18th announced:

I chatted in person with native German speakers today: Reinhard and his son, who both teach at the college. Now I know how to pronounce your name - I like it even better in German.

Three days later, I mentioned my former professor again:

BTW: I found out Reinhard is going (coming?) to Germany this

summer. Believe me, if there were any way for me to tag along, you know I would!

My Thursday message continued:

Another BTW: Monday is a holiday here; it's Memorial Day, to honor those who died defending the country.

As I encounter both by-the-ways, my eyebrows crease and my pulse ticks up - the reason why still vague at best.

I wrote that the day before my decision weekend - but our emails had not mentioned meeting since the third week of April, when Thomas repeated it wouldn't happen that year. More baffling still, no hint of it came up in our 22 missives spanning Friday through the Monday holiday.

The reference to Reinhard's Germany trip is a clue - although I did not, in fact, tag along with him. Curiously, for as much as I tend to read *into* our old emails, I believe I've found an instance of my deliberately planting a foreshadow at the time. It's in my response to a Saturday paragraph from Thomas where he explained a change in public transit schedules. I asked how long it takes to get from his town to Cologne, with this aside:

(I have a strong feeling that someday somehow I'll get to come and see what that's like.)

An intrigued smirk lifts my expression; I hold the remark in reserve as I keep going through the printouts...

Aha - here's the Big Reveal!

It's in the message I wrote the morning *after* Memorial Day. Our 249th email, sent Tuesday around noon and reaching Thomas at 7 that evening, carried the subject line, "Better sit down for this..." Following my German greeting ("Hallo Thomas!"), the dispatch consisted of a single paragraph:

> *Here's a distraction for you… Are you sitting down? Believe it or not, I've come across an opportunity to come to Germany for a few days in July or August. JSYK [just so you know], I'm not assuming anything. Tons of open questions, I know. Any thoughts?*

I signed with an unembellished "K."

This is the key! Myriad thoughts racing, I hardly know how to continue; first I need to catch my breath.

So the impetus was all mine - what an epiphany!

That I presented it to Thomas as a happenstance travel opportunity reminds me of a scrap I haven't told you of yet. At the front of the May folder is a half sheet of unlined paper, torn-edged and scribbled with notes I hadn't been fully able to decode. Among its jottings is the lone word *opportunity*; nearby is the phrase *him as an added feature*. It isn't until I come to the end of the month's printouts that I can make sense of this.

Remember, from the memory-narrative, my consulting with a counselor before the trip? These are obviously notes I took during that phone call. The scrap's phrases also include: *eyes open…safety plan… don't see a problem…go for it…have a great time!* The scratchings point to steps I took before letting Thomas in on my idea.

I now think my inner urgency a chapter ago was telegraphing the enormity of what this means. The visit happened when it did because *I* catalyzed it, out of a boldness my much younger self could not have acted on. The crux of the story, before I ever went to meet Thomas - an amazing and beautiful epoch all its own - was about meeting *this moment*, a whole new level of living out who I was becoming, of seeing how far it could take me.

By now you must be curious, as I was, about Thomas's reaction. Curious doesn't come close to describing my suspense.

No Better To Be Safe
Than Sorry

M oves I made toward a possible Germany trip took place outside of conversation with Thomas - the revelation stops me in my tracks. A strange sensation of having finished telling the story passes through me, makes ephemeral sense to my deeper self.

It was true, as memory held, that I'd set Memorial Day weekend as decision time, determined to render a verdict by Monday evening. But that telling was oblivious to the private percolating; I hadn't yet brought Thomas into my contemplations of traveling.

I'd done legwork as to economic feasibility, even looked to a trusted counselor for moral backing. It's all clear to me again! Now, going into that weekend, I looked *within* - not just asking, Should I go for it? but, Can I *handle* going for it? I reckoned I could. Was I convinced enough to present the idea to Thomas?

I was well aware that even if I felt capable and ready it might not work out, for any number of reasons. If my confidence were to falter, I could back off and wait for Thomas to come the following year. At the core of that weekend's deliberating was this either/or: let the chance pass, or take the leap.

I leapt!

In the email to Thomas, my words were charged with barely contained exuberance and uncertain hope. His reply - just two hours later - began by alternating my short sentences with his rapid-fire comments:

"Here's a distraction for you..." Just a quick one...
"Are you sitting down?" Rhetorical question?
"I've come across an opportunity..." Thass a big surprise!

I nervously read on:

Is it only up to you whether you come or does it depend on something/someone? Where in Germany are you going to?

What an interesting opening question. I started to feel better when he asked:

Do you need a bed? Or three? Three would require some arrangements.

I rapid-fired my reply:

"Thass a big surprise!" Thought it might be... Surprises me too. As a result of developments as recent as this afternoon, turns out it's almost all up to me. Well, to be accurate, it depends on you some.

This begins to put together - reading between my own lines - the first mention of Reinhard's trip with my later intimation about a train ride to Cologne. Some is coming back, some isn't. My original inspiration must've been to approach my professor about accompanying him, and that discussion must've raised the feasibility of going on my own instead.

I continued:

I would land in Düsseldorf. If I do this, it's not going to be an extravagant sight-seeing type of trip, and only for 6 or 7 days (probably mid-week to mid-week). So far, I'm not expecting to join a tour. This all came about in a string of unexpected convergences of circumstances, and there's still some flexibility.

Apparently Reinhard recommended Düsseldorf. (Cologne's airport would've been closer for Thomas.) As for beds, I answered:

Just one, and I'm still not assuming anything. Thought you could tell me how much lodging in your town would cost.

Next came my rationale:

So, I know you're surprised, but... You'd be ok with me visiting you? Would you like me to come? This is a chance for me to "get my feet wet" as a first-timer with international travel. That's a big wonderful step for me. Aside from that, I'd be coming largely to meet you and to experience a world outside of Wisconsin - are you comfortable with that idea? Or do you think that's too crazy?

I took into account Thomas's normal obligations:

I know you'd be working at your jobs - I'd come up with adventures while you're busy. I know I'll be *thrilled* with Germany and that I'll want to plan an expensive tourist-y trip some other time. But this current possibility feels like one that if I let pass by, I'd regret it! If you're ok with that last paragraph, would you be able to meet me at the airport?

His response was reassuring:

You can have a room and a bed - breakfast and meals are negotiable (if you help me cooking). I'd take at least some days off while you're here. I can meet you in Düsseldorf.

With gratitude, I let Thomas in on how I framed my apprehensions:

That was my number one worry, so that's a great relief. I do have fear about being in an unfamiliar country where I don't know anyone or know the language. I like the idea of being both bold and wise, but that doesn't mean I won't be a little afraid. It's bold for me to fly that far alone, and it's wise for me to have someone there to meet me, rather than to have to figure out how to catch a train to your town by myself.

Ah yes, now I remember that *bold and wise* formulation, part of my decision-making grid.

I accepted Thomas's terms, saying I'd love to help cook. Hardly able to restrain myself, I showed him a sliver of my amazement:

I gotta tell ya, for me to even take seriously the thought of actually *traveling is a bizarre feeling. I've known for a long time that I *will* someday, but I couldn't picture it being possible in so near a future.*

Carried aloft by those words, I can't contain my beaming grin as I shake my head in fresh disbelief.

Watch Me Go, I'm A Happy Girl

The train had left the station, in a manner of speaking. My preliminary machinations about visiting were now out in the open, and Thomas was receptive.

The May folder has lived up to its promise. A single soliloquy I emailed as the month drew to a close showcases my earliest trip contemplations, and widens the window into the state of mind behind this life-altering move:

The way this progressed from a distant, probably impossible thought (starting with maybe tagging along with Reinhard) to a 'hey, wait a minute - it's not impossible after all' idea, to actually putting the material things in place, is a pretty cool story. (Can't take time to tell it here.)

When I come to that aside I literally utter, "Dammit." I want to know more! I'm likewise in the dark as to details behind this:

The funds won't come out of my normal household budget; that's why it's possible at all (that's another story). And I didn't set out to make it happen, just sort of checked into it little by little. Several factors were unexpected but seemed to fall into place (with regard to money and time off work) that aren't likely to come around again for a while. When I wrote the short message suggesting this, I first *typed it and then just stared and stared for a *long* time before sending, cuzz I couldn't believe the whole idea had come that far.*

I was already both hedging and celebrating:

Anyway, I still could choose not to do this. Going through the motions as if I actually have this choice has been valuable in itself - exercising a part of myself that can now look past the old limits of my life. Instead of assuming it can't happen, which is how I lived for years, I can knock on doors until there's a compelling reason not to. Well, one of those doors was finding out what you thought of the idea. I wasn't sure you'd be ok with it, cuzz it does seem like a crazy thing to do.

I pushed for a more definitive take from Thomas:

Sounds like you're cool with it, but would you indulge me in asking you to be specific about how it really hits you? Need is a strong word, but I think I need to know exactly where you're at on this. I'm not saying there's one certain thing I want to hear, just whatever's true...I can't tell and don't wanna presume.

He answered:

I love the idea to have you come for a visit.

I could reread that sentence all day and never tire of it, like a happy girl writing it again and again on a chalkboard, as a reward.

The exchanges that followed exhibited more lightness than ever, as Thomas and I discussed preparations and possibilities. Here's one delicious nibble, a suggestion from me:

This may sound silly, but you know what I'd like to see? The music store you mentioned in Cologne - I think it'd be hilarious to buy music there (maybe Rock Me Amadeus?).

Thomas:

I read years ago that this shop was #4 amongst Cologne's tourist attractions (Cathedral was #1).

My heart leaps reading these debut appearances of our later exploits. His next sentence:

Hey! This all sounds to me as if you're coming in 8 weeks time with a probability of at least 90%.

Guess he was feeling some amazement of his own. I joined in:

WOW!!!!!! While I leave it to computer scientists like you to actually *quantify* it, I think you've got that about right! I hadn't wanted to say anything until I'd checked out the feasibility, so from your end it might seem more sudden than it is. Actually, it's only been a little over a week since it first occurred to me to check into it, so I guess that's sudden enough after all. I admit, I'm still a little in shock over it!

I borrowed his favored sign off:

<CU> (sorta takes on added meaning now…)
P.S. We could still meet in Spain if you prefer. <g>

I'm in the same shock again - and crying the same joyous tears.
Time and again, disinterments of buried treasures stun me at first, then settle into familiarity in the daylight of the fresh encounter.

Now, in place of the near-overwhelm at the outset of this batch, I feel effervescent! Here, in affirming detail, is the most essential rediscovery yet from those enchanting months so embedded in my identity: how, faced with a preposterous opportunity, *I leaned in.* As the illumination filters through, it almost feels as if I've known this the whole time.

But not quite. I'm gobsmacked to think how far from recall it was before now. It could only have become overshadowed by its even more profoundly heart-enveloping consequences.

☿ CHAPTER 35

THE WAITING IS THE HARDEST PART

It takes time to absorb the effects of bringing all this back to light. As I make my way through the Box, the emails tamper with memory and pummel my feelings. For respite I revert periodically to arid analysis of page counts and time spans. I can now report the interval between inklings of Someday Meeting and talk of Me Going There was nine weeks.

Exactly as many weeks would elapse from the day I hit Send on that jolt of an email until United Airlines Flight #952 would lift off from a Chicago runway, whisking me over the ocean to meet for the first time someone I already knew and loved.

Our impending encounter dominated May's remaining correspondence - and carried us on clouds into June.

My late May messages told of advance groundwork and up-to-date developments:

I decided before I heard back from you that getting a passport wouldn't be a wasted thing to do, even if this trip wouldn't work out (and it's a good move for me symbolically :-) .) I jumped through all their hoops, and I'll get it in the mail by early July...I've started checking with airlines for prices. I'm looking at July 29 to August 5, but they tell me flights are filling up fast.

Thomas expressed concern about whether such a brief stint would be worth the airfare and jet lag, and I responded:

Are you kidding?...a chance to travel overseas, see another country, meet a friend?

One week seemed ideal to me, with so little travel experience and because my boys had never been away from me that long.

On May 28th I reported:

Was able to reserve a round trip flight today...Took a lot of finagling and phone calls to different travel agencies. Get this: including several dates on either side of the ones I reserved, I got the LAST seat available for the flight there and the LAST seat available for the flight back!!

On June 1st, I cautioned:

My flight is reserved but not paid for yet - if I don't do that by

Wednesday, I'll lose my seat. Was hoping to have child care in place before I risk the airfare. Worst case scenario is I don't come at all if that part doesn't work out. But I'm still optimistic at this point. As someone I know once said, "We have to wait and see..."

I kept Thomas apprised of the drama in nailing down care for the boys - I did end up paying the airfare while that was still up in the air. (Unintentional, I promise.) Two days later, restlessly awaiting an answer from a promising lead, I observed:

Trying times reveal ourselves to ourselves; my anxiety is once again showing me how much this trip means to me.

That email's next page contained this mid-message eruption:

HOLD THE PRESSES!!! Just got the call from Deb's neighbor family - THEY'LL TAKE CARE OF MY BOYS! EVERYTHING'S SET! I'M SHOUTING!! I can't believe it - now I can run through the streets shouting "I'm going to Germany!" Boy is my heart pounding!

Such elation - I must have walked on air for days, probably all through the two weeks until I announced:

Got the call yesterday that my airline tickets have come in, so I have to go down to the travel agency to get them and have the agent explain all the details I'll need to know (such as, Don't forget your passport!).

That extended process - phoning airlines, visiting agencies, reserving flights to pay for later, picking up paper tickets in person - sure sounds foreign now, doesn't it?

Fragmentary trip details from my shoebox mementos are corroborated, explained and enlarged upon in June paragraphs to Thomas, making me even more jubilant. Up to now, I've emphasized the recovery of the forgotten; that doesn't diminish a parallel satisfaction - seeing the tangible proof of what I remembered.

It will always feel strange that the kernel of how the trip came about faded into oblivion. But I never forgot the lightness of spirit I lived in as the weeks toward departure counted down.

Mundane travel info from Thomas - such as Europe's electrical system requiring an adapter for U.S. appliances - fed my exhilaration and helped convert the trip plans from dreamlike to concrete. So did discussions of splitting expenses and settling up at the end, freeing me from having to carry German currency. His stated aim:

Just want to make your stay as a "stranger in a strange land" as comfortable as possible.

Always so thoughtful. I had an aim too, a concern underlying pragmatic considerations:

I'll be dependent on you to some degree (especially in terms of language). I'm not saying that's a bad thing; it's just something I'm watching for, so that (taking it to extremes) you don't begin to feel burdened and I don't begin to feel helpless.

I didn't see myself as a typical tourist:

I want to see what Germany is like in a deeper way; that's why it makes all the difference that I get to meet you there. I've already met a German and I'll get to live a tiny bit of what his life is like. I don't mean to sound like you're just any German. But you already know that. Friendship first - tourism, the incidental fringe benefit. :-)

Although I framed the visit around the international travel I'd dreamed of, you know very well what most lit up my being was the thought of meeting Thomas.

Uncomfortable Shoes and Dangerous Dresses

It was time for some research. Where else to start than using Thomas's internet access to look into visiting Thomas! I also consulted a travel guidebook from the library, called *Let's Go: Germany*. This depiction stands out now: "Germans are formal and reserved in public and you won't see many smiles or displays of affection." (Guess I forgot about that at the airport.)

Among our most delightful June exchanges were those in which Thomas offered commentary on tidbits of research I ran by him. Several etiquette tips elicited Thomas's satiric rebuttals. Here's one I emailed:

"During introductions, older or especially formal gentlemen might take the woman's hand and kiss it." How quaint! That sounds like a charming little custom.

Thomas responded:

Go to Vienna or to dance schools to experience that!!!

Ha, a rare triple-exclamation. The same decidedly gendered etiquette list stated:

"While walking, the man walks closest to the curb."

Thomas didn't know that rule, he said, then spoofed its antiquated perspective:

I know that ladies walk first going upstairs, but gents walk first going down. That's because ladies always wear uncomfortable shoes and dangerous dresses, so they are at a tremendous risk of falling down the stairs, and therefore the gents are always below to catch them.

As he continued, I was chortling:

The curb rule probably is meant to stop women from falling under a car or getting hit by one. That's because ladies always wear uncomfortable shoes and dangerous dresses, so they are at a tremendous risk of falling even without stairs.

I'm elated to see his zany diatribe. He wrapped up his spiel: *Nice that dance school rules survive - as cliches in tourist guides.* A practical inquiry from me arose from my research:

"Keep the tines of your fork pointed down during meals." Am I correct in assuming you take a "hands-on" approach to pizza? (After all, "tines" change. <g>)

He hadn't heard that guideline either and, to the contrary, expressed his preference for what he termed "the fork-and-knife approach," prompting me to assure him:

While at the Mr. ___ place, I will do as Mr. ___ does. :-)

My reminiscing skips forward; I clearly remember conforming.

Another resource included pointers on "how not to look as American." Thomas flatly contradicted one, repeating the tip first:

"No light t-shirts. (Germans wear t-shirts in darker, more subdued colors)."

I normally wear light t-shirts.

It was, as you know, the only shade I saw him wear.

A list of "tips for women travelers" armed me with the German phrase for "Leave me alone!" Thomas helpfully elaborated:

"F*** off" and "p*** off" are also widely recognized in Germany.

That line is a favorite Strand; I roared back then and never forgot it. Thomas offered a take of his own on tourists:

Some tourists need to be reminded that the benches in the Cologne Cathedral are no place to make a picnic.

The remark stirs up Cathedral reflections, in waves and layers. A hazy flashback to my complete ignorance of the landmark now undulates through ponderings on its enduring place within.

A few tears break free as I come back from this meditation, and then are urged on by what I see next - my silly aside to Thomas about the travel guides:

As far as etiquette, they don't say what's appropriate for email friends greeting each other for the first time at an airport.

LOVELY THINGS

The age of personal emailing being in its infancy, my quip about proper social behavior at an airport landed in a way it wouldn't now. Traveling to meet a person you'd corresponded with by digital means alone was virtually unheard of; these days it's normal. I like to think Thomas and I got in on the ground floor of that.

My unsophisticated background left me ill-equipped to envision what sightseeing would be like. But Thomas and I made homier plans too, inspired by a shared interest instrumental to our friendship. In my June 7th email (our 283rd), I returned to the subject of music and compatibility:

When I mentioned appreciation of music, I didn't mean common taste necessarily, but rather feeling similarly about its capacity to add so much pleasure to life. I'm sure your taste and mine overlap only to a degree.

Thomas harmonized:

Even if you enjoy only 10% of my records, we may still enjoy discussing some of the rest.

And I intoned:

Looking forward to this!

Here was an activity I *could* envision. Of course, I couldn't picture the surroundings - the way I am now. Once again, fond reveries intertwine anticipation with remembrance.

How incandescently scenes come back of Thomas and me listening to music in his home - moments forever embodied in specific songs and bands from those priceless evenings. Lifelong experience tells me other tracks we played are probably so cleanly erased from those same scenes that I wouldn't know they're lost at all.

The notion of keeping and losing comes up again in an alternate musical context; this time I know all too well the key piece that's gone. In a thread touching on the singing duo with my sister, I told Thomas about preparations for an upcoming performance:

Finished writing a new song last night; I'm excited about this one. It's about a woman who sees her scars from what she's been through as no longer ugly but beautiful, cuzz they remind her she's come a long way and she can make it to where she's headed. It's called Lovely Things, and it'll be one of the new songs we perform on the 26th.

 Lovely Things

This was the HeartSong farewell concert I recalled - but the song is forever lost, as they say, to the mists of time. I wish I could hear my creation now.

One more musical exchange gives me back a memory-jewel I didn't know was lost. When Thomas first received the cassettes I sent in May, he remarked only on my recorded voice. In June he commented on the songs. Well, just one song - well, just one line. He wrote:

Hey! I took the time to listen to your music tape. The line that struck me most is, "To love somebody foolishly can happen once..."

I replied:

True story: I really suspected that line would hit you. Another that always gets to me is, "To love somebody hopelessly can hurt so much."

These are from Van Halen's *Not Enough,* a stirring and poignant composition about loves that don't work out. Just now I go read the rest of the lyrics online - and everything has to wait while emotions quake their way through.

Before encountering this today, I wasn't sure whether Thomas ever wrote a response to the song tape. It's as though I've recovered a long-lost locket, tiny and delicate, bigger on the inside. It holds words in place of a lover's image.

The bauble contains multitudes; I could count the ways. It leaves me pensive about what I have yet to confront - in the Box and in myself.

Say What You Need to Say

Our music passages were broken up by tangents about international events. The World Cup competition, in full swing that June in France, prompted regular reports from Thomas. He brought back his half-serious reminder that *football* referred to soccer; succeeding variants turned it into one of our growing number of callback lines.

Also garnering worldwide attention was the approaching millennium, with alarm over its potential technological disruptions. I happened to raise the subject before Thomas did, citing my go-to news source's first mention:

> *Been hearing about the doom and gloom of the "year 2000 problem," when all the computers in the world will become useless because they won't know how to interpret the 00 year. This week's Time magazine called it the "Y2K glitch" - a handy label I thought.*

Thomas replied:

> *The clock in my computer will switch back to 1900 - but my computer will run if I set the clock manually to 2000. Dunno what DOS will do with 1900 - file dates begin 1980.*
> *I bet all problems will be solved when the new century begins on January 1, 2001. <g>*

My techie friend didn't sound terribly worried, and I liked how he snuck in the technicality about when centuries and millennia actually turn over. I responded:

> *Good point! This is only slightly related, but half an hour after I got your msg, I heard this: "Meanwhile back in the year One..." Recognize the song?*

The descriptions of Y2K worries sound faintly comical now, since the world's computers didn't crash after all. And lyric coincidences like that one (from Jethro Tull's *Skating Away*) never fail to charm.

With the weeks counting down, more vital conversing was underway too. The pragmatic considerations of staying at Thomas's home melded with a return to full-on relational talk, settled and absent from our emails for a couple of months. Now our frank and affecting dialogue examined in depth what we each intended, expected, hoped for and accepted about the whole scenario. What exactly were we about to do here?

True to my bold side, I kicked off the fresh round - by looking back:

About this upcoming trip o' mine, we have 8 weeks to discuss some things before I come. Allow me to quote you...

Next I inserted his lines from March about what could happen if we were to meet, and suggested:

Of course, you wrote those when we weren't expecting to meet for a *long* time. But the sooner we talk about boundaries and expectations, the better I'll feel, since I think it's fair to say I'm risking more than you are by making this trip, and if we do discover differences, it won't be at the last minute with no time to discuss them in advance.

Here's our old risk topic revived in a more tangible realm. I didn't remind Mr. Not This Year that he had also said, "Ne'er say ne'er." Thomas replied:

You're my cyber-friend, but you're also a stranger in many ways. When you lodge at my home, you'll have access to many private things. There are potential risks, namely loss of privacy or loss of

*property. I think neither is probable in your case (I wouldn't have
invited you if I was scared about that).*

I agreed:

*Ditto. This is one oddity about email - in some ways you know
more about the other person (than face-to-face), but in other
ways you still know *less*. I'm SO glad you brought this up - I
totally understand!!*

I meant that emailing had a way of drawing out inner selves we
might be more guarded with in person. As for privacy, the issue cut
both ways. Thomas elaborated on his offer:

*You'll have a separate room which you can lock (from inside or
outside). You can also lock the bathroom from inside. After your
morning arrival you'll still have 8 or 10 hours to decide whether
you'd prefer a room in a hotel.*

This answered questions I'd been gearing up to ask. Clearly we
were like-minded as to commonsense concerns.

A corresponding degree of circumspection was called for in aligning
perspectives on more profound matters.

Don't Try to Live Your Life In One Day

When Thomas and I had last explored feelings about meeting, it
was in soft-hued *someday* territory. Now we examined them under the
bright light of an actual plan, just weeks away. It's impossible to describe
the effect of that crossover on me, the glistening dimension it added to
everything I wrote, everything I felt inside.

It meant, among other things, questions of trust were no longer

theoretical. I was candid with Thomas about my concerns and the fallback plans I was formulating - while assuring him he'd given me no reason to worry. He was in sync with the rationale I put forward:

> It's just that it's unrealistic and foolhardy to trust someone too far at this stage, all the cyber-promises in the world notwithstanding.

Proceeding to make just such promises, I enlarged on my working principle:

> I wouldn't dare tamper with anything at your place, much less take anything, and will respect your privacy to the utmost. I appreciate the trust you feel is warranted so far. Trust must be earned, must have a basis, and should be extended in degrees appropriate to the friendship's context, and no further. I expect you won't take offense at my not trusting you past a certain point; I don't expect you to trust me past a certain point either.

I cited an example from our beginnings:

> When we first started communicating, I was careful not to name the town I lived in, only that it was "an hour south of Green Bay" (when I still thought you were in the States). But by the time you were ready to send the diskette, I decided it was safe enough to give you my address.

My closest friends, I explained, were naturally a little less trusting:

> The original consensus was that my coming there is somewhat foolish. One worries for my physical safety; two are worried about my heart's safety. But they all trust my judgment enough.

Thomas's reply:

Your friends know where you're going, and I would be suspect #1
if you didn't get home on time.

He was being less serious than it might sound; I won't rattle off the surrounding jokes. OK, just one, from an exchange about undisclosed criminal backgrounds. I wrote:

My record is squeaky clean so far. :-) You may not have a police
record, but I already know you have Police records, so don't try
to deny it. <g>

Of course, before I would have a chance to steal anything from Thomas, we would need to find each other at the airport - the next arena for implementing my bold-and-wise maxim.

In the third week of June, I wrote:

Haven't decided yet on a back-up plan for one particular contingency
- I need to consider what I would do if for any reason you're not
there when I land. I know that's not likely, but I still have to have
a strategy. What do you think? We should decide on an amount
of time to simply wait before I do anything. And then...?

My flight was scheduled to arrive at 8:30 a.m. He planned to reach the airport in plenty of time (without sacrificing more sleep than necessary) and "typed out loud" for several paragraphs, calculating variables and working out through his keyboarding fingers a range of potentialities. Arriving at the just-in-case recommendation that I wait at the airport until 11, he finished with:

If everything works fine, I'll be waiting at the gate.

You'll forgive the cliche: the sentence is still music to my ears.

AM I MISSING SOMETHING?

We succeeded in resolving logistics well in advance and without a hitch. Weightier affairs remained. It was essential that Thomas and I be clear about our relational expectations.

Of those expansive in-depth conversations, I can give you barely a sampling. From various springboards, we dove into views on compatibility, personal qualities we considered essential, definitions of relational terms, and even conjectures about a post-meeting future. This time, we did run into a snag or two.

Now that I'm this far through the paper artifacts, and in view of the luminescent imprint left by events they chronicle, I haven't abandoned trying to detect (or impose) a pattern as to what lodged for good and what evaporated. While I willingly yield to the human frailty of random access memory (what the RAM in your computer stands for) for minor deletions, I crave a grand unified theory as to erasures of consequence.

I'm especially stymied by memory's treatment of our June discourse on all things relational. Snippets and Strands of little moment - revered only *because* they remained - flank obliterated passages of monumental impact.

As history would have it, by far the most startling and revealing utterance from Thomas was nearly lost to me *at the time* - before I ever saw it.

It wasn't unusual for him to ruminate before responding, so I hardly noticed when he didn't take up the expectations thread as soon as I raised it. The next email from him to hit my inbox, dubbed with a fresh subject line, pursued other themes about the mechanics of the trip, with German language lessons thrown in and lots of joking around.

I didn't needle or nudge him - but I did give him a hard time about an acronym he'd debuted a few messages before. As a segue between ordinary updates, Thomas wrote:

ANFSCD: Got the spell checker installed again. I guess that'll filter 25% of my typos.

The usage was unfamiliar. In my next email, I ribbed:

Well, good for you, but did you really think I'd be able to figure out that acronym? Please, clue me in. :-)

Without decoding it for me, he deployed it again:

ANFSCD: Recently I listened to an old record I've had for at least 15 years. I know the lyrics and have been singing along to the record many times. Now I heard it again after a rather long time - and somehow the words got a new meaning.

I relished the thought of him singing, and completely related to the musical experience he described, but was still clueless:

Interesting... No offense, but was that supposed to help me with that acronym? :-)

Do I detect, or only imagine, a trace of exasperation in Thomas's response? He wrote:

I explained that acronym: And Now For Something Completely Different. 'Twas in my May 31, 23:58 message.

I stood my unruffled ground:

Not meaning to be difficult, but I have two msgs from you dated May 31, one at 8:09, the other at 13:28. In the second, I see you used the acronym but didn't explain it. Then on June 1 at 20:49 you used it again. AFAIK, I haven't seen it explained until now. :-) Did I miss it somewhere else perhaps? It's a great one, BTW.

Detail-oriented, right? It more than paid off in this instance. His next email consisted of a single sentence that introduced a forwarded message:

I s'pose you didn't get the message below...

The forwarded header showed he'd hit Reply to an email of mine days earlier, titled "getting brighter…" Sure enough - there was the Sent time of 23:58. Mystery partially solved. It was there he had clarified:

And Now For Something Completely Different: I notice I often use BTW when I actually mean ANFSCD. A comedian from Austria sez this is typical for Cologners - using 'apropos' to change the topic.

British comedy buffs, by the way, will catch the Monty Python reference. I didn't.

I've brought you a long way to explicate a minor thread, but for good reason. Were it not for the unrecognized initialism - how perfect that an acronym was the tip-off! - I would've remained unaware of the missing message. And *that* would have left me oblivious to a disclosure from Thomas of colossally greater import.

I replied immediately, extending his forwarded subject line with: "missed it alright!" How could his Sent message not have been Received in my inbox?

As you've put together by now, the missing message held Thomas's thoughts on relational expectations for my visit; he had responded to my suggestion within hours. His words border on poetic and merit quoting in full, in his exact formatting:

We had agreed that our relation has to be platonic.
Well - for one week it doesn't have to be…
…but after that one week it will have to be platonic again for many weeks (or many months) to come.
Never say never. Caterpillars to butterflies. Can't be done? Poof - it's done.

One week is long enough for a romantic Hollywood movie - but
life goes on, and movies always end in the middle.
I think we shall try to keep it platonic.
I think we shall keep it platonic.
I hope this answers your question without disappointing you.
I do hope I don't disappoint you - I want to be honest, but not
brutally.

Do you hear the desire, the self-talk, the sweetness? More than any other passage, his verselet has me falling to pieces, wishing I could have him back in my life.

Butterflies

A digital message gone missing, the plot twist I imagined many chapters ago as if to rev up drama: I had no clue it would prove prescient. But as I've stressed to you, this is not a constructed tale. It's a reconstructed one, authenticated by the printed antiquities.

The shared state of ignorance, while Thomas and I stitched with other threads, lasted three days - no meager stretch given the frequency of our emailing. Sent a few urgent hours after learning of Thomas's vaporized message, my response insisted it had not arrived and asked if he could tell how the drop occurred. I told him I was reeling at what I'd nearly missed out on, and bemoaned the inescapable implication that his sweet, earnest reflections had been brushed aside.

Those intimations of his laid bare something I had not known about: his own tug-of-heart about us.

I answered his raw poetry with the same bare-hearted candor, and from there a river of dialogue rushed, carving deep and wide. All we had were typed words on a glowing screen, yet to me it felt as though we had just then stopped to look up from our keyboards - and met each other's eyes.

The platonic restraint had come up months earlier, even before imaginary notions of someday meeting; it hadn't since. Now with my visit on the near horizon, his musings hinted at an exemption. I was thunderstruck.

His doesn't-have-to-be line catches on something inside, like the sudden tension on my yarn that signifies a knot needs unsnarling before I can keep knitting. I read the sentence again - it comes back to me more keenly each time I do. How could the memory of it have gone away?? This one *really* matters.

I responded:

I love the underlying assumption there - that we would want to and get to meet again after this visit. :-)

You can see me equivocating as I took in what Thomas could be implying:

I'm pretty sure I understand what you're saying, but we are approaching the point where, to really understand each other, we have to define our terms more specifically. Maybe our definitions of platonic match, maybe not. We also agreed there's no way of knowing what will happen until we do meet.

Now more than ever, we needed precision in our language. To Thomas's next level of never-say-never-ing, I replied:

Wouldn't dare try to guess what the future holds, but I'll say this:

I've been witness to a whole lot of butterfly transformations in the past several years. :-)

I told him I loved what he said about movies:

I'm glad we're both old enough to know life ain't often like romantic movies. I've said before we've learned a lot about each other in four months. Now we need to realize there are important things we *don't* know yet. And there are conversations we'll have that can only be done face to face.

I'm allowing that last sentence to engulf me, letting out a soulful sigh. Appraising my 30s-aged self, I'm gripped by the levelheadedness of my words to Thomas, considering how caught up my heart was. I hadn't let go of the reins.

Neither had he, his words made plain. I'm moved again by his thoughtfulness about their effect on me. I responded:

It's your honesty I so appreciate. It warms my heart to hear your concern. You haven't disappointed me, and you sure haven't been brutal. :-) Only dishonesty would be brutal and disappointing.

You can see the caution and caring from both of us.

Further in the thread, Thomas wrote this handy encapsulation:

We (both or individually) could get into a dilemma between head, heart, and "belly."

He was efficient with his analysis even when it came to heart talk. He followed with an "appellation," then curved onto another avenue:

I'm looking forward to your definitions of platonic, romantic, and

other words you might like to define in this context. You said your
Mr Right would be a lot like me, but Mr Right would live in the
midwest - and I don't!

I could hardly wait to dig into those. The second sentence was as much an invitation as the first, whether Thomas realized it or not. As a start, I inserted a rambling thought about my own expectations for the visit:

What I want and what I expect may not be the same thing, and
what I might feel like I want and what I think I ought or ought
not to want may not match either. I was thinking about this before
I received your last msg, and then - how about that? - there you
are saying exactly the same thing with your "dilemma between
head, heart, and belly." It amazes me how you manage to sum
things up sometimes.

Thomas wasn't the only one wrestling inside and self-talking.

We both had to contend with thoughts tugging one way, feelings another.

The Head and the Heart

Tension between the rational and the emotional is no unfamiliar trope when it comes to affairs of the heart. I harbored, though, as yet unuttered grounds for mine. So did he. These were not at all alike, as I would soon learn - and they hovered in the ether as the conversation turned to definitions.

I went first:

If I'm not mistaken, I'm hearing you use "platonic" as equivalent

to non-sexual. It includes that, but I would add non-romantic -
"romantic" to mean a special private love between two people; it's
exclusive, in contrast to friendship, which can be open to including
others. Though closely related, to me sexual is not identical to
romantic.

This provided a gateway for me to remind him of a March exchange:

If I remember right, you first used the word when you said "our
relation is platonic because it has to be." I've never told you this
but, while I agreed with you, I wondered about your exact reason.
Well, if I'm right about how you're using the term now, there's no
question why it has to be. But by my slightly broader definition,
a letter-writing relationship can have a romantic element even
though it can't be sexual or even physical.

That last sentence, in a key paragraph, is undeniably central to this
whole experience. I'm catching something hiding behind my assertion
too: the matter of Thomas's relational status with Gretchen by that time
lay quite dormant in my thinking.

Being unambiguously unattached myself, I turned next to Thomas's
assertion about a potential Mr. Right (I hadn't used the term). You can
hear me sounding tentative again:

"You said your Mr Right would be a lot like me..." Seems like it.
More precisely, Mr Right could be a lot like what I know about
you so far. Remember when you asked about smoking? Well, that
one's no problem, but I can think of one or two other things that
could get in the way (deeper issues than smoking).

While in concert with his premise, I sharpened it for accuracy's sake (if not clarity's) - and then persisted:

"But Mr Right would live in the Midwest..." Can't agree with you there. He could be from anywhere. The open questions are how will I come across him and how would we decide where to settle down. I don't expect to stay in the Midwest. So... you wouldn't ever move somewhere else?

With this and other exchanges, I'm getting a kick once again out of our little dance - foxtrotting among hypotheticals in really-about-us steps.

As usual, Thomas was first to abandon the pretense:

Moving to America would be a big step. I'd have to live with you to find out if moving to America is worth it. And I'd have to move to America to be able to live with you. OK - maybe one week is enough to find out we don't fit - maybe not. This is the "mechanical" problem.

He rightly construed my speculative nuance, then roundly slammed reality onto the table in front of me. Not for the last time.

Thomas's very next lines:

And I still have that ambivalent relation with Gretchen. It is getting loose - and it's fine for me. But it's not broken up completely. This is only my problem. I think this is another reason to expect our relation to remain non-sexual and non-exclusive (though it already is rather deep, I think). At least for the time of your visit here.

Ouch.

I was grateful he provided the facts so I could face them. And he wasn't done disclosing. He referred to the assumption we'd want a second meet-up as a "worst case scenario" - then backtracked:

Not really worst case, but remaining good friends would be easier.

When I come upon this today, at first I chuckle lightly at his way of putting it. Only at first.

I heartily seconded his "already rather deep" characterization. Confronted now by the forgotten paragraph he'd tucked it into, I'm transported back to the emotions it elicited: a jumble of intoxicating felicity tempered by gravity.

A neighboring snippet - one that never left me - draws forth the same emotional jumble, this time stirring me to tears. It's his dictionary definition of platonic, the source of the shoebox clipping. The magnet-affixed fridge display (a retro form of social media post?) not only fed my joy over the friendship, but kept me in mind of facts to keep unmuddled about. You can see me facing them in my next email:

"But it's not broken up completely." Been wondering about this...
Couldn't decide if or when I wanted to bring it up, so I'm glad
you did.
"This is only my problem." Not necessarily.

Well, I'm corrected yet again. Apparently the matter, long absent from our emails, wasn't sidelined from my thoughts entirely. Still, I maintain it wasn't top of mind when I asserted that letter writing could be *non*-platonic.

Our theater of the theoretical returned with a turnabout I posed:

Last time you mentioned Mr Right... Well, you've opened the subject, so now I get to ask: what will your Ms Right be like?

That his current "SO" wasn't his Ms. Right I relegated to subtext, I see. It's clear now what I wanted from him by asking this (fishing much?). I'm sure it was plenty clear then too. In any case, he didn't play along.

BETTER LEFT UNSAID

For all of June's serious talk, frivolity was never far away. Leave it to Thomas to slip some right into the middle of the heavy stuff. With the girlfriend subject back under discussion, he titled his next email, "Some things are better left unsaid." Primed for some mildly startling complication, I gave his fairly long message my usual rapt attention. Nearly all of it concerned mundane travel information until just before his signoff:

"Some things are better left unsaid..." I think this is from a song. Sounds deeply meaningful - and has nothing to do with this message!

He sure had me going, I recall, side-smiling. My reply added to his subject line: "...maybe you shouldn'ta said that."

I say "nearly all" because his message opened by addressing my Ms. Right question:

Hard to say that! I can tell Ms Wrongs - sometimes within minutes,
sometimes within months - but I cannot say what Ms Right has
to be like. I think it's normally easier to say why you don't love
somebody, and difficult to say why you love somebody.

Well, if I hoped he'd come back naming even one trait of mine, that was strike one. (For what it's worth, this doesn't sound like someone in the throes of affection for their SO.)

I countered:

Hmm. I don't have many bottom-line "requirements," but I can
easily think of qualities I do enjoy. For me it's not hard to describe
what I love or appreciate about another person.
Maybe that's a better question: what qualities do you most enjoy
in a woman?

There's my second swing. But this got him musing about the practicalities of living with someone, until he concluded:

A relation includes give and take. But how could I describe that
extra bit that makes the difference between friendship and love???

I wasn't expecting this methodical down-to-earth techie to be stumped on specifics - whereas I, in my lofty fancies, could effortlessly reel off commonalities that attracted me. I touched on these (hypothetically) in my response:

When it comes to musical sensitivity, humor, world awareness, *and reflectiveness, if a man doesn't share these, maybe he couldn't conceive how important they are to my own personality (been there, done that!!). I'm *not* looking for someone exactly like myself; I'm saying there's no chance for permanent relationship where each person can't truly appreciate (even if they don't share) the components of the other person's whole being.*

He replied:

I can sign onto that.

Next I gently placed reality on the table in front of him:

There must be some reason you keep reading my msgs and writing back, beyond the fact that I keep showing up on your computer display. What do you enjoy about our exchanges? We agree there's a basis for friendship; how would you describe what that is?

His reply still didn't give me what I *thought* I was after. But I loved what my laconic, playful cyber-friend (finally!) said:

Well, any friend of my screensavers is a friend of mine! <g> I enjoy reading your messages - and I enjoy sending you messages. Our friendship works coz there's so much we want to tell each other.

My oh so clever response:

Well, any creator of those screensavers is a friend of mine! <g> And... I think that's a very interesting and succinct way to put it. :-)

In his understated way, Thomas covered the essentials - and in the end, I delighted in *not* having succeeded in manipulating him. He was probably toying with me, perfectly aware what I was pulling for. Then again, hard to say.

Several pages ago I alluded to running into snags; I had in mind the nearly lost message and the reappearance of Gretchen. Now that I've aired them out, I'll retract the term because neither foiled our preparations to meet. Both instead clarified them.

As for expectations, I decided to assure Thomas of one more thing:

Wanted to say I wouldn't try to change any boundaries you set for yourself, just as I know you would honor mine.

Verbalizing this seemed especially called for in light of head-and-heart tussles we'd both confessed to.

His obviously had to do in part with Gretchen. I hadn't yet divulged what was behind mine: it was easy to envision Thomas and me being affectionate in person - and encountering a cultural difference as to physical intimacy. My boundaries were closely tied to religious beliefs; both were important to me. But given our upfront platonic designs, why go into it by email?

Perspective

After all, we had so much to talk about, loads more stories to sketch with words.

While I appreciate the visual arts, I don't share a talent for creating them. I've never forgotten, though, my fascination learning in middle school about perspective drawing. I remember a pencil sketch depicting train tracks coming to a point to create the illusion of dimensional depth. The image comes to mind as I consider where we are in this story.

Approaching the moment when I would be *present* with Thomas, lines are converging toward that single dot in the distance.

In the interval, I would sketch for Thomas in great depth the most personal facets of myself - expansively written soliloquies on old backstories and new awakenings. My relationship with him brought these out, inspiring me because he showed he valued them.

In our 307th message, three weeks into June, I wrote:

A phrase I often use when I think about my personal renaissance is how things come "full circle." Here's one I'm getting a kick out of: on August 1st, my 20-year high school reunion will be held, which I'd signed up to attend with my sister. When I scheduled the trip and saw that I would miss it, this rhetorical question came to mind: Would I rather look *forward* or *backward*? It was a no-brainer.

Remember the "pretty cool story" I didn't have time to write in a May email? I found time in June! And I'm completely blown away by it, on several levels. Here's part of my lead-in:

I'd been thinking about whether to just talk about it when I get there. But since I have all this quiet time, I'm writing it now. Be warned, it's long...

Treasure of treasures - the epistle spotlights a watershed moment in my self-view, one which ultimately led me onto that ocean-crossing airplane.

I'm calling it the Happy Girl story. It began with a recollection, prompted by old photos, of my "happy, free and self-assured" feelings in the year before getting engaged at age 18, and of losing them in the years after. I fast-forwarded to 1998, when I hadn't yet made the trip decision, and relayed a recent episode of driving alone on country roads, late for a lunch meeting at an out-of-the-way restaurant - and getting lost. Working through the predicament brought about the epiphany that I *could* take on the unfamiliar with boldness and wisdom.

Such sweet nostalgia washes over me reading the blotted out event. Now I remember hearing *Happy Girl* on the radio. Imparting it to Thomas, I didn't recognize that, rather than being merely verbose or oversharing, I'd written a self-contained personal essay. It prefigured a throughline to the book in your hands, to the realization I could legitimately consider myself a writer. And now the train-tracks drawing comes to mind again, with new perspective. This time the lines I wrote to Thomas are coming to a point decades beyond the trip I was then planning, connecting at the dot where I am writing - and you are reading - about all of this now.

Thomas's response to my story stunned me - and leaves me now almost without words:

I really appreciate your restaurant story. Thank you for giving me such a deep insight into your heart.

He *thanked* me - and engaged next-level by naming what the narrative represented to him.

These passages get at why I've always maintained we knew each other before we met. I'm amazed to the point of tears at the depth of our experience in June alone.

Thomas and I were now less than a month from adding the next dimension to our relating. One final batch contains emails we wrote before meeting.

Folks usually have a tale of how a friendship or love arose out of nowhere, of some random moment which began it all. The dawn of this one holds unfailing charm for me. I loved Thomas - from afar, and ever since - and I love the *story* of how I encountered him.

It left a permanent heartprint.

You've seen close to six months of its flowering as we near the July folder, whose pages comprise the countdown. I've said the adventure overlays a kind of organizing principle onto my life-view; the email records catch me in the act of organizing. A trivial aspect of that process reinforces both.

I didn't bother to tell you the Box's chronological contents had been arranged newest in front. On retrieving each folder, I reverse the order of printouts before settling in to read, which strikes me as an obscure hint at a larger truism. I'm thinking of the perspective on our own life from its middle, set against the perspective we gain nearer to its close - and can't help but summon Kierkegaard: *Life can only be understood backwards; but it must be lived forwards.*

The understanding July's emails bring comes from blockbuster discoveries that present themselves in more compact form.

ϒ CHAPTER 39

PLANES, TRAINS *UND* AUTOMOBILES

I n the busy weeks leading to my departure, Thomas and I sent fewer and briefer messages, sometimes in bursts, with subject lines like, "I think, therefore I spam" and "one spam thing after another." More substantial missives perpetuated the nuts-and-bolts planning. One extended discussion centered on whether to rent a car.

I catch myself grinning, newly charmed at the ease with which we debated over such decisions, as we focused on making the most of our eight days together, mere weeks away.

Remember my bold-but-wise guiding principle? In the confab on modes of transportation, I find an instance where boldness overtook wisdom. You may be able to spot it.

Deliberations began with tips I picked up online specifically for Americans traveling to Germany:

A section about car rentals said to reserve a car even before you get there, especially if you want an automatic transmission, since they are in short supply. I would much prefer an automatic... any comments? (If we use a standard, it would take me some practice to get used to it - it's been years and I've never used one regularly.)

I'm not keeping you in suspense long - that's the unwise bit right there. It was a little crazy to consider driving a stick shift car in so unfamiliar a place. I'd learned how with no difficulty, years before, but I'd only practiced a few times, and never outside of a parking lot. (To this day, when someone asks about driving manual, I say, "Sure I know how, but I've never done it.")

When Thomas offered to look into reserving a car, I replied:

I guess I'm pretty concerned about it, yeah. The more I've thought about it, the more I think I *really* better try to get an automatic, so if you really don't mind, I'll take you up on your offer - tnx!

There it is already, the course correction on my part.

Sightseeing ideas under discussion included packing in some quick visits to neighboring countries, partly for the sake of collecting passport stamps. Thomas speculated whether rail or car rental would be more efficient:

We can easily ride to Aachen or the Netherlands by train - the Rhine-Holland-Express drives thru my town. If you really wanna go country hopping (Belgium, Netherlands, Luxembourg, France), then we'd better go by car.

I replied:

Yeah, I really would like to do the country hopping thing, if you're into it. From what I'm gathering from you, most of the other things I'm hoping to do can be done by train.

Thomas:

Country hopping reminds me of certain tourists - they visit several countries, but they only see the highways most of the time. I'd rather go by train, but since I won't have to do the driving, it won't make a big difference for me. It's your holiday!

Both of us were considerate and flexible, but not overly timid or deferential - as my earlier self would've been prone to. I replied:

I'm glad you mentioned this. I thought you said we'd be better off with a car for some reason. If you'd rather go by train, that's really fine with me! Well, yeah, it's my holiday - and tnx - but it's also your home you're opening up, your time away from work, your money for your half, and your country!

Thomas distilled the issue further:

Going by train could be cheaper if we know where we're gonna go and plan carefully. That is, if visiting one city in Belgium or the Netherlands is enough for you. (Even better if you say that making the best of only Germany is OK for you.)

I reconsidered:

It sounds fun but it's probably goofy to cross borders for the passport stamps, just to say I've been there. I'm not so tenaciously attached to the idea that I couldn't let it go, if there are better ways to use the time as well as money. I'm all for making the best of "only Germany"! It's your neighborhood, so let's do stuff we both wanna do!

That settled it: we'd travel by train.

Another preparatory step for me was learning more of the language, cramming with a 12-part CD-ROM course and practicing on Thomas. I didn't need to, but studying German delighted and energized me; I'm astounded to see the progress I made.

Two weeks before leaving, I told Thomas of an impromptu opportunity to try it out:

My coworker invited me to breakfast at a little diner. I suspected by our waitress's accent she was from Germany, and I was right. I told her about the trip and as I was leaving she asked in German when I'd be going - and I understood her! AND, I answered her in German, and she understood me!

In July messages peppered with German words and phrases, I counted on Thomas for corrections. Occasionally I'd realize a mistake before he had a chance to point it out:

I'm sure I made language errors in my last msg - please correct me! One I thought of is, I probably should have capitalized "Ich" even though it wasn't the first word of the sentence, since it's a pronoun, right?

In this case, I was mistaken about my mistake. Thomas explained:

No... I think I told you this earlier (but you wouldn't remember
since you weren't learning German then). It was part of the "i for
an I" discussion. We only capitalize "You" in letters, but never "i".

His cleverly worded reference went back months to our exchange
about my uncapitalized i's.

Before long, capital-I would be speaking to him face to face.

When You Come Here

A pair of major life developments, independent of Thomas and the
trip, meanwhile continued to percolate. News bits about my hoped-for
job change and Deb's impending move out of state made it into emails
to my faraway friend.

Lakeland College (which became Lakeland University in 2016)
formalized their job offer early in the month:

Been in email negotiations with my new employer over hours,
money, and starting date. I've accepted the new job but won't
start until after I get back from Europe, the following Montage
10 August.

It's funny I presented the date European-style and knew the word
for Monday, but didn't look up the word for August.

Thomas applauded:

So you're moving smoothly from one job into another. Great for you!

He'd changed jobs two weeks before our emailing began, and had
described a similarly smooth transition.

My next paragraph (in our 349th message) told of an upcoming
public appearance of sorts:

Am Donnerstag, meine Schwester has a crucial court hearing that may determine whether the judge will let her move her children to Seattle. Her lawyer called me to request that I testify.

At the time, I wouldn't have needed my German dictionary to write the words for Thursday or sister; today, however, I had to confirm (in seconds, online) which weekday this was. Days later I sent Thomas a summary, taking a stab at titling my email in German. I tried to write: "a long time in the courtroom." Predictably, it required fixing from Thomas, but first came more cheering:

"A good try!"

Thomas expressed keen interest in the proceedings, with questions that probed what had precipitated the case, laws regarding parents' rights, and whether my sister's positive outcome bore significance for my future plans. He noted as a point of contrast:

I can live and work anywhere I want to - but I don't have children.

Well, since he asked… I filled nearly two pages with my response, beginning with:

It's all about the children…

My sons were younger by a few years than Deb's daughters - an important factor. I answered Thomas with long-term hypotheticals:

If I were to decide to move farther than 150 miles from here, I would face a challenge from their father. Things that would strengthen my case: a career choice or job offer, and/or a marriage or well established intimate relationship. These would argue for family stability for the boys, and for sufficient means of transporting them for visits.

You can hear in my wrap-up my hunger to see the world:

When the boys are grown, I'm going anywhere in the world I want!!!!!! (And I hope to have visited lots of places by then.)

Yes, six exclamation points.

My connection with Thomas was a flint that sparked the latent yearning for travel. A commensurate longing - for him to someday visit me too - peeked out hopefully between my lines, in a smattering of deft allusions to "when you come here."

The screensavers responsible for our attachment delighted me all the more as I drew closer to meeting their maker. Along with bulletins informing the programmer which eye-catching design I was using, I reported sporadic oddities of how they interacted with my system. He appreciated knowing how his creations behaved "outside the lab," even the trivialities. To one such notice I tacked on:

You can look into it when you visit here. ;-)

I described the quirk without noticing how it related to a problem we'd dealt with long before. Thomas noticed:

I guess that's the same effect that established our contact!

Wow. Nothing about this ever gets old.

It could've been that exchange which inspired yet another feat of retrospection from me. I wrote:

Well, here's yet another chance for you to think I'm crazy; last night

I read through a month's worth of old msgs again (mostly from February.) Dunno what brought that on - a mood thing, I guess. Read all the stuff about you offering me use of the web. It's funny now how arduous the process of getting me on CompuServe was!

As you've seen, I did this sort of thing several times.
On a grander scale, I'm really just doing the same now.

I Don't Wanna Wait

An opening line from one of my July messages was:

Do you still smile often?

Thomas unquestionably recognized the throwback to his March assertion. Since then, another 270 messages and 13 weeks had passed. Only a few weeks remained before I would see that smile for myself.

Playfulness and poignancy maintained their coexistence while we waited. One day Thomas wrote:

Today I left my job a little earlier, so I have some time to answer you.

I replied:

I think I'm honoured or something. :-)

His relentless attention to detail couldn't leave it alone:

I hope the "so" is correct: I wanted to say I had time to write coz I left earlier… not that I left earlier to have time to write (so much for the honour).

I'm smirking the whole time I'm writing about this. I responded:

Aw, you're so honest. I was just being playful with the other interpretation (I even used the British spelling on purpose). Your use of "so" wasn't incorrect, just slightly imprecise. I took it as you meant it - apparently I know you well enough for that.

Yet another reminder of the *knowing* I keep taking joy in.
In mid-July I told Thomas of a personal observance:

Tomorrow is another anniversary for me. I know I seem to keep track of these kinds of date-oriented things a lot, but this one is pretty important. I call it my Freedom Day cuzz it marks the date I started out on my own again - tomorrow makes six years. :-)

I loved sharing these curios with Thomas. With time *together* on the horizon, I could almost taste the sweetness of being able to talk about such things in person - the experiences and aspirations most profoundly bound up with who we were.

There wasn't room for that in July's email communings. After telling Thomas of "one of the most insanely busy days I've had in a long time," I wrote:

Well, it's a little hard to have a conversation when we're this busy, ain't it?

I was commiserating for both of us.

One Friday I let Thomas know the boys and I would be away for the weekend visiting out-of-town friends, and that he wouldn't hear from me for a few days. (No cutting-edge laptop for this single mom.) It was good to hear, when he wrote the following Friday, that he was getting a break too:

*I'm AFH, but not AFK! [away from home / keyboard] We arrived
yesterday at the outskirts of Berlin for a small vacation. I think
I'll check for email every day, but since I try to limit connections
to one per day, messages may overlap more often.*

The parties covered by "we" were politely left unnamed. I was sure
if it were anyone other than Gretchen, he would've said so. By then both
my mind and heart had settled into our framing of special friendship,
so this didn't affect me much. I couldn't have known the significance
his passing reference to Berlin would take on - much later. And I'm
nowhere near ready yet to explain.

LEARNING TO FLY

B oth of us, in those final two weeks, remarked on the heavy
demands on our time. To Thomas's vacation heads-up, I replied:

*It's kinda funny that we're each away for consecutive weekends
too.*

The following Monday I wrote:

*Back to the routine, eh? Me too. I'm guessing it's gonna be a heavy
work week for you…? I wish we had time to get back to some
slightly deeper topics again, but such is life. I wonder what you're
thinking and feeling about this upcoming visit o' mine.*

With no comment on this in Thomas's brief intervening messages, my next email acknowledged he "may have too much going on to answer that." While I waited, I tackled the question for myself:

> On one hand, part of me still can't seem to really believe it's gonna happen, even though every detail is already in place. But at the same time, enough of me must believe it cuzz I'm so happily excited about it that I don't sleep well. Interesting how the human mind is capable of both simultaneously.

Then I opened up more:

> I'm also feeling more fear than I expected. But I think that's at least somewhat related to not hearing from you much lately. Six months into this, and I still tend to worry... My feelings are fighting my brain big-time; can't quite explain it or help it. The closer the trip gets the more I feel like I *need* to hear something personal from you, such as that you're looking forward to it, in order to feel more calm.

I'm watching myself, once again, working out my emotions through writing about them:

> Actually, my mind is pretty settled about most aspects and expectations; it's my feelings that are a little turbulent, as this trip is a momentous undertaking for me. As you said, you are my email friend, but you are still a stranger in some ways. Some fresh encouragement from you would lessen my somewhat irrational fears.

The first sentence of his reply sure cleared one thing up. About being back to routine, he wrote:

No, I am still near Berlin. We're driving back on Saturday.

I can almost hear my prolonged "Ohhhhhhhh…" I shot back:

Silly me. Obviously, when you said "small vacation," I mistook that to mean just the weekend. Around here people take weekend trips "up north" all the time.

Well, that was one way to discover a cultural difference. He continued:

My place is no hotel, but I hope you'll find the comfort you need. Gonna have to do some preparations on Monday and Tuesday.

Given the feelings I'd bared, that sounded detached - but after all, he was on vacation.

This was mere days before my departure. Fifteen minutes later Thomas wrote again:

Don't get me wrong: I am looking forward to your visit and I expect that we'll both have a good time.

That helped a little. I replied:

Me too. Thanks a million for connecting an extra time to say so… :-)

What helped even more, radiating through hasty messages in the final countdown days, was the obvious delight we each took in nailing down details for the airport rendezvous. How would we find and recognize each other?

Just now as I'm typing, my whole world stops - and I exclaim, wide-eyed and beaming, *I can't believe I did this!!*

In the middle of my keyed-up messages, I meet an unexpectedly peaceful passage, whose clarity and resolve stuns me. I told Thomas:

Something inside changed for me earlier today, since I wrote you last. Not sure what precipitated it (nothing I did consciously), but I seem to have crossed a threshold in my feelings about the trip - I'm not experiencing that fear anymore!

I proposed an explanation:

Maybe it has something to do with the trip getting close enough now that I don't have trouble believing it anymore - actually seems pretty natural now. Anyway, I'm feeling VERY happy and excited and yet relaxed and unafraid. Not that there won't be moments of trepidation, especially if anything goes wrong, but it's a turning point for me and I thought you might be happy to hear of it.

The context makes clear this was unrelated to anything Thomas said. It's notable too how closely this matches my memory-narrative: *As I readied myself to board the plane, I felt, excited, confident, sparkling, awake - and completely unafraid.* How touching to my core to ponder the reliability of my recollection for that unparalleled scene.

I was set to leave home on a Tuesday. The Saturday before, Thomas wrote that he was headed back, and had just learned his home phone line (needed for emailing) was out of order:

I'll try to send an email to you as soon as I can after my arrival home. In the worst case, I won't be able to send and receive before Monday afternoon. So don't worry about that!

I'm having trouble typing this out without it seeing it play in my mind as a movie scene. I replied:

Your phone not working is a greater inconvenience to you than to me, so I don't mean to make light of the nuisance when I say: it's getting almost comical how little we're communicating now that we're about to meet each other.

That Monday I received the following single-line message at 2:30 a.m. Wisconsin time:

When you read this message, then my phone line must be working again.

Four hours later, I sent a single line too:

Congratulations - your phone is apparently working again... :-)

I haven't ceased glowing for several pages now. Reliving this run-up brings indescribable pleasure.

Send Me On My Way

These days it's hard to imagine life without cell phones. Neither Thomas nor I had one when I was set to arrive in Germany on July 29th, 1998. We did have home answering machines - his came into play as part of our backup plan that day. I completely forgot about this (a familiar refrain, I know).

In one of my last few messages I reviewed the remaining time window for emailing:

I'll be leaving my home about 10:30 my time on Tuesday morning.

So the latest you could email me something in time for me to reply before I come would be your Tuesday at 1300. Don't hesitate to tell me even a hundred times that you'll be there at the airport! :-)

Of course, I was ecstatic at the opening lines of Thomas's reply - his first substantial message since returning from vacation. I could tell he was more relaxed:

I'll see you Wednesday at the D'dorf airport. If my memory is correct, we agreed I would take the train scheduled to arrive at 8:38 - and that you will wait at your arrival gate wearing a sign with your name around your neck.

LOL! My comeback:

Well, your memory is partially correct! Yes, I'll wait at the arrival gate. If you think I'm gonna wear a sign, then you better have one on too!

Thomas continued:

Trains don't always arrive on time, so don't worry before 10:00!!! Here's a phone number where you can leave a message for me: 02xxx-xxxxx. After waiting 20 seconds you'll be prompted to leave a message. I'll plan to check this message box if I haven't found you by 10:30, so I suggest you go and look for a phone if we still haven't met at 10:00 and leave a message where you are.

Brilliant!

Nine hours before I would power down my computer, I received an email from Thomas to confirm the airline and flight number, in which he mused:

I dunno wot I'll wear tomorrow. But if you could let me know what you'll wear on arrival, it could help me identify you: Einstein T-shirt and baseball cap, you said? <g>

I snarked:

Oh sure, ask *me* to commit to an outfit when you won't decide until the last minute.

Maybe he considered donning something special for the occasion, but his indecision is laughable in retrospect. As you know, he wore his signature outfit on that day and on all the others I was with him.

Nodding to my expected weekday arrival, his final email title was "April, Spring, Summer, and Wednesdays" (helpfully noting it was a Status Quo song). My penultimate subject line was "Waiting for Wednesday" (by Lisa Loeb). The last sentence of the last message I received from Thomas before I met him was:

Weather forecast for tomorrow: 23 degrees C, showers possible.

My final message to him - titled "departing soon!!" - evinced a bit more excitement, and confirmed my sartorial choice:

Here it is already, my departure message! Can you believe it?! The boys are all set up at the other family's house, my ride will be here soon, and this is my last msg to you before I see you. Should get there in about 15 hours. I suspect we won't have any problems recognizing each other, but just to make it easier: I'm wearing a bright blue dress (and it's not dangerous <g>)... ¡Dios mío! I'M ON MY WAY!!!!!!!!!!!!!

After six-plus months and some 380 email messages - not a single phone call or live chat - it was really happening!

You might think this a perfect place to bring to a close what I call the story's pre-trip era. I would never again exchange an email with Thomas without the knowledge in my being of what being present with him was like. On that day, I was so ready to leave for Germany - but I'm not quite ready to leave this chapter.

I haven't said much about this batch's music banter. I won't now - except to point to one song. Thomas was a fan of The Who. When I described hearing a song of theirs which was new to me, he replied that he owned the album; the song was *Getting In Tune.* In the couple of decades before I opened the Box, hearing it has always evoked my fondest, most deeply moving memories of listening to it together at Thomas's home.

Finding the song title in our July messages gives it a less pleasant association now. The exchange containing its mention fell during the week I lamented to Thomas about not hearing from him much - unaware the explanation was his getaway with Gretchen. I wasn't as in tune with him as I thought. Sometimes a spotty memory can have its upside.

The subject merits a few observations before I move on from my email-only relationship with Thomas.

Resplendent in Dignity

You've seen me use collective language for Thomas and me - when it's backed by the email record, that is. As to Thomas's undivulged thoughts, I can only speculate. And when I do, it's most often related to Gretchen. Only because I saved the printouts do I relearn their status at the time: separated but not over. Was Thomas conflicted, while he was still involved with her, about our emotionally intimate email friendship?

I think this conflict shows in what he wrote, but I can't go further than that. I can, however, give *my* take, including my own waverings in the present. It's plausible to me that as Thomas and I got closer through our email sharing, he became persuaded their relationship was at its end, as he himself all but stated in the Missing Message. And... I can't know whether their small vacation the following month reinforced or contradicted that outlook.

I do know my recent discovery of how close to my arrival their excursion took place disturbed my sleep, as I worked through this in order to write about it. Could I have been confused about the two of them because Thomas was? I keep turning over in my mind the question of what I thought or knew about their status at the end of my week with him, during *our* last night together. It still *feels* like I believed they were broken up before I got there, but that's not what the emails show. I must have believed it by the last night, right?

Before I left for Germany I convinced myself, in light of our profound connection, that abiding by platonic trappings would be both doable and enough. When I think of *denial,* I think of refusing to face hard or negative things. But if I was in denial then, it meant I was instead minimizing something beautiful and true and good: *my* non-platonic love.

When I come across her name in the emails, it catches in my ears, hits a sour note, for a medley of reasons. It would seem I idealized Thomas's and my intentions to such a degree that I couldn't conceive either of us would do this, would waltz into a complicated relational situation knowingly. But - I'm telling you - we didn't *do this*. Oh wait, thanks for reminding me: *I* didn't do this.

I can't speak to Thomas's experience. For my part... I guess I slipped and fell into something of theirs - but out of confusion, not out of carelessly discarding my convictions. One conviction that has not changed is this: while he was evidently working through his own relational dilemma, I don't believe Thomas intentionally misled me.

That kind of honest love we *did* have.

As must be quite obvious, I wasn't expecting so much of my exposition to be about Gretchen. I don't want it to be - even now that it's written. I see it as a byproduct of how I chose to approach this writing endeavor. First you heard the tale I remembered, and here you are, still with me for the Sherlock-Holmes-ing into the printouts.

Now, along with the airplane headed for Germany, the story taxis and takes flight to new territory, the consummation of months of epistles.

Spoiler alert: you've already read what it was like for me to lay eyes on Thomas. For that moment and the eight days that followed it, we're forced to rely on my memory alone. You've seen too that I departed *from* Germany carried aloft by a rapturous love which levitated my whole being.

The stage of the Thomas story following my return, with the eventual unraveling that brought me back to earth, was - fortunately or not, we'll see - again documented by emails.

Again the printouts become a panel of light against which I prop x-rays of heart-memory, to examine them for what may need piercing in order to correct. I think the treatment is going to hurt this time.

It won't work to describe for you right now my rueful smile, as lips quiver and eyebrows tighten. By the time the sentence is typed, I have ruptured.

The tears commingle ecstasy and regret. They glisten too with resplendent wonder - that it happened at all, and that I am telling you about it.

As I explained early on, part of me resisted letting the emails reupholster the story. I knew they would reshape contours I had caressed and sheltered through many years. But in the process of showing you both memory and record, something quite unexpected is becoming attainable.

I yearned to know what happened.

And I wanted to remember the forgetting.

What a shock to find I can do both.

PART SIX

The Emails After

HEAD OVER FEET

Your book page doesn't look much different from the end of Part Five until here in Part Six. But between them, I traveled to Germany and spent a glorious yet wrinkled week with Thomas. Also between the two parts, I perused the Box's remaining printouts. In contrast to my earlier method, I decided to masticate on our post-trip correspondence in one chunk. I'm solving my mysteries - most of them anyway. And I feel quite changed by what I've read. But we have far to go before I explain.

As I sit down to show you what happened, I feel an urge to run away from the laptop and do something easier, less fraught, like organizing a closet. Well, maybe that's not a bad metaphor for what I *am* doing. It starts off messy - *I* feel messy - yet there's hope I'll be able to bring some order.

You already know my emailing with Thomas began in mid-January 1998, and that I went to meet him in late July. I've suggested the increasing bulk of the monthly folders could fashion a 3D representation of our story arc.

Here's the sculpture after my return: swollen files of printouts for August and September, October's a little slimmer. November's and December's messages are few enough to combine into one folder, and a skinny file finishes off schnibbles of contact into 1999. Together these post-trip emails number far fewer than those before it. Even so, there's an awful lot to deal with here.

It isn't only the potpourri of emotions that makes these tough to get through. There are defects in my storage techniques that weren't present with the earlier folders; they require extra concentration to sort out, and add distracting perplexities to already disconcerting and difficult conversations.

You'll recall my hand-inked green digits on the pre-trip printouts are absent from those after it. It shouldn't be a problem (for ease of reference) to add numbers now, right? Nope, not that simple. A switch in email providers that autumn resulted in an alteration in time stamp systems - in short, greatly complicating the sequencing task with multiple messages in a day. (Both accounts are long gone.) Attempts to trace our labyrinthine discussions, themselves occasionally tedious, reveal I filed many messages out of order and missed printing some altogether. I'm taking the time and tedium now to sort and number the printouts with sticky notes.

On top of that, my method of storing oldest in front makes things harder than they need to be. Yes, just as I sometimes did in the conversations themselves.

The incidental metaphors aren't letting up.

Remember my sneak peek at the tech support plea when I first opened the Box? I do the same now with our first exchange after my return - and blubber like a baby at the sweetness. If, after the glorious final night with Thomas, our contact would've gone silent for no reason, I would've wanted our last message ever to be the one he sent for me to open upon my arrival home.

The woman who returned to Wisconsin overflowed with unadulterated, uncontainable glee. I experienced a pure ecstatic dancing in-love-ness unlike any before or since. This would morph all too soon, in fits and starts of hope and disappointment, into a jumble of distress and confusion I didn't know what to do with. The emotional tangle I read in these emails feels weird, hard to grapple with. My most persistent expression as I pore over them has my intensely scrunched eyebrows almost frozen that way.

For as euphoric as I felt when I got back, it's startling to see how little time we had before things between Thomas and me became difficult.

Before I go there, it's essential to reiterate yet again a central wonder of the entire adventure. The person who greeted me at the airport in Germany, the person with whom I spent the wondrous week that followed, thoroughly accorded with the Thomas I'd experienced in our purely digital friendship. The longer I live, the more convinced I am of how noteworthy this is. Nothing about our later difficulties altered that.

My hastily scrawled notes during that week supply but a meager resource to bolster recollections of what took place there, and you've seen my faculty of memory prove imperfect. Call me a somewhat unreliable narrator. To the rescue, however, come emails Thomas and I exchanged in the weeks after my return. In our resumed correspondence, as we began to contrive ways to build a future together, we also reminisced about the time we'd just spent in each other's presence. Another resource! The scenes we replicated in writing bring a wealth of particulars I never would've known.

Among the enlightenments, our earliest threads demystify a key inquiry from the memory-narrative. I wanted to understand a miscommunication we had before my plane even lifted off from Germany. And now I do.

But first, the sweetness.

In Your Wildest Dreams

Back in my apartment on Wednesday, August 5th, I powered up my computer - and found an email from Thomas waiting for me:

Hi! When I start to write this message, you are probably back on the ground.

He described stopping off in Cologne on his train ride home from the airport. On a whim, he'd swung into the Saturn store and bought a replacement of the Slade CD. What a pearl: the very first memory-confirmation from my time in Germany features that gift!

Only a few paragraphs long, his inaugural post-trip message included these declarations:

You said this was the nicest week of your life. We had such a fine week…Now we'll get back to writing email.

It feels so grounding to read my sentiment through the prism of Thomas's emailed words. Our frequent "you said" construction

- repeating in type spoken words from our time together - fills in a considerable number of blanks from that week.

Here's another lifelong memory authenticated. His message was signed:

Luv, TH

That first-ever sign off makes me swoon again now. My rapturous response began:

Good birthday afternoon, my sweet Thomas! How I miss you!

Sent the day following my return, this tells me there's already a printout missing - the note I would've emailed the prior evening to let him know of my safe arrival. My next sentence is further evidence:

I told you I had lots of time to reflect on the plane ride home - wrote pages of notes between giving in to the tears.

This clarifies too the timing of some undated notebook jottings.

My Thursday message's four stapled pages contain several stirring and invaluable corroborations of memories - as well as lost tidbits like the name of the coffee drink (Rüdesheimer Kaffee) I sipped during our cafe talk, "a highlight among many highlights of my time there."

I described in detail the surrounding deluge then in progress:

Our back field is completely under water, as it was when I wrote you about a similar situation this past spring. Actually, this is already quite a bit more serious. All the streets are closed, and Deb said her basement is already a torrent.

From local news I moved to music tidbits - which song I awoke with in my head, which CDs I planned to buy - then to more personal musings.

How affirming to meet this contemporaneously recorded vignette:

After we said goodbye, I started to miss you as soon as I started walking down that hall. On the plane, I was able to turn toward the window and finally let out some of the emotion that had been building up for all those hours. After a while, I couldn't cry anymore - and don't worry about it all being sadness, cuzz it wouldn't have hurt so much to leave if it hadn't been so joyous to be there.

The deeply seared window-seat scene remains unfaded; I had no idea there existed backup testimony to it.

An accompanying detail about the return flight stands out:

Coming into Chicago we had to circle above the airport for an extra half hour because of bad weather.

I have zero recollection of this; it's jarring now because I happened to use the metaphor in the memory-narrative to describe our final evening's conversation.

Here's backup for the supreme comfort I remember:

It was strange to be back in my apartment, because your place was home to me for the longest stretch of time I'd ever been away. Being back here made me realize even more how at-home I'd felt there.

My attachment to the country makes an appearance:

I said goodbye to Germany as the plane rose on take-off...Then
a cloud blocked the view under the plane and it was all gone.

I'd forgotten the cloud's rude interruption - now the recollection is crystal clear. Again nature presaged a metaphor I would later employ, this one evoking the same breath-halting sensation as the white wall of leaving Thomas.

He'd paraphrased my words about our week together; now I paraphrased his:

You said you enjoyed "every minute"...I can't say emailing is like
going back, because now when I read your msgs, I can hear your
voice and see your face.

Nothing would ever be the same as before.

Naturally, remembrances I wrote about our last evening pierce the deepest:

I simply can't describe how deeply wonderful it was for me to
spend those long sad hours together just holding each other. And
when you looked into my eyes, it was like you could see there was
nothing else in the world I would rather be doing than looking
right back into yours. Later when I dozed off on the plane, I awoke
wondering if that night was something I'd only dreamt.

I hadn't merely idealized the scene in retrospect - though I've never really doubted that.

Some of Thomas's words that night are refracted back to him in what I wrote:

Early during our last evening together, you said you had a comment you might not say cuzz it might make me even sadder. It was about how you'd feel on Thursday and whether you might wish I'd never come at all because of how it might be easier never knowing what you'd be missing. It didn't make me sadder cuzz I knew what you meant; it made me happy. And I sure would like to know how you feel about everything today.

The paragraph hits me hard with its knotty sincerity, its touch of shadow.

How Precarious

My early emailing with Thomas could not have been a greater delight to write about. It's not like that now. Entering this segment of the adventure is as emotionally harrowing as I knew it would be. Wow, does this hurt. Its ups and downs are difficult to explain to you - because they're difficult to explain to *me*. Tears, frustration, angst: all roil and pulsate. But the worst of the inner storm barrels through, ultimately allowing the pain to dissolve into a measure of tranquility. I'm finding out what I so desperately wanted to know.

Already in my first long message after settling in, a mix-up of meanings began to emerge:

I loved how you said to me at the airport that I could tell Deb I stayed safe and that my heart was safe too.

Thomas replied:

Now I'm not so sure anymore that your heart was always safe.

I elaborated:

Looking back, I can say my heart was mostly safe, and where I felt it to be at risk, I knew what I was choosing. When I'm with you, I feel very comfortable about being myself. That makes my heart feel safe and it's an incredibly valuable gift you give me.

Thomas started to wonder:

Maybe there is an idiomatic obstacle. In German, you "lose" your heart if you "give" it to somebody. I'm afraid I lost my heart to you when I met you. What do you mean when you say your heart was safe most of the time?

And I confirmed:

That puts a different slant on what you said to me at the airport and partly explains why I didn't completely understand your feelings that morning. My meaning is almost opposite of yours. To me, safe means safe from getting broken, whether one guards their heart or gives it. I've told you I had feelings for you before I ever saw you, and when I said my heart had been safe there, it meant I could give it to you knowing you wouldn't hurt it.

This was taking us beyond mere linguistics. I continued:

So when you said at the airport that my heart had been safe, I took that to mean you would never hurt me. And when I wrote about my heart being safe "mostly," I meant that in giving it to you, I never felt it to be in danger of being broken (except when I thought maybe you and G still wanted to be together).

I roped in an earlier thread:

This goes all the way back to eight weeks before I came there. When I said my friends were worried about my heart's safety, that meant they were afraid I would give it too easily, and then somehow find my love disappointed.

Our crossed wires about safe hearts - how wild they arose from the language/culture difference! - became the inroad to uncovering a misconception of even greater impact.

In the message that greeted my arrival home, Thomas had said he wanted "to sleep over" his emotions before sharing them. In his second message, he said:

I knew how it feels to be alone when you love somebody who doesn't return your emotions. Now I love somebody who returns deep emotions - and still I'm alone. Well, not that alone! It's a great relief to know you and your emotions and to keep in contact with you…I expected I would feel sad because of the hopes that got smashed, that you and I could live happily together ever after.

I wasn't entirely clear on his smashed hopes, though it was true we couldn't be together right then. He added:

P.S. We never kissed each other. I wanted it so much, but I think it's good we didn't coz I would miss you even more if we did, though I don't know if you would've allowed it.

I replied:

I also wanted it so much and was a little scared of the same thing. I would've not only allowed it, I would've welcomed it. Maybe this is like a romantic movie - just that we're only in the middle of it so far. Do you think you really could come here, and when?

His reply began:

Good morning, sunshine of my life! I think I could come in May, June, or July for 3 or 4 weeks...Not so long ago you told me we couldn't live together coz I didn't meet your requirements. You sounded very firm and assured.

Whoa, there it is! Ignoring for the moment how abrasive "requirements" sounds, this (to tweak Leonard Cohen) is the crack that let the light in.

Thomas was alluding to our evening conversation, when my thoughts hadn't come out the way I meant - and I didn't know it. In my narrative from memory, this part was especially hazy. Now I'm squeezing back tears again.

DON'T STOP BELIEVIN'

Neither of us realized our sadness at parting came in contrasting shades. Like greenery sprouting through sidewalk crannies, the disconnect made its way to sunlight in our emails.

Without waiting for an explanation, Thomas's next message took to machinating over how to bridge our geographical distance. You can hear his elated agitation:

> *I loved you before I saw you - and love you even more now. But will our love stand the strains of everyday life? Only time will tell. Do you want to try it? Do I want to try it? Dare I?*
>
> *I think "lovesick" is not the correct word. My love wasn't disappointed! But still I am in a state of confusion - unable to concentrate on my work, and always thinking of you.*

His closing included info about arranging a phone call - I'd told him I hated that his voice in my mind was fading, that I needed to hear it. He signed, "Your confused lover."

My reply brooded over what I might've said in our talk that gave him the wrong idea:

> *I remember many details of that night's conversation, and that*
> *I sometimes hesitated and stumbled over my words. I feel badly*
> *for leaving you with confusion. You asked what I thought possible*
> *obstacles might be; I think I mentioned a few things I'm scared*
> *about, but didn't know how firm I sounded. I do know I feel quite*
> *in a happy daze now, hardly able to concentrate on anything either,*
> *even though the future is uncertain.*

It wouldn't be the last time I expressed uncertainty - or regret for causing him trouble.

Years before, I'd determined my "bottom lines" for a prospective partner (the term came from comparing lists with friends), among them no alcohol addiction and willingness to wait until marriage for full lovemaking. On that night in Germany, face to face with the man I'd fallen in love with, I was reflecting on them aloud - for myself as much as for him. The two I just named had presented no problem for Thomas. Now in my email going back over the talk, I told him I really hated the requirements label, and arrived at this nutshell:

> *I haven't written about any obstacle yet that is insurmountable.*
> *Difficult, yes, but not insurmountable if we both would wanna*
> *take huge chances. There's one thing left that I mentioned that*
> *night, and that is, to put it dryly, our belief systems.*

Here we go. I continued:

I hope that whatever confusion I may have caused for you, at least you felt my acceptance of your journey. A long time ago you sent a definition of platonic love that described the two people as "searching for truth and beauty." And I remember how it warmed my heart to think of you as doing that.

It might sound presumptuous to refer to his journey - it does to me now - but I was basing it on that phrase about searching. After all, it was Thomas who'd sent it.

I was almost done:

Years ago I read a description of life-long love that's always stayed with me: The love starts out with two people looking into each other's eyes, but lasts as they both look in the same direction together. That idea resonates deeply with me. Another way to say it is to ask whether we are both looking in the same direction.

Passages that suggest I was trying to influence what Thomas believed are among the most difficult for me to work through. (I was less subtle in later messages.) I can't deny it's what I was doing. I wouldn't do it now.

I don't apologize for where I was on *my* journey, but I vehemently regret causing him sorrow because of what I couldn't have yet comprehended about it.

But the excerpt above comes as some consolation in what it reveals - to me! - about *why* I was insistent. Yes, as I would later explain to Thomas, I came by the convictions I held through hard challenges, but wanting him to share some version of them wasn't as tied to my specific belief system as it sounded. Rather, I was utterly persuaded our relationship would run into trouble down the road if we went into it knowing we didn't elementally "face the same direction" (whatever that means). Underlying my urgings was a desire to forestall needless heartache.

I know now that how I chose to handle it didn't, in the end, save either of us one iota of anguish.

To my lengthy explanation, Thomas responded:

My sweetheart! I'm afraid we had a miscommunication! Took more than 3 days to get it straight. I think Wednesday would have been different if it hadn't been for that misunderstanding. No point asking who's to blame. But in order to clear the miscommunication I tell it here how I see it.

Now it was his turn to review our crucial conversation:

We had been talking about insurmountable obstacles and bottom-line requirements, when you said you "couldn't imagine to live with somebody that didn't believe in being with you after death." I thought this was still a requirement, and this one really would be insurmountable.

Oh now I remember! I felt such uplifting relief at his exposition. My feelings now are more mixed. (He hardly sounds open-minded on the life after death point, I notice.) He continued:

After Wednesday morning I thought there was no chance for us to live together because of "belief incompatibility." If you found some of the stuff I said confusing during that day and since, this misunderstanding may be to blame.

His closing remark makes me a little stomach-sick:

I think I would have kissed you if I knew then what I know now - well, maybe I would have not. But it's sure that the misunderstanding made the farewell more sad for me!

Here Thomas sounds less absolute, yet another of his maybe-maybe not's.

Sometimes hindsight has a blind spot. Who can say what might've been - yet it bruises my heart, as fresh tears testify, to think not just of missing a kiss, but to think this was the reason.

As I compressed it for you from memory: *Thomas didn't realize I was open to staying sweethearts. I didn't know he thought I wasn't.* Guess I nailed that one.

I opened my next reply:

Hello, my love! Wow, I'm just staring at my screen for minutes not knowing where to start. There, I've finally started...

Nothing's Gonna Stop Us Now?

As of my third day home, Thomas and I were back on the same page. We'd sorted out the miscues - and we were desperately in love. Only four thousand miles and the divergence on faith imperiled our being together. Only.

The message I was staring at on that August day was our 387th. Staring now at its printout, I am once again overwhelmed by this process and its emotions. Time to take a slow breath, regain my balance. That's better; now I can go on.

I thanked him, and expounded:

I understand everything much better now. Until we started emailing,

I never expected to become this attracted to someone who believed
so differently about the soul. I'm sure I was unclear and confusing
to you because it has really shaken me up! I'm having a long-
standing standard of mine be sorely challenged. And I'm finding
it's hard to make life-affecting decisions when one is in love.

I couldn't move on without apologizing:

I determined to never be careless with your heart by not dealing
with obstacles out in the open, but it looks as though, in my own inner
confusion, I've done just that without meaning to, and I'm so sorry!

He'd said he didn't blame me - but I blamed me.

The thread continued with each of us elaborating on our beliefs,
attempting to move toward common ground, while in another thread
we worked on plans for his visit.

As usual, Thomas summed things up nicely:

I'm less confused now!...So it's up to me to put my money where
my mouth is and try to overcome the distance - if we get the belief
question settled.

Science doesn't have all the answers, he wrote, but enough to
convince him the Bible isn't a reliable resource. He added:

I believe that when I'm dead I'm dead; I don't think I have an
immortal soul. I'm not trying to convince anybody (coz this is
only what I think - I'm not sure about it) - nor should anybody
try to convince me.

You can see he makes some allowance in the parentheses, then
retracts it. He wasn't bothered by differing on belief; to him the obstacle
was mine to surmount. He was right. (Here again, though, he doesn't

sound very searching.) It was on me to work out my bottom line. Before closing his message with updates on arranging vacation time and renewing his passport, Thomas said he wanted to give me all the time I needed - exactly as I would later say to him.

I echoed in reply that "we still have that big if," and explained:

I draw a huge distinction between personal faith and religious behavior, and I hate religion and religious behavior. ("I will not be led…"). I think there are reasons to believe the Bible does contain revelation, but much of it isn't straightforward and has been distorted and misused.

Evangelicals may find the dichotomy between religion and faith familiar. He'd made clear his connotations with faith came from institutionalized religion - so here was a tiny patch of common ground already.

I reiterated I wasn't out to change him, and celebrated a commonality:

I believe in living life fully and deeply, always questioning, embracing its highs and its lows and its mysteries…unlike those who skim the surface and shut down part of themselves to avoid pain or uncertainty. One of the first things that appealed to me about you was seeing that same willingness to struggle with life.

It was my own constant questioning, staring down uncertainties, which years later would lead me away from what I told Thomas I was so sure of. How could I have known that then?

It was Sunday, less than a week since we'd been in each other's arms, and I closed that August 9th message:

If I haven't put you off by anything I've said so far, how soon can you come? Can you make it by tomorrow?

We were off and running and hopeful - working to narrow the spiritual gulf and the ocean between us.

Both kinds of distance loomed, barriers that needed demolishing for our impassioned dreams to survive.

The Power of Love

With every waking breath, I could hardly wait to be with Thomas again.

Pages and pages of August and early September emails were devoted to making that happen. We might never have tried for togetherness had our farewell misreading remained undiscovered - just as we'd have never met were it not for the screensavers. Life brims with such if-then's. Some are harder to let go of than others.

Try we did. It was a time of ecstatic hope, our captivated hearts frantic over trying to make *us* work. And yet, in our August 10th exchange, I see us already inching toward an impasse.

To his "take all the time you need," I replied:

You are so sweet and kind. I'm still sorting it out some. I hope this doesn't sound offensive to you: if you see yourself as a searcher for truth and beauty, I'm prepared to beg you to consider whether you could possibly be open to ever coming to accept a belief different from where you've come thus far. And I say this only because I love you so much!

Wordy again, and frantic indeed. Thomas responded:

I cannot change my belief - at will. I never thought I could live with someone who believes in resurrection. Never thought about it, but I can handle it. Please say as soon as you can whether you can live with me despite the different beliefs. You can have all the time you need to think about it. It took me very long to write this short message. It's not easy to write about - as this turns out to be the key problem for our relation.

There he is again giving *me* time, with a little "as soon as you can" thrown in.

His paragraph opens my eyes - at this moment - to a crucial insight. The actual locus of our stalemate over belief involved the role of the will. To me, faith was something you chose (or rejected) after examining its claims. He made it sound like something you wait around for to happen to you.

Thomas also wrote:

I would say that our beliefs are compatible because I respect your belief, and you appear to accept my belief.

This I wholeheartedly agree with now. I so wish I could've just gone with it back then.

Instead, the complication hovered - relegated to background, to work at individually - while we charged ahead. Call it a mini-reprieve.

Our next stage was like an elaborate logic puzzle, interlocking parts attached at the base to getting Thomas here. Conundrums and their solutions branched off from "seeing how it goes when we're together in a few months." In his August 13th message, he wrote that he was eyeing a round-trip flight for December 13th to January 8th.

Now, follow me on this… We loved each other madly yet aimed to be clear-headed, knowing our story wouldn't imitate fantasy forever; we would move toward real-life couplehood in steps. If three weeks of family life in December confirmed we'd like to make it permanent, we'd familiarize ourselves with the bureaucratic hoops for him to emigrate to the U.S. (Alternatively, we puzzled over taking turns living and working partial years in each other's neighborhoods, bringing added complications regarding my sons' interests.) This would mean leaving his job, looking for work here, renting his own place at first, maybe even in my building. To honor my preferences, Thomas was willing to marry - which would entail consulting an immigration lawyer about a fiance visa. Before we knew it, we found ourselves exchanging preferences about a potential wedding - and I hadn't even been back three weeks.

Also in the mix was a brief but serious consideration of Thomas purchasing my sister's house. Among the printouts is an email exchange directly between him and Deb.

Talk about logistics! How very simple it sounds now to think back on planning for our single week together at his place.

No wonder August's folder was difficult to sort - we were writing constantly, in dense detail. The emails confirm we spoke briefly a few times by phone, and that we didn't use the calls for this scheming. It's mindblowing what we were again able to accomplish by email alone. An outside reader would find these messages overwrought and convoluted; at points, our matching detail-orientation now even drives me crazy.

All of this was taking place, as I said, with the contingency about beliefs now mostly off to the side. But soon factors related to distance would conspire to force the faith issue - making us confront what we might otherwise have been content to let ride indefinitely.

Were it not for the Box, I wouldn't have known how swept away we became right after my return. My retellings through the years emphasized his planned December visit. They never included being engaged; we plainly were.

In this hopeful phase, Thomas wrote on August 15th, in our 400th message:

> *It is irrational to expect to find a lover on the Internet - but I found you and I love you; it's irrational to believe that we could live together. But there is a difference between impossibility and improbability!*

And I replied:

> *Well, I already left my heart there with you when I left Germany. I've never loved anyone like I love you, and I know I've never been loved like you love me. If you are willing to walk into this with eyes open, risking relational pain, accepting there are no guarantees, well then that's exactly what I am willing to do. Shall we give it a whirl?*

AGAINST ALL ODDS

Thomas didn't take emigrating lightly, of course. He admitted it would be difficult, and more than once called himself a coward about it. Amid this August precariousness, a message from him began:

Question: Will you marry me?

Answer: Definitely maybe!

Question: Will I emigrate to America?

Answer: Definitely maybe!

I think that's all the certainty we can expect at this stage of our relation.

Weeks later, his relief was palpable when he hit on the idea of living with me part-time instead, so he could keep his home and job. He calculated the amount of days we could be together each year, based on both of us using accrued vacation time for extended overseas visits - and estimated how many years this might be necessary, based on when my sons would be old enough to be independent. Then he asked:

> *Do you think it's worth starting a marriage like that? For me the marriage would be a sign - for us and the world - that we belong together even if we are not always together.*

How many times, how many ways can I say my heart is melting, tears welling?! I'm telling you again. I replied:

> *Well, ask just about anyone and they'll agree we haven't done hardly anything typical in this relationship yet! Why start now? :-) We have no options that fit into the category of "easy." Maybe we should be calling it a "virtual marriage."*

Neither of us downplayed the obstacles - both of us highlighted hope.

By early September, Thomas was exultant about the progress in working around the geography, while I'd privately been gaining clarity as to the spiritual chasm. When I returned to the subject, with new specificity about my beliefs and hopes - this is important - it was with the mindset that he was a searcher who *wanted* to know and would consider them.

But instead of clearing the way, our efforts along the twin tracks would bring about a collision.

Remember when I told you of disliking a side of myself in my April messages? I knew I'd feel that again at this stage, put off by my passages arguing for faith. But in these September messages, there's something

I did not see coming: I'm also dismayed at *not catching on* to where Thomas was really coming from on the subject.

Some of that oversight owed to my reckless optimism, some to his not being direct enough. These qualities in each of us became accentuated - because we loved our love for each other so much.

As the sky clouded over, this passage from Thomas left me both lifted and downcast:

> *I know I love you. One certainty amidst the ifs, maybes, buts, fears, doubts, uncertainties! My love is like a rock - but a constant stream of water can wear a rock down.*

In his subsequent message he apologized for sharing his foreboding, and assured me nothing specific I'd said had brought it on.

In an exchange about a particular take on the Christian story I found compelling, Thomas said he found it interesting and would think on it. Well, here was some grounds for hope - I even mailed him the book I'd taken it from. But that verbalization of openness was far outnumbered by statements with a certain passivity to them. Although he'd initially said he would "take the challenge" of reading the book, he also said he didn't think a book could change his belief - and never acknowledged receiving it. He restated, in various iterations, the following sentiment several times over those weeks:

> *I don't say I'll never change my belief, but I can't change it at will. And I think it's highly unlikely I will.*

At the time, I clung to any shreds of hope I could read into his words. Now I see the fixedness and incuriosity plain as day.

Also clearer to me now is this: Thomas was given to speaking in probabilities, hedging with tactful language. Had he stated flat out he had no inclination to dig deeper, and/or asked me to drop the subject, I absolutely would have - though it would undoubtedly have hastened our ending.

I myself tend to err on the side of tact, gentleness, hedging. But I know they can prolong discomfort rather than ease it when directness is called for. I had always thanked him before when he did state difficult truths plainly.

As for my role, it can't have been easy on him that I kept professing my ardent and undying affection while insisting we couldn't be together unless something about him changed. It really does pain me most of all to think of conveying that mixed message.

I agonized over where to land. When I did land, I told Thomas I didn't see how to avoid an either/or predicament:

Either I decide to give up what has always been a solid commitment to myself about marrying someone with whom I have at least a core belief in common, or you happen to become genuinely persuaded toward a faith similar to mine.

I reminded him I'd already investigated atheism for myself, but he hadn't investigated my belief. It took me too long to realize he wasn't interested in doing that.

Maybe if we'd have met and lived in the same town, we could've managed some sort of holding pattern for a while. As it was, imminent decisions to be made about flights and visas would afford us no such luxury.

Both of us waiting for the other to give ground was not sustainable.

On September 7th (in our 464th message), after reiterating the unlikelihood of his beliefs changing, Thomas wrote:

Faith is no hurdle for me - but it could be a big problem for us.

That single sentence is highlighted in purple - the only time I did that on any printout. Now I write a sticky note and affix it to that page: *the beginning of the end.*

We would never be in harmony again.

The Tide Is High

I am tragically over-simplifying a tragedy. There was a baroque beauty in what we tried to do, beauty even in the unraveling.

Thomas and I were headed for a collision, I told you. Now I'm rethinking the metaphor. September was tempestuous and difficult, but I felt the final impact in slow motion - and I wouldn't call it an accident. With a love genuine and profound, we *really* tried to move toward each other. And we did! We took *who we were at the time* as far as our individual integrities could then handle.

In the throes of the trying messages of early September, I told Thomas I felt I'd already compromised (in the positive sense) quite a lot - as much as I could while remaining true both to my convictions and to my love for him. I said one of the many things I loved about him was how he challenged me, and that it seemed the faith issue was one arena in which I challenged him too.

Thomas replied:

There are cases of people changing their belief at a late stage in their life - so I don't say this won't happen to me.

See what I mean? I couldn't detect a corresponding *effort*, leaving me stymied. And in his same message, here was the kicker:

I think we should stop talking about marriage while we still have a potentially insurmountable hurdle in our way. And I consider rescheduling my vacation in USA to a different time (maybe Easter) to avoid the trouble of traveling in winter.

I stopped breathing. When I replied (with the title, "Truly, madly, deeply, sadly"), I begged him not to postpone his visit - and tried to find silver linings:

I would venture to say for both of us this is sad, difficult and painful, precisely because we love each other so much. I guess we knew from the start potential obstacles could bring us to just such a crossroads. And we knew the further we got, the more of our hearts we were putting at stake. S'pose if there's any good to be found here, a positive side may be we've never been more clear about where we're at - nothing foggy anymore.

Thomas responded:

It seems that our relation will remain platonic for a long time now. This is something I have to accept - after being rather confident about marriage recently. But I also need time to eat that.

In the midst of all the heaviness, I smile weakly at that last wording. He noted that with three months before our planned visit, he had "a fortnight or two" to decide about booking the flight, and closed:

I think I'm too sad now to make rational decisions. Good night, my love!

With the subject line, "Love Hurts - but it's *not* a lie!" I replied:

This whole thing is sort of freaking me out too. I'm glad you don't mind continuing to talk about our thoughts and feelings, even though there's been an earthquake. Calling our relation platonic will not change or lessen my deep, intense, passionate, more-than-platonic love for you, no matter what riding this storm out will be like.

I wasn't ready to relinquish the slimmest sliver of hope.

No point dragging this part out. There was more to the unraveling, but I've given you the gist of it. And I don't need to think up a metaphor - Thomas's would be hard to beat:

Programmers would call this situation a deadlock - you're waiting for a change in my belief; I'm waiting for a change in your belief. And it can't be said if or when either of these will happen.

He wasn't *quite* giving up either - but it wouldn't be long.

The span between flying away from Germany and receiving his deadlock message was five weeks to the day. The truly final reprieve was truly over. You wouldn't know it from my next message:

How I wish that I could be with you right now! I miss you with such an ache - my heart is still there with you, and I can't stop thinking about you. We've come to an especially difficult phase, but I look forward to us being able to laugh again.

The next day he said:

I feel like I need time to think - a whole lotta time. We'll stay in contact but probably we won't meet again this year. Please don't urge me to come at Xmas.

I gasp as my hand jerks toward my mouth. My god, there they are - those six crushing words I told you my reaction to from memory.

Eventually I got up off the floor, dried my eyes, and replied:

I will try to be patient, and won't try to change your mind anymore about when we meet again.

Thomas:

I don't want to make you cry. I'm afraid we both woke up from our dreams now. And it hurts.

I swallow hard.

On the first read-through, these scenes completely shredded me, left me awash in chest-heaving tears to the point of incapacitation. I keep pulling myself together to keep telling you the story.

Rereading those six words from Thomas gut-punched me a second time. It's the only Strand I've carried crystal-clear from the post-trip emails. Well, that's if you don't count a minor mystery solved. In an August exchange I mused about introducing Thomas to my friends, and he responded describing himself as "terribly shy." I didn't make it up after all!

There… In the same way I just used that paragraph to defuse the story's tension, I can feel my inner experience of the story's distress beginning to tilt toward peace, wobbling toward the equilibrium I've needed.

The words Thomas and I wrote, all fourteen hundred pages, will never lose their inherent force and splendor for me. Now as the panorama unblurs, the old adventure is finding a place of rest inside, a home where writing about it (fittingly enough) dissipates some of the emotional intensity it has held for me all these years.

I have only a little left to tell.

With or Without You

It was mid-September and a change of seasons was coming.

Thomas and I voiced our intent to hold onto friendship, and I looked ahead hoping to recapture the spark and delight from before.

Our messages were still full of affection, with sweet, pained greetings and signoffs, as we acknowledged arduous realities. I told him:

There was nothing wrong with dreaming. Something very real happened that was good - and I dream with my eyes open. As I see it, in actuality we have been wide awake to something wonderful all along.

It was a towering height we were coming down from.

Soon the pace of our emails slowed, the fervor in them cooled - his sooner than mine, as you might guess. It didn't take long for them to become lopsided; his shorter messages engaged less with longer heartfelt thoughts I wrote. At the end of September I described feeling "at a loss" about the state of our correspondence:

One thing I still want from this encounter would be to be lifetime friends. I can still look forward to much enjoyment and contentment to think you'd want that too. And then my life will be so much richer than it would be without you.

The next day, with no intervening response from Thomas, I decided I had more to say. It was time for a sort of manifesto, a summation of my perspective on our adventure, to mark the occasion of our shift back to cyber-friendship.

As I'm about to tell you of it, I hear an internal record-scratch, alerting me about a subject I've unconsciously skipped over. I need to go back and tie that together first. You'll recognize the irony - since it has to do with Gretchen.

In Thomas's second message after my return - the one with his smashed hopes - he said in the same paragraph:

There is something missing between Gretchen and me. I knew that before your 1st email. I felt it stronger when our cyber-friendship became so deep and intense. I feel it yet stronger after your week here.

I replied:

I didn't realize you knew this so long ago. I guess I'm a little relieved by that, cuzz I wouldn't want to have been the cause of the demise of an otherwise OK relationship.

A few messages later (after our miscommunication was resolved), I wrote:

During our last night together, you said something changed for you during our coffee conversation at the cafe. The first time we really talked, during my second evening there, you said you still wanted to see where the situation with G would go. At the cafe five days later, you said you'd like to try living with me but weren't sure you would move to America. Then, that last night, well, wow, that last night…

Inquiring as to what had changed, I pursued:

Doesn't this also put you in a difficult position in terms of what you will tell G, if you don't mind my asking?

He didn't mind:

I don't love her anymore. But still I don't want to hurt her. I didn't know what I should tell her before you came here. Should I have told her it's over? Should I have told her something was going wrong in our relation and that we should work on it? It can be hard work to keep a relation; I have to learn to talk about problems in relations.

You won't be surprised to learn I blocked all this out - but it's back big-time now. He continued:

Maybe it would've been better if we would've met next year, not this year. Before you came I was almost certain that my relation with G was done for - and that's where I still am: almost certain. I think it's morally wrong to continue a relation after the love is gone; but it's easier to bear than being alone. My love is with you, but I cannot be with you; but this is what I would prefer most of all! I feel I have to make two important decisions this week - what I'll tell G and if I should fly to America in December.

By then, this thread ran parallel with our wild and ecstatic planning and dreaming. As for not hurting Gretchen, I replied:

Of course not. I barely know her and wouldn't want to hurt her. I only meant to acknowledge this will be difficult for you, cuzz from what you've been saying, it seemed hurting her was inevitable (maybe even if I hadn't come along at all).

That paragraph was written August 14th, a week after my return. It would be two more weeks of indulging our own flights of fancy before Thomas mentioned her again.

Are you seeing what I'm seeing?? Contrary to my protestations in earlier chapters, the record shows I knew exactly what I was doing. Busted.

To borrow Thomas's phrase: now I have to eat that.

November Rain

I've long claimed to favor facing reality over living under illusion. But it seems I've been perfectly fine with a *retrospective* illusion. How effortless it was for my subconscious to gray out the Gretchen factor over time.

Thomas told me at the end of August that he'd broken the news to Gretchen. His wording was less than direct:

I spent yesterday evening with G, after avoiding her for several weeks. We didn't talk much about our emotions, so I don't know how surprised she is, or to what extent she was expecting or fearing this.

As he later explained, he told her he didn't love her and informed her he was considering emigrating to be with me.

Well, you've seen what became of that idea. By the end of September, as you know, Thomas and I were attempting a clunky adjustment back to cyber-friendship.

On the first of October, I composed the manifesto. It began:

Dear sweet Thomas!

I'm overflowing with thoughts and emotions at this transition we're facing. This message is not exactly a short one, but that's either your good fortune or misfortune for falling in love with a writer.

I told him my pleased relief about remaining friends alternated with "deep, wrenching grief," and that I regretted causing him pain by not being sure of my faith boundary sooner:

I've sometimes worried I've made life very hard on you. All I can say is I've been, in every minute with you, as well as apart from you, as honest as I know how to be. I know now if I don't live by what I've come to believe through my challenges, then I lose my identity, lose what has made me me - and thus can't offer anyone else integrity, and I go back to being anchorless in the wind and waves of the storms of life.

Alongside the regrets was jubilation. In the following words my most profound lifelong takeaways are substantiated, bringing me much needed comfort in this moment:

You happened to meet me at a happy and special time in my life. What you did for me on top of that was to add *immeasurably* to my happiness and my enjoyment of life, and I will always be grateful to you for that!! My week with you in Germany is and

I expect always will be a highlight of my entire life. You, and Germany, will always be a cherished part of who I am now. Nothing can change that.

Although I expected to stay in touch, I wrote this to honor the sunset of our Romantic period:

This romantic movie hasn't gone the way either of us hoped for, but still, thank you for being so good to my heart. You can always know that someone OTOSOTP loves you and will never forget you.

Thomas did not acknowledge or reply to the message.

And then, after three days of silence, this:

Hi luv!

Gretchen told me a fortnight ago that she is pregnant - 4th month already.

He even signed it, "Luv, Thomas." In the skimpy paragraphs between, he said he didn't want to live with her, adding:

But she received my child - weeks before you and I met - and I have to take the responsibility now.

He noted, helpfully, this would tie him further to Germany. (And he was stretching that timing a bit.)

It was a body blow, but I had no grounds for resentment. Not only were we supposedly "just friends" before my visit, our ensuing romance had been sidelined by the time of Gretchen's announcement.

Of course, given the processing he would've been doing, I'm not surprised he didn't tell me right away. He could've chosen not to tell me at all. It's the minor tidbit of unnecessary honesty I don't know what to make of - why bother telling *me* he'd already known for two weeks?

I replied:

Whew. You've certainly had a whole lot more on your mind than I suspected - and that's not likely to change for a long time.

We continued to converse about the development - lightly, as friends - alongside trivial threads. Before I leave this passage, though, I have one more memory confirmation to tell you of.

Thomas hadn't said how Gretchen felt about the pregnancy. A week after the announcement, I wrote a P.S. consisting of four extremely wordy yet halting paragraphs. It took me all that to come to this:

What I'm nervously trying to say is this: if you still don't see things working out between you and G, and if things could ever work out for you and me, and if there is any thought on her part of not keeping the baby…I just want you to know I would want to raise the child with you. There - I've said it.

Over-bold and bizarre, granted - I asked him to say if I offended him - but the idea came to me because of his saying more than once in our early correspondence he'd like to be a father someday. The Offer happened to be in our 500th message.

As a P.S. to a page-long email about German pop star Falco, Thomas replied with this couplet:

I am not offended by your proposal. But Gretchen wants to have that child.

I didn't regret offering.

Do You Believe In Life After Love?

Our emailing became more sporadic and less emotional through the end of the year, as you'd expect. We were friend-like, but the laughter never came back.

Thomas's emails felt perfunctory, as though he went through the motions out of respect for our history more than from genuine interest. The qualities of his that had so sparkled in spring had retreated. I didn't think mine had changed, but he no longer seemed charmed by them. He complained in almost every message of being crazy-busy - job, side hustle, impending fatherhood. Yet he apparently didn't want to let go completely of what to me had become the husk of a friendship.

I understood he didn't have the bandwidth, but the Thomas I knew in our glory days would've found a kind way to come out and say that. Instead what I felt from him was detachment. The third week of November I wrote:

> I knew our October transition would change things, of course. For whatever confluence of reasons, what we have now is a different kind of distance. I feel almost completely disconnected from you. Not sure anymore how to write in view of that.

Five days later he responded:

> I don't want to lose your friendship. I know I have to spend time to keep it.

I pointed out he no longer responded with personal thoughts or feelings, and I described how it felt to keep writing him:

> It's like reaching out to shake hands with someone and finding

only air - you're just wagging your own hand up and down. Or like leaving a pretty package on someone's doorstep and then never knowing whether the recipient bothered to take it inside or just kicked it off into the bushes.

I couched my entreaties in apologetic language, accompanied by expressions of understanding and well wishes. I wouldn't have kept sharing deeply if I'd been certain he didn't want to hear it. Once again, it took me too long to catch on. I should've taken the cues, rather than waiting for directness.

A later paragraph in the same message absolutely blows me away:

Remember the Monday evening I was there? After the three of us came back from the cinema, I stayed up in the bedroom so as not to interfere with you two. What I never told you was that I cried for the first ten minutes I was alone, before I adjusted and opened the door so you'd know you could come in if you wanted. Metaphorically speaking, I have felt like I'm back up in that bedroom again.

Ok, this is making me wobble again. Now I'm remembering those tears. And to think I wrote as if he wanted to know.

This time it was seven days before I heard back - again, with no acknowledgement of the feelings I'd poured out. He spent two pages on fatherhood matters (but not his feelings about them) and programming work. Well, there was this:

I spend more time with G now than I did before I knew we would have a baby. I dunno how our relation will develop, but she is less demanding, less possessive, less commanding, less annoying

now than she was before. Time will tell what comes of it. I was
95% sure I wanted children - I do wish I'd have that child in a
happy relation.

He didn't sound happy - and we'd clearly lost our connection. But I
wasn't willing to stop writing. In light of their reigniting, I felt the need
to assuage a concern weighing on me. On the last day of November, I
titled my message, "Cold November Rain," and wrote:

There's a little something I'd like to clear up cuzz I'm not certain
you know it. I mean, in hindsight now, it looks like I came onto
the scene in the middle of a long-standing relationship that may
not have been the best but was still an exclusive relationship, and
then complicated things for all of us. I feel foolish now. I have a
defense...

I cannot adequately convey to you what it means to come upon this.
I have in my hands, in the ensuing paragraphs of that message, a full
recounting of how I saw myself in relation to the Gretchen question,
from the very rise all the way through the fall of my Thomas adventure.
My defense began:

I'd told you from the start I wouldn't interfere with a relationship
you already had going, and I meant it. I may not have ever told
you this (or perhaps referred to it at the cafe), but here's the crucial
point: I did not realize until *after* I arrived (and after I was
already loving you) that you two were still "together." Stupid me:
when you told me in February that G had moved out in December,
I mistakenly took that to mean you broke up.

This intrigues me, because it means I had even then ignored data in messages leading up to my visit. Oh look, I acknowledged that next, in so many words:

> *True, I s'pose I should've figured it out when you told me about the trip to Berlin a week or two before I came. And I did try to caution myself, but I was also still telling myself I was only coming there for friendship.*

We both did - try to caution ourselves, that is:

> *My second day there you told me you thought you ought to give that relationship one more shot because of the years already invested, and I still understood that to mean you had broken up but maybe would try to get back together. It didn't sink in that you technically were still a couple until I saw you two holding hands. Which did come as a surprise, and I tried to back off, as you know.*

My god, that's right! I remember them holding hands at the movie. No wonder I was in a muddle:

> *Then, well, I got so caught up in you by the last evening (not without encouragement from you, I might add) that I was totally blocking out this factor by the time I left. And then you said later that I hadn't needed to back off, that it was over with her anyway, and that you just hadn't given her the news yet. Well, now there's 'new life' in your relationship, and I just wanted to be sure you had this complete past perspective from me.*

That muddle was not of my making alone.

IT MUST HAVE BEEN
LOVE

Thomas had a defense too. A week later he answered and gave it:

> When G decided to move to an apartment of her own last
> year, I really thought it was over. All in all I didn't mind coz
> I felt free - no nagging, no demanding, no commanding.
> Well - then I met you. And it was a painful process to find out
> what you want - what you really really want.

That's him riffing on the Spice Girls, by the way. His long paragraph described the rollercoaster he said began for him with the hopefulness of our cafe conversation. (Not a word of this email oration, though, addressed their status during my visit.) He closed:

*I took the plans we made seriously. But I also think the distance
and the ups and downs made me a little bit cautious not to take
my hopes for reality. I think I didn't get over you completely.
I think I love you, but neither of us should expect more than
cyber-friendship.*

I remember how much I appreciated that he finally made time to
write about us. And yet… Call me picky, but with the benefit of years
I can't help but notice Thomas didn't actually own up to anything, or
acknowledge my feelings, or wish me well. Should I be angered by that
now? Or chalk it up to his dealing with all this imperfectly, just as I did?

My clearing-the-air message also contained newsy updates, including
this:

*Deb's house hasn't sold yet - and, BTW, in one of life's meaningless
little ironies, the apartment downstairs from mine became available
this month.*

And my P.S. is amazing. I inserted a single-frame comic - a sketch
of the characters from *Casablanca* facing each other up close, captioned,
We'll always have email. That's the clipping on my refrigerator today.

Now I see my tendency to minimize the Gretchen factor was in play
from the start - and so was Thomas's! Our denial is key to the story,
despite my beliefs being what shelved our romantic hopes. As Thomas
intimated back in spring, "Remaining good friends would be easier."
If we'd have waited to meet until the following year, we probably never
would have. Fatherhood likely would've kept him from coming here,
and my special opportunity to go there would've passed.

When I interred the printouts in the Box by the end of the century,
I must've interred along with them the more vexing details of the story,

out of shame. If I barely admitted to myself what I'd willingly stepped into, why would I admit it to others?

It's crazy to think I wouldn't know it *now* if I didn't have the old emails to explain me to me.

You might wonder how I responded to Thomas's rollercoaster wrap-up of our romance. So do I. His was dated December 6th; my reply is missing. Just then my PC suffered a dreaded hard disk crash, leaving me (because of a perfect storm of local techie difficulties) without a computer for three full weeks.

By the time I got back online at home, it was the 29th of December. When I wrote Thomas that day, I told him that as part of resetting my equipment, I arranged my own local internet access ($8.33 per month). No need to access his CompuServe account anymore.

Thomas's full-page reply, on the last day of the year, consisted of his own techie updates and tips for me. He remarked that losing his hard disk data would be the worst thing that could happen to him, as he was "a bit floppy about backups." He signed, "CU."

I replied the same day - New Year's Eve at 8 p.m. My boys were with their dad overnight, and I was feeling pensive:

Well, here it is, New Year's Eve; there went another whole year! It sure was a momentous one for me. I look ahead and instead of eager, excited anticipation, I just feel sortuva calm, tinged with a little melancholy. Things will be alright, I guess. It's very quiet here, and I'm just drinking tea and processing words. I'm already in for the night; it'll be just me welcoming myself to the new year.

What a lovely note to end on. And I can't ignore the symbolism of being back on a smoothly running computer system, with my own internet account, to close out the year.

That was pretty much it.

The best part, anyway. We corresponded in dribs and drabs for a few more months. I helped him beta-test new screensavers, he helped me with minor computer questions, the baby came, Gretchen moved back in.

Bittersweet Symphony

I didn't just roll with his fade. Periodically I confronted him about what he wanted out of staying in contact so thinly. In late January (a year after our beginning), I told him it might be better for me to do without writing him at all for a while. He replied:

> It's sure that writing to me wasn't very rewarding for you recently because I didn't have much time to write. Apart from the workload I'm in a difficult situation because I will be a father soon - and I don't know if I can handle that.

His acknowledgment of my experience was refreshing; so was his admission of anxiety. I answered:

> While my suggestion had to do with shielding myself from disappointment and acknowledging reality, I also thought it might come as a relief to you. I'm uncomfortable with the notion of myself as a "hanger-on" in the presence of signals that the friendly interest may be one-sided.

After two weeks, his response was:

I admit it was a long time since I wrote. Sorry, but got a lot of work piling up.

Weeks later I gave it another shot, with a single newsy page. I tossed in, "I miss you, Thomas." His reply was surprisingly warm:

These words touch me. We exchange only few messages these weeks, but you are more than a friend for me.

In my notes today, I jot a remembered reaction: *Who knew?*

Those words of his were an aberration. They turned out to be his final sweetness, and they make my final reply to him all the more poignant:

I haven't wavered on my determination to return to Germany. In fact, I know I'll be back, whether I get to see you while I'm there or not. It's important to me to know that Germany, our music, the Cathedral, the Rhine, are in a certain sense my own. (And I have you to thank for giving them to me - thank you.)

I closed with, "Heard any good jokes lately?"

How perfect is that?

Epilogue

Let Your Amazement Grow

In a world of technology, people make the difference. That was a 1990s tagline for a telecommunications company; I quoted it in a P.S. to Thomas in spring of 1998. We were good, then, at connecting. The unconnecting, a little less so. It has taken all my available hard drive and memory to go back over the emails and to comprehend that.

By the time Thomas and I parted ways - such a gentle phrase for it - we'd stayed in contact just shy of a year after meeting in person. I've learned from our emails that *I* made the visit happen when it did, but not the relationship itself. He was as initiating as I was.

On the way *into* the Box, I remembered above all the heights of delight and the urgency of affection… and that the breakup was on me… and that fatherhood would've kept us apart anyway. Now I know the nuances. When I finished with all the emails, it felt like I'd made it to the other side of a vast tree-shadowed place. Slivers of sunlight cut through foliage along the way - but I can see clearly now. Epiphanies happen on the way out.

I looked back in order to move forward; clarity makes me happy. Even back then I sensed the episode's enduring impact, as seen in this October message of mine shortly after Thomas and I reverted to cyber-friendship:

It's been 12 weeks since I was in Germany. I think I will always feel a strong sense of connection, almost belonging. This is more permeating in my thinking than I expected the experience would be. I'll say it: in a certain sense, it changed my life. Whether I ever see you or Germany again, everything I remember of life on my own will be either pre-TH or post-TH.

That summer (to rephrase the Pogues) became the measure of my dreams.

I experienced my love for Thomas as deeper and more real than I'd ever conceived of. My notion of romantic love would be impoverished had I not known him. For all that each of us could've done better, at our height it was the best parts of our souls and selves that meshed.

I carried regrets into the Box. Some got accentuated, some alleviated - and some have shapeshifted. There was grieving left to do; facing my own words in the old messages is what it took to get it out. I wrote this to Thomas, near the end of our contact:

I think there are at least two kinds of grief: a) the sadness in response to something bad happening, and b) the sadness of having lost or become separated from something good. I know both. And so do you.

I was showing Thomas my pensive self again:

Anyway, you've heard this Tennyson quote before, but probably not often with all four lines of the quatrain:
I hold it true, whate'er befall,
I feel it when I sorrow most,
'Tis better to have loved and lost,
Than never to have loved at all.
It hit me this morning how it's really the second line that's the most

striking - and I've consistently found it ever so true whenever I'm
feeling the second kind of grief.

I can't say, of course, how Thomas grieved. But I do know we approached *anticipated* loss differently. The contrast in a nutshell:

Him: Let's not kiss, in case we lose each other.
Me: Let's kiss, in case we lose each other.

I still want that kiss.

Now that the whole story is exposed to sunlight, this book is my way of placing the experience into its proper folder - so I don't need to be questioning, misremembering, sorry anymore. I wouldn't call it trauma, despite the pain of its ending - there was too much ecstasy - but it did need to be filed. Now when I weep, I weep from amazement.

I said earlier when you work with layers of memory, almost everything looks like foreshadowing. The timing of when we tell our stories, I also said, influences how we perceive where endings are. Now I say: most everything comes with an ellipsis.

When I reflect on loving Thomas, I think of these words from the philosopher Montaigne about his dearly loved friend:

"If I am pressed to say why I loved him, I feel that I can only express myself by answering, 'Because it was he, because it was I.'"

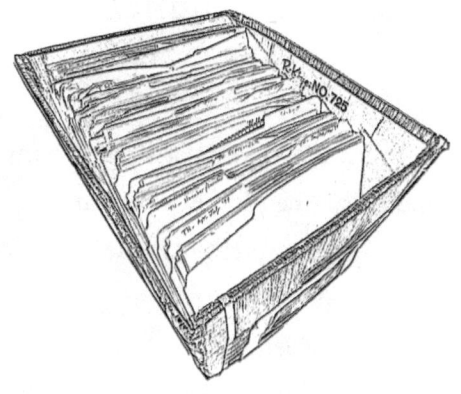

Afterword

I've said the shape of our stories is influenced by when we tell them. This one didn't end here.

After ten years of 'radio silence,' Thomas and I came across each other again online - again without trying - and met in person a second time after 23 years. I hope to tell that story in a future book.

Acknowledgments

I am inexpressibly grateful to my sister Deb, to my sons and their sweethearts - Sam and Kelsey, Ben and Ryanne - and to other family and friends who graciously and supportively made room for the obsessing it took to get this written.

A special thanks to dear friends Kris Harmelink and Eric Weiland for unwaveringly nourishing this project from seed-speck to fruition.

I'm indebted to the following manuscript readers and editors, who at varying stages of its development offered insightful feedback, suggestions and relentless cheerleading: Jonathan Thorndike (my former literature professor who became my friend), Jamison Stokdyk (friend and designer of the author website), author Danell Parker, Laurie Scheer of the Wisconsin Writers Association, and beta-reader Tayler Otten.

About The Author

An essayist and music lover living in Sheboygan, Wisconsin, Katherine is fascinated by life's lyrical absurdities as well as its patterns and through-lines that connect us as humans. Before beginning work on *A Confluence of Rivers: A Memoir Through Digital Love Letters,* she wrote essays since 2014 for her blog (ahansenchronicle.com). See her author website at: KatherineSHansen.com